Understanding early childhood

Second Edition

Understanding early childhood

Issues and controversies

Second Edition

Helen Penn

 Open University Press

Open University Press
McGraw-Hill Education
McGraw-Hill House
Shoppenhangers Road
Maidenhead
Berkshire
England
SL6 2QL

email: enquiries@openup.co.uk
world wide web: www.openup.co.uk

and Two Penn Plaza, New York, NY 10121-2289, USA

First published 2008

A catalogue record of this book is available from the British Library

ISBN 13: 9780 335 22550 7 (pb)
ISBN 10: 0 335 22550 0 (pb)

Library of Congress Cataloging-in-Publication Data
CIP data has been applied for

Typeset by RefineCatch Limited, Bungay, Suffolk
Printed in the UK by Bell and Bain Ltd, Glasgow.

The **McGraw·Hill** Companies

Contents

Preface

When one considers how many facts – habits, beliefs – we take for granted in thinking or saying anything at all, how many notions, ethical, political, social, personal, go to the making of the outlook of a single person, however simple and unreflective, we begin to realize how very small a part of the total our sciences – not merely natural sciences, which work by generalizing at a high level of abstraction, but the humane, 'impressionistic' studies, history, biography, sociology, introspective psychology, the methods of the novelists, of the writers of memoirs, of students of affairs from every angle – are able to take in. And this is not a matter for surprise or regret; if we were aware of all that in principle we could be aware of we should swiftly be out of our minds.

(Isaiah Berlin 1997: 15)

I wrote the first edition of this book as a result of teaching courses on child development to undergraduates taking an early childhood degree at the University of East London. My students were mostly mature entrants, non-traditional students many of whom come from ethnic minority backgrounds. They were usually women under pressure – holding down a job, bringing up a family and fitting in their studies. They had often been out of education for some time, and had returned to it with some trepidation, and sometimes with unreal expectations of the studying they would need to do. So I tried to make my courses as clear, practical and as interesting as possible. But partly prompted by my South African family, I was also keen to get my own thoughts in order. I had become interested in issues of culture, identity and diversity, and I wanted to try to understand the impact of wider socio-economic conditions on early childhood, especially in poor countries. Teaching helped me extend my knowledge and clarify my arguments. So I was very grateful to the students for being so patient with me as I explored my ideas – and prejudices – with them.

Life has become still more difficult for the students of early childhood. What happened only five years ago now seems a luxury. University education – at least in the UK – costs more, and it is easier to get into debt. The Government has funded a wide range of cheap, semi-vocational training narrowly aimed at workplace competency. In particular, the government is anxious about the lack of skilled and qualified staff in early years and has targeted many of its training initiatives at them. Foundation year degree courses in early years outnumber all other foundation courses. Women working in childcare and early education are frequently being offered sub-standard and franchised part-degrees, using pre-digested on-line modules with prescriptive answers. Or else they are crammed into large classes in twilight hours, so as not to erode work-time. Much of the course content is dull and circumscribed. Students are being taught in a hurry. They have to know *what* to do instead of *how* to think, almost certainly an unwise strategy in a fast-paced world. A university, of all places, should provide an opportunity for open-minded debate. Students need time to explore and reflect on new ideas and stretch their thinking muscles. It is questionable whether these 'foundation degrees' and other short, part-qualifications are transferable, that is whether they have any value outside of early years – or even within it, especially when they have been created so quickly and franchised so readily.

But I do not mean to sound too pessimistic. Anyone lucky enough to attend my colleague Richard Harty's module on writing children's books, for example, is in for a treat. The students are encouraged to write and illustrate their own stories and in doing so explore what appeals to young children and why. It is both practical and profound. There are still lots of good courses like this being delivered by dedicated teachers, and students are still inspired by them, despite the many difficulties.

This book, then, even more so in this second, enlarged edition, is a *how* to think book. It focuses outwards, not inwards on the limited, politically dictated courses that now dominate training for work with young children – at least in the UK. It tries to explore a range of ideas that might be useful in understanding young children and how we treat them.

The first two chapters explore general ideas about memory and about epistemology – what do we think we know and how do we come to know it? How do we organize our knowledge and balance our experience against what we are taught? What counts as fact and what is convenient invention? What is research and what can it tell us?

At the core of the book is a discussion of child development. Knowledge of child development is frequently put forward as the fundamental, underpinning framework for working with young children. It is true that as a discipline child development focuses uniquely on the extraordinary shifts in behaviour and understanding as human beings grow from babyhood to adulthood. Many important insights have been gained through this intense focus. These insights are explored in Chapter 3. But the central idea in child development is that age is *the* crucial variable in explaining the differences between children. All too often the findings gained from careful and very diverse observations and experimentation are crudely reduced to the all-pervasive idea of 'ages and stages' or 'developmentally appropriate practice' that underwrites so much policy and practice in early years.

On the contrary, there is so much that the discipline of child development does not explain, and probably cannot. How does the brand new nano-technology of the brain sciences and genetics tie up with what we know about children's behaviour? Ideas about genetics and neurosciences are cited all the time as evidence for particular aspects of child development, but what is the basis for such claims? This is explored in Chapter 4.

Children live in many different situations. The discipline of child development has not had the scope or methodologies to take account of the majority of the world's children – the 60 per cent who live in conditions of chronic poverty – and the effects of the circumstances in which they live. More seriously, it ignores the relevance of these very different contexts for current American and European psychological traditions. This distortion presents us with ethical as well as theoretical problems. It is important to know how children lived at other times, and even more importantly, to know something about the variation in their circumstances *now* in other countries. People's expectations of children and childhood have been – and continue to be – very different, and those differences are worth exploring. Chapter 5 reviews ideas about culture and identity that challenge some of our own implicit values and understandings about normality and morality.

Our history shapes what we are and what we do, even if we do not always choose to acknowledge it. Chapter 6 explores the history of ideas about provision for young children, and shows how ideas shift and are forgotten, only to come full circle again. The first edition of this book stopped at the end of the twentieth century. This time, perhaps rashly, I attempt to bring the history up to date, and explore the very rapid developments in policy, as governments – not only in the UK – struggle to accommodate to new perspectives on the workplace, women's role within it, and children's place outside it. Above all, recent history is the story of the expansion of the private sector in providing for young children.

I have dropped the chapter on health, not because it is not important, but because I do not feel I can do it justice in this book. Allyson Pollock (2004) tells the story of how the National Health Service has become privatized in all but name, and services are shaped by the concerns of the private sector. Medicine is highly technical and medicalized and – as anyone who is on a hospital waiting list in the UK knows – highly rationed. At another level, health interventions are required when the main need is to improve circumstances for the whole population – for example, public health measures like immunization. At yet another level, health interventions are closely tied up with family welfare, trying to make sure that the most vulnerable individuals, especially the very young, are supported within the community, and provided with minimal standards of healthcare – a rationale a century ago for providing nursery schools. Angela Underdown has written a book about health in the early years, which admirably covers the subject.

Chapter 7 addresses child rights, again another area where ideas have been rapidly developing. Drawing on the previous chapter by Priscilla Alderson, I bring the book up to date on some of these developments.

In this second edition, I have included a new Chapter 8 on the economics of childcare and early education. Inside and outside of the family, ideas about what children are worth, how that worth is rated against other expenditure, and what kinds of proofs of worth are necessary, are crucial in any arguments made for more, or better, provision for children. The position of those who care for and educate young children, the support they offer in the home or out of it, also has a value within the economy. These cost calculations are rarely discussed. Some of my own recent research has been in this area, and I feel more competent to discuss it than previously.

In Chapter 9 as before, I discuss practice. In the UK, the government has sought to control the curriculum very tightly, but this is not the case in other countries. The discussion of practice takes in a very wide range of examples of practice.

The final chapter summarizes the themes of the book, and draws together the theme of interdisciplinary thinking. This book then takes a broad perspective about the contexts in which children grow and change. It explores some of the ideas, micro and macro, which may be of relevance in thinking about children and childhood and in working with young children.

The first edition of the book was dedicated to my students. This second edition is for my colleagues Lynn Ling-Yin Ang, Paulette Brown, Richard Harty, Helen Masterton, Kevin Morgan, Abiola Ogunsola and Carolyn Silberfeld, who daily undertake impossible tasks with almost undented cheerfulness. Eva Lloyd bailed me out again and again. And, as ever, Veronica Burton was always there to help. I must also thank my editors at the Open University Press, who remain imperturbable and supportive in the face of my delays and prevarications with delivery dates.

1 Remembering Childhood

Around the hamlet cottages played many little children, too young to go to school. Every morning they were bundled into a piece of old shawl crossed on the chest and tied in a hard knot at the back, a slice of food was thrust into their hands and they were told to 'go play' whilst their mothers got on with the housework. In winter, their little limbs purple mottled with cold, they would stamp around playing horses or engines. In summer they would make mud pies in the dust, moistening them from their own most intimate water supply. If they fell down or hurt themselves in any way, they did not run indoors for comfort, for they know all they would get would be 'sarves ye right. You should've looked where you wer' a-goin!'

(Thompson 1939: 40)

This is an extract from a well-known book by Flora Thompson, called *Lark Rise*. She was writing about her childhood in an Oxfordshire village in the 1880s. The childhood she describes sounds abusive to our modern sensibilities. But she did not think so:

They were like little foals turned out to grass and received about as much attention. They might, and often did, have running noses and chilblains on hands, feet and ear-tips; but they were hardly ever ill enough to have to stay indoors, and grew sturdy and strong, so the system must have suited them. 'Makes 'em hardy' their mothers said, and indeed hardy they became, just as the men and women and older boys and girls of the hamlet were hardy, in body and spirit.

(Thompson 1939: 40)

Literature is full of rich accounts of childhood. The Irish writer Frank O'Connor describes his childhood in a way that is so funny and charming, that you seem to catch a glimpse of a magical time when he thought the world should rearrange itself about him:

> In the afternoon, at mother's request, father took me for a walk . . .
> Father and I had quite different notions of a walk in town. He had no
> proper interest in trams, ships and horses, and the only thing that
> seemed to divert him was talking to fellows as old as himself. When
> I wanted to stop he simply went on, dragging me behind him by the
> hand; and when he wanted to stop I had no alternative but to do the
> same. I noticed that it seemed to be a sign that he wanted to stop for a
> long time he leaned against a wall. The second time I saw him do it,
> I got wild. He seemed to be settling himself forever. I pulled him by
> the coat and trousers, but unlike Mother, Father had an extraordinary
> capacity for amiable inattention. I sized him up and wondered, would
> I cry, but he seemed too remote to be annoyed even by that. Really, it
> was like going for a walk with a mountain! I had never met anyone
> so absorbed in himself as he seemed.
>
> (O'Connor 1963: 22)

There are also vivid accounts of non-western childhoods. Camara Laye
wrote about his life as the child of the local goldsmith in a rural village in
French West Africa. He was brought up in a compound always full of people,
visitors, relatives and his fathers' apprentices. He describes his first impressions
of school:

> Once in school we went straight to our seats, boys and girls sitting side
> by side, our quarrels over; and, as soon as we had sat down, we
> became all ears and sat absolutely still, so that the teacher used to give
> his lessons in impressive silence. I should just like to have seen what
> would have happened if we had so much as stirred in our seats. Our
> teacher moved like quicksilver; he never remained long in the same
> place, he was here, there and everywhere. His flow of talk would have
> bewildered less attentive pupils. But we were remarkably attentive,
> and we found it no strain to be so. Young though we were, we
> all regarded our school work as something deadly serious. Everything
> we learned was strange and unexpected; it was as if we were learning
> about life on another planet; and we never grew tired of listening
> . . . an interruption was out of the question; it simply did not occur
> to us.
>
> (Laye 1959: 64)

Camara Laye admits later in his story that this attentiveness was under-
written by corporal punishment. There were frequent beatings from teachers.
There was also bullying by older pupils. But in his recollections, he said that
learning was so precious to him and to his friends that they learnt despite, not
because of, the threat of beatings. The physical punishment was cruel and

unnecessary but endurable. 'Our love of knowledge had to be ineradicable to survive such ordeals.'

Some of these reminiscences about early life describe unimaginable childhoods such as that of the orphaned Russian writer Maxim Gorky; or the Serbo-Croat-Jewish writer Danilo Kis, who spent part of his childhood in a concentration camp; or Bessie Head, the South African writer abandoned by her white mother for being black; or the abused black American writer Maya Angelou. Their childhoods were so comfortless, so full of pain, hunger, despair and longing that you wonder how they ever survived and made good. Books about difficult childhoods have topped bestseller lists. Such books are popular perhaps because they are testimony to the resilience of the human spirit; they demonstrate that early experiences are survivable however extreme they may have been. They also illustrate the unpredictability of experience. In general, 'bad' childhoods harm children, and vice versa. But 'in general' is not the same as 'in particular'. On an individual basis it is almost impossible to make predictions about what kind of adult a child will become. As Boyden (2007) has pointed out, resilience is a much abused concept; it is not an identifiable quality that some children possess, but not others. Instead it is highly contextual phenomena, only identifiable after the event.

There are lots of stories about childhood, by writers who think in some way their childhood critically shaped them. They trace the development of the person they are now by trying to remember and make sense of the past. Their narratives construct a continuity of self and experience. But are they useful in helping us – people who work with young children – understand a new generation of children? Childhoods are so very diverse and unique that, looking back, adults sometimes seem surprised at the person they have become. Can a gifted writer looking back truly describe the experiences of being a child, especially being a young child?

These stories raise questions about memory and experience. What kinds of things do we take into account when, as practitioners, we make judgements or take decisions? Technically skilled professionals such as surgeons or accountants dealing with highly specific phenomenon will draw almost exclusively on their specialized training in order to act. But in working with young children – or other people – we may draw on our memories and feelings in making judgements as well as on our training. In fact, we'd be inhuman if we did anything else. This relational aspect of work, the internal resources we draw upon, is often left unexplored or unvoiced. In our study of nursery nurse training, for instance, we found that student trainees drew again and again on their memories and experiences, the 'naturalness' of what they did as carers, despite the formal, and rather different, requirements of their training (Penn and McQuail 1997).

Child development rarely deals with rich internal monologues, the kind of speculation, self-questioning, nuancing, recalling and re-shaping of everyday events in our minds, although the eminent psychologist Jerome Bruner claims that such narrative processes are the very stuff of psychology. A good writer, however, can bring these processes to life and perhaps enhance our understanding of situations as a result. Our memory is an essential – perhaps the most important – aspect of our self-identity. It ties our past to our present and enables us to imagine the future. Without it, you are unanchored, like someone with Alzheimer's disease. But where do childhood memories fit in to this construction of self? Is it only important things that we remember, those events that made us feel deeply at the time? Or do later events add a layer to those earliest memories, so that what we remember is an amalgam of many events, what we did, when we did it again, mixed up with what our parents told us we did? The Martinique writer Patrick Chamoiseau writes about this jumble of memory. 'Childhood is a treasure whose geography you never clearly reveal. In it you mix up eras and ages, laughter and the illusion of having laughed, places and sensations that weren't even born there' (Chamoiseau 1999: 3).

How do you remember: in pictures, or in words, or by ideas or by a mixture of all three? The writer Vladimir Nabokov, in his autobiography *Speak Memory*, describes his memory of the process of consciousness:

> In probing my childhood I see the awakening of consciousness as a series of spaced flashes, with intervals between them gradually diminishing until bright blocks of perception are formed, affording memory a slippery hold.
>
> (Nabokov 2000: 18)

Children seem to remember things more vividly than do adults, and their memories are more often *eidetic*, that is photographic. But if we remembered everything with such vividness, we could not cope. We have to filter what we see and hear as we grow older. In experiments it is common to find children with photographic memory, but it is rare in adults. We lose it along the way. We learn instead what it is important to pay attention to and what not, which memories it is important to store and which we can forget. Steven Rose (2003), in his book *The Making of Memory*, suggests that there are several kinds of memory besides eidetic memory. There is *procedural* memory, that is, remembering how to *do* things with our bodies, such as riding a bicycle or swimming. There is *declarative* memory – remembering what things are called, people's names, the titles of books, and so on. There is *episodic* memory, that is remembering the order of sequence of events in one's life. There are also other ways to categorize memories. Rose queries whether the brain deals with memory in different kinds of ways; different kinds of memory setting up different neural pathways. This is discussed further in Chapter 4.

Nonetheless, from a psychoanalytic perspective, some people argue that we do indeed remember most things, at least the sensations and feelings of crucial emotional experiences, and that if we are helped to dig deep enough, we can retrieve those earliest agonizing or blissful memories. Others have argued that what babies and very young children experience is 'blooming, buzzing confusion'. A baby experiences life as chaotic, fragmented and disordered and she has to learn about the patterns and meanings of the events that happen, and latch onto the things which seem important, like the voice and smell and feel of the person who most often cares for her and feeds her. Even if babies see and hear much more than we once thought they did, and they very quickly begin to make sense of the 'blooming, buzzing confusion', how does such recognition turn itself into memory, especially if young children are continually re-evaluating their experiences to try to make sense of them? Other psychologists would argue that very young children, at least, cannot possibly remember details from their early life, because they would not have had the cognitive capability to identify, classify, sort or retrieve those memories.

We all think we can remember some events from our childhoods. Writers such as Flora Thompson and Frank O'Connor may have very clear childhood memories, but they are also very good at embroidering and reordering their memories to turn them into an entertaining story. Can we use such stories as a source of information about childhood? Do we really learn in a straightforward way from our own experiences, by analysing our memories of childhood? Can we, as adults, get an inside feel of what childhood is like for a child? How important is a sense of narrative, and where does it fit into more conventional theorizing?

The systematic study of childhood

So far I have argued that there are many different ways of remembering childhood. Our own and other people's memories of childhood are a powerful, if complicated, source of understanding. Memories are forceful but subjective; we have all lived through childhood but just how much can we generalize from our own childhood or that of someone else? But if not our own memories, what other insights into childhood can we use? Is it possible, through systematic experimentation, to identify universal, age-related traits that all children have in common, and use these as the basis for developing a science of childhood? Or, at the very least, accept that age is the most crucial variable in understanding development. This, after all, is what psychologists claim to be doing. Can young children themselves describe clearly or accurately what they think and feel, or do we have to observe them and make informed guesses based on what we know about children in general? Psychologists claim that child development adds to personal expertise and understanding. 'A broad scientific framework can enrich [our] understanding of development, add intellectual excitement to the learning process, and guide the practical applications of our work' (Cole and Cole 1996: Preface).

Child development is the discipline that is commonly supposed to offer a systematic, objective and scientific study of childhood. A familiarity with 'the facts' of child development, so it is often argued, will help practitioners be more skilful and knowledgeable. But there are problems in understanding and interpreting the everyday world of children (or anyone else). These problems can be summarized as follows:

- universality versus particularity;
- continuity versus discontinuity;
- objectivity versus subjectivity;
- competing disciplinary frameworks;
- translating theory into practice.

These themes run through this book, each chapter considering them from a different angle. First, however, we take an overview of the different positions.

Universality versus particularity

What you feel about your own experiences is unique (although it is always good to find someone who seems to share your experiences). The world is also full of surprises. The Greek historian Herodotus in the fifth century BC wrote about the extraordinary twists and turns of life in different places, the sheer oddness and idiosyncrasy of each existence. Man is the victim of fortune, he thought, and human happiness never remains long in the same place. So, can the idea of 'ages and stages' be superimposed on the quirkiness of individual experiences and the luck of the draw?

The notions of 'child development' and 'ages and stages' are odd, given the great variety of human life and experience. Biological changes such as rates and patterns of growth, skeletal, muscular and physiological development, can be measured and charted (although even these are not so straightforward as many manuals would have us believe). A doctor or a forensic scientist could give a reasonable estimate of someone's age by looking at their body or their bones. But social changes are another matter. Do living, thinking, feeling people really change in the same identifiable ways and at the same identifiable pace? And if children are changing very fast as they grow, does that mean we should not take their feelings or views seriously until they are older, and the rate of change has slowed down? Does it make a child more or less of a person, depending on which stage of life he or she has reached? If children are 'developing', what are they supposed to be developing into? At what point does a person's developmental stage become of less importance, compared with their rounded persona as an adult? We may talk of a typical 7-year-old, but can we talk of a typical 17-, 27-, 37-, 47- or 57-year-old? Human beings are exceptional in the animal kingdom for their very long childhoods – but why is childhood so long, and how important – and time related – are the changes which take place? Some of this speculation about why childhood exists at all is considered in Chapter 4, in the section on evolutionary psychology.

Young children do change a great deal, and they change rapidly. This rapid pace of change means that our assumptions about what a child can or cannot do might quickly become inappropriate. We would not expect a 2-year-old to pronounce perfectly grammatical sentences, but we would expect an 8-year-old not to use babytalk. People, especially people working with young children, may feel in need of some guidelines about what kinds of behaviour to expect. The findings of child development can be used as a basis for such advice. The difficulty is that values and beliefs about bringing children up are not constant; they vary enormously over time and in different places.

For example, the education given to well-to-do children, girls as well as boys, in Tudor times makes amazing reading; a de luxe Renaissance education expected and routinely achieved the most prodigious accomplishments in children. Edward VI (the son of Henry VIII) by the age of 11 was writing, in French, a substantial treatise on papal supremacy – in exquisite italic handwriting. Elizabeth I, Edward's half-sister, was also extremely well educated, spoke several languages fluently and also had perfect handwriting. The historian Diarmaid MacCulloch (1999) has suggested that study of educational methods in Tudor times, best described as a system of apprenticeship to scholars, would reveal some extraordinary assumptions about children's ability to learn.

On the basis of these historical variations, another historian, Michael Zuckerman, argues that theories which suggest regular and predictable patterns of development hinder and obscure our understanding of childhood. Psychologists, in his view, spend too much time trying to simplify and to make generalizations from particular lives. They ignore the messy, contradictory realities of everyday life.

> We can hardly do the most elementary empirical work, let alone the more theoretical exercise, if we do not address these questions of competing realities, or at least competing claims on reality.
>
> (Zuckerman 1993: 239)

The historian of childhood, Paula Fass (2007) also claims that there is a necessary 'mental remapping' in most disciplines, as new material from the past comes to light, but also as globalization takes hold, and diverse peoples are brought into ever closer contact through trade and migration.

So one set of arguments concerning child development, or the uses it is put to in policy and practice, is that it oversimplifies. It condenses all kinds of complexities into simple and straightforward patterns. Nicolas Rose has argued that the 'normal' child is in fact a curious mix of statistical averages and historically specific value judgements. The most striking aspect of the 'normal' child is how abnormal he or she is, since there is no such person in reality and never has been. The advantage of defining normality is, in his view, that it is a device that enables those in control or in charge to define, classify and treat those who do not seem to fit in.

Continuity versus discontinuity

The discussion at the beginning of this chapter was about memory. Is the child we dimly (or clearly) remember in ourselves the same as the person we are now? Jerome Bruner (1990) in his book *Acts of Meaning*, argues that we are continually adapting and re-adapting our own personal stories to make sense of them, to make them hang together in a coherent narrative. Children, especially, try to make narrative sense of their experiences. Some children whose life at home and life at school are very different, for reasons of language or religion or social class, try very hard to fit these different experiences together to make sense. We make narrative patterns out of our experiences vertically (over time) and horizontally (over place). No wonder, in the highly mobile, very diverse societies of the developed world we have some difficulty in establishing a solid sense of self. The sociologist Ulrich Beck has described contemporary society as 'risk society'. Traditional boundaries and constraints have broken down, and people's life trajectories are not tied to those of their parents. Each individual young person 'must therefore learn, on pain of permanent disadvantage, to conceive of himself or herself as the centre of action, as the planning office with respect to his/her own biography, abilities, orientations, relationships and so on' (Beck 1992: 135).

Children, then, are actively creating their own (dis)continuities. So does it make sense, in the face of this complex, creative process, to adopt ages and stages as a framework for understanding children? The psychologist Piaget hypothesized that there are logical stages in learning to think. He put forward the ideas of 'accommodation' (getting used to new ideas) and 'assimilation' (making these ideas part of thinking) as a way of understanding the changes from one stage of thinking to another. His concept of stages of thinking has been widely extended to explain the development and progression of many other kinds of behaviour. Piaget made a very good job of trying to define thinking processes, although his work is now dated, and probably not compatible with new thinking about the brain (Edelman 2006). But defining the stages of any kind of learning or behaviour in a watertight way, and then explaining how children progress from one stage to another, is extremely tricky. Just how tricky is explored in Chapter 3.

Objectivity versus subjectivity

Another theme is the idea of 'objectivity'. Could a more scientific approach, using the rigorous experimental methods of the 'hard' sciences such as physics, help us understand children better? Are precise measurements and observations and clever experiments more 'accurate' than our own 'common-sense' memories and understandings? Most textbooks argue that such methodologies provide a degree of objectivity. They can and should be used to analyse behaviour. Such methods, they claim, enable researchers to stand aside from their own assumptions and prejudices in order to minutely record the events and experiences of childhood. These questions about scientific methodologies are discussed in Chapter 2.

Some of the fears about making people in general, and children in particular, the object of scientific scrutiny concern manipulation and disregard of feelings. These concerns have become greater as issues about children's rights have become more prominent (see Chapter 8). Observations and experiments concerning children may be carried out in a very kindly way, but they raise questions about the autonomy of the child. Can you observe what a child does without enquiring into what he or she feels and thinks? And can you guess what he or she feels or thinks if they do not choose to or cannot tell you? Is it even important to know about feelings when investigating behavioural change or highly specific aspects of cognitive development? Can you ignore your own feelings if you are the experimenter or observer, observing children behave or perform in certain ways? An adult taking part in a research project – or even being observed by an inspector in a classroom – might be very critical of the person who is judging her behaviour. Are children oblivious to it?

Many experiments using children as subjects are conducted 'objectively'. The investigator may be very kind to the children taking part in the experiment, but the feelings and thoughts of the children themselves are regarded as being unreliable, hard to establish, or irrelevant. The investigator also rules out his own feelings as any part of the experiment. What matters most in a scientifically conducted experiment is how carefully the experiment has been set up, how meticulously the procedures have been followed, how much data there is, and how accurately the data is being measured. Much of the information about child development comes from experimental data. At least one critic, Erica Burman (2007) says that the overwhelming majority of psychological research on very young children is concerned with methodology rather than with actual events, precisely because it is so difficult to measure very young children's behaviour.

Observation is the most familiar method for carers and teachers trying to familiarize themselves with children's capabilities and preferences. It is, perhaps, a way of getting around the fact that young children are often not very verbally articulate about what they are doing. To make sense of their behaviour you have to watch them for some time, to tease out their intentions and estimate their capabilities. But observation is a method that also has its pitfalls. It is difficult as a practitioner to observe a child in a nursery or other childcare setting without prior expectations about what the child should be doing. In English nurseries much observation is designed to assess children's performance, for instance, in the key areas of the foundation stage of education, that is, seeking proof that the regime of the nursery is working. In addition, observation may be perceived by children as surveillance. Corsaro (1985) has suggested that one way to observe children – at least as a researcher if not as a teacher – is to take the role of 'least adult'. This means trying to be a friend of the children involved, to act as a very large boy or girl in the peer group. Not surprisingly, it is a method that has not caught on.

Scientists consider that it is important to have data that is collected in as neutral and as reliable a way as possible. Other scientists or researchers can then check the results by repeating the experiment, and they should get exactly the same results when they do. There are many debates about scientific methodologies. The metaphor of science as an unstoppable march towards more detailed information and more accurate prediction of the world in all its aspects has been vigorously questioned. Scientists have been described as belonging to an exclusive club, where all the members share the same paradigms and discourses; that is, they have ideas and assumptions in common, they check them out only with one another, and are very unsympathetic to anyone outside the club who introduces new paradigms or discourses. Science, too, has its fads and fancies, its blind alleys, its grand theories that get superseded by other grand theories, its overenthusiastic and intrusive methods.

Scientific methodology has its roots in physics, chemistry and mathematics. No one denies that the progress of mankind in many ways is dependent on the progress of science, but there have also been plenty of mistakes on the way. There have been mistakes in understanding the factual evidence and, as importantly, mistakes in ethics; the problems about applying new evidence and facts. The genetic manipulation discussed in Chapter 5 is a case in point. Can scientific methods, and the positivist assumptions behind them (that is, that science will eventually reveal all), be transferred easily and directly to the human sciences, especially to the study of childhood?

In the field of early childhood there are certainly ups and downs, and reversals of 'scientific understanding' about childhood. Christina Hardyment (2007) has written about the history of advice manuals for parents on bringing up children. Many of these claim to draw on the latest 'scientific evidence' yet the advice they give invariably reflects the time at which they were written. It is possible to argue that in the field of child development, the theories of childhood tell you more about the theorist and his time and place than they do about childhood itself, since the behaviour of very young children is essentially ambiguous and unknowable. We inevitably impose our own constructions and interpretations on what we observe. How detached can you be in collecting evidence? This quotation from the psychologist Nicolas Tucker illustrates both the limitations and the ambitions of psychologists:

> The psychologist is usually working only within his own culture and time. With his nose pressed hard up against the evidence in this way, it is not surprising that broader trends in child development may escape his view, even if he could think of ways to measure them . . . Nevertheless, accurate, intelligent observation of children is still the basis for a great deal that is known about them, and is particularly valuable if it produces ideas that can later be tested in more controlled situations . . . Psychology is still far and away the best tool we have for understanding children.
>
> (Tucker 1977: 35)

So how do we understand childhood, especially early childhood? What actually happens in these first few years? We know enormous changes take place, but how do we account for them? Who influences what? How can we investigate and explain these changes? Can we use them to inform practice in caring for and educating young children?

The arguments about how to apply science to the study of young children are essentially about the problems in measuring the complexity, diversity, unpredictability and irregularity of everyday events; events which are being not only observed but actively experienced by those being observed. The educationalist Carol Fitz-Gibbon said of education that, 'in all but the most simple systems, there is complexity beyond the reach of most theories and predictions' (1996: 49). She argued that such complexity can only ever be gradually and partially unpicked, but we should start on the job by using rigorous investigative scientific methodologies. The sustainability of this argument is explored in Chapter 2.

Competing disciplinary frameworks

Another theme to appear in this book concerns disciplinary frameworks. Which ones are most appropriate for the study of young children? Child development may be regarded as a crucial topic for those studying to become teachers or carers of young children, because it focuses exclusively on children. But there are other important sciences too – biology, physiology, genetics and neurosciences. There are also social sciences such as sociology, anthropology and history, and increasingly, economics. Which sciences are most useful in understanding childhood? Where do we draw the line? Is the 'scientific' methodology different depending on which subject you study?

Each discipline operates within a particular set of paradigms or discourses (or ideas or assumptions) about what constitutes its foci and its boundaries. Erica Burman in her book *Deconstructing Developmental Psychology*, closely examines the paradigms of developmental psychology, that is the particular ideas or assumptions held by the scientific club of developmental psychologists. She argues that the studies of infancy are dominated by discussions of methodology, because it is so difficult to attribute intentionality to infant behaviour. In order to achieve results, these methodologies concentrate on what is measurable. The result is 'the indeterminate, ambiguous non-instrumental features of infant behaviour are suppressed' (2007: 43). For example, studies which show how babies repeat and echo their mother's facial expressions may leave out a great deal of data which is simply uninterpretable. Babies wrinkle their noses, flick their eyes or open and shut their mouths for no very obvious reasons. Erica Burman goes on to argue that the notion of the child at the heart of developmental psychology is one of dependency and inadequacy. A child may be very attractive – especially to its parents – but at bottom we fear that it is an aggressive and primitive being who needs to be shaped and educated.

Much research nowadays is interdisciplinary. There are many books – like this one – which argue that we have to try to map the edges and the overlaps between a series of disciplines in order to better understand childhood. Martin Richards argues that any theory of development should be 'epigenetic', that is, it should try to combine a range of understandings about development from the genetic to individual reflections on personal experience *and try to work out the connections between them*. He, too, argues that human activity is immensely complex. Any attempt to understand and explain it must take account of the effects of feedback and readjustment to feedback at many levels: genetic, physiological, psychological and social:

> [Epigenetic theories] begin with a notion of a system in which there are multiple interconnections and which is hierarchically organized into multiple levels from societies through individuals to cells and their chemical constituents. Mutual influence is to be found at all levels.
> (Richards 1998: 143)

Nevertheless, he still thinks it is worth trying to find a psychological theory of everything.

Richards argues that while development processes continue across time, and like 'Time's Arrow' are unidirectional (you only get older and not younger), starting and endpoints are usually arbitrarily fixed. For instance, should you take a person's genetic inheritance into account in trying to understand their development? And if genetics is important, how far back do you try to trace the genes? Is the genetic information actually any use? The most well-known genes are 'faulty' genes that cause major disruption; genes that cause serious dysfunctioning such as Huntington's chorea can be traced across generations. However, as the genome project (see Chapter 4) shows, genes which show a clear association between behaviour and genetic make-up are unusual. In general, the hope of linking particular behaviours to particular genes is a vain one.

So where do you start? Genetic inheritance is still important, because it is one set of – always interrelated – factors which shape us. Similarly, where do we stop? Do people go on developing until they die? (Or perhaps even carry on after death, as the poet Dante suggested, moving through circles of purgatory until they reach heaven.) Many psychologists now talk of lifespan development rather than child development. How do we set the framework and draw the limits of what we call child development? When does a child stop being a child? It certainly varies from place to place. Even in the UK we contradict ourselves. A child may not vote; you are only old enough to vote at 18. But you can marry at 16, and be tried and imprisoned – like the children who killed James Bulger – before you are a teenager.

Richards ends his article by claiming that new and promising avenues of research lie in focusing on 'the diversity of cultures and of individual experiences of children. This work raises exciting new challenges which demand a new perspective' (1998: 145). The sociology of childhood is a relatively new area of study which focuses on what it means to be a child in an adult-dominated and orientated society. It takes children's own views of their situation as an important source of evidence. Richards considers that this avenue of investigation will offer useful insights in understanding the phenomena of childhood, especially when linked with other disciplinary areas of study.

Translating theory into practice

There are many textbooks or handbooks for practitioners working with young children that try to distil a range of empirical and theoretical findings about child development into a set of handy prescriptions. The best-known of these handbooks, *Developmentally Appropriate Practice*, is used all over the world. It is produced by the National Association for the Education of Young Children (NAEYC) in the USA. It is discussed in more detail in Chapter 9. There are many other practice handbooks. They reinterpret a range of evidence, mostly from child development, but also from genetics and the neurosciences, to inform practice with young children.

Often the evidence they use does not justify the extrapolation to everyday practice with young children. A leading example of this eager overuse of highly specific and limited findings is work on neurology (Rutter 2002). Even the most enthusiastic of neuroscientists admits there is no general theory of brain functioning. Some even argue that all the recent focus on the brain is misleading because the body works only as an organic whole – or to put it very crudely (much more crudely than the authors would probably countenance), there is no brain without a digestive system and other body parts, and there is no such thing as consciousness (Bennett and Hacker 2003). There are many diverse, highly complex and sometimes contradictory findings about different parts of the brain. But we are a long way from understanding how they add up or can explain or predict behaviour. Yet practitioners have been led to believe that these findings have great significance for practice. For instance, it has been claimed that reading books to a child before the age of 2 years stimulates neuron development and enhances the child's subsequent progress; yet there is *no direct evidence* which would support such a claim. The misuses of findings from the neurosciences and genetics are discussed in Chapter 4.

Popular magazines such as the UK *Nursery World* carry frequent articles that refer to child development. Consider this article, for instance, part of a series:

> Test your understanding of child development by following the pro-gress of Jasmine over the following months. Each column will note specific milestones and allow comparison of Jasmine, a healthy full-time baby, with developmental norms by way of demonstrating how individual growth rates vary among 'average' babies. Each column will include questions about important points in the development of a healthy infant.
>
> (*Nursery World*, 15 May 2000: 23)

Hidden in this extract are a number of common assumptions: that normality can be measured as acceptable deviation from a statistical average; mental development is the same as physical development; and development can be compartmentalized into stages with identifiable signposts or markers.

Nicolas Rose has also suggested that in practice the function of psychology has been to sort out the sheep from the goats. It defines what is and what is not acceptable behaviour, and identifies those who deviate from it. In Rose's view, developmental psychology has been regarded as a popular and useful subject because it has enabled institutions – especially educational and childcare institutions – to compartmentalize children so as to manage and organize them better. There is some truth in this, although practitioners themselves might express it in a different way. They are more likely to say that knowing what to expect enables them to help, encourage and shape young children's behaviour and learning. How ideas translate into and shape practice, explicitly or implicitly, is another major theme of this book.

Students' memories of childhood

Individual childhoods are so specific and unique, and yet so much part of their time and place. Any explanations of child development must allow for this diversity and complexity of experience, as well as teasing out what children might have in common at different times and in different places. The many different circumstances of childhood in other countries, especially in countries of the developing world, are considered in Chapter 5. But even in a rich country like the UK, children's experiences are likely to be very different from one another. As a recent UNICEF report suggests, there are enormous differences between the experiences of children from rich and poor families (UNICEF 2007).

In urban areas many nationalities come together, and many languages are spoken. Population mobility is much greater in urban areas – children move around much more with their families. There are also many refugee families, whose children are likely to have a very bad time. As Suzanne Hood (2001) has pointed out, refugee children have considerable difficulty in accessing even standard services such as education, let alone more specialized services.

I asked a group of early childhood students to explore their memories of childhood. What were the events that had stuck in their minds? How influential did they feel those early experiences had been on the way they thought and acted now? Below are some extracts from their replies.

> I was born in England but my parents originate from Pakistan. For the first three years of my life I was brought up in West Yorkshire. We lived in a small terraced two-bedroom house. The climate up there was very cold and it was an extremely hilly area. The town was exceedingly quiet and the people there had more of a quiet lifestyle . . . At the age of 3 we moved into a three-bedroom house in London . . . Everyone seemed very busy. It was very noisy. My religion, which is Islam, was practised by my mum but not as much by my dad. From a young age we were sent to the mosque to read the Qur'an, which Muslims hold to be a divine revelation. We also dressed in a certain way by wearing a headcovering called the hijab and not wearing revealing clothes. My parents set down the limits and told us what was right and wrong. As I got older I started to practise my religion more. My parents did not force it upon me; it was just something I felt I wanted to do. I thought if I was going to practise my religion I might as well do it properly.

> I remember my plastic doll, because I used to put it in my back and tie it with a wrapper. Myself and my sister, we used to play together, and we gave ourselves funny names like 'mum and dad' and 'fish-seller' and so on. We used to do cooking play, we went into grandmum's kitchen and pinched some of her cooking ingredients, then we went outside into the bush and plucked some vegetables for soup. Sometimes we ate the soup, sometimes not. I also remember feeding my grandmum's goat. Goats always like people who feed them. We had a

cat. My grandmum used to say that a cat's back never touches the ground. I always wanted to experiment. I will hold the cat's four legs, then I will try to get his back to touch the ground. But those cats are very clever. Their back never touched the floor, truly.

My father worked on the railway until I was 2 years old then he got a new job at Ford's. This meant we had to move so my dad could travel to work and my mother was near some of her own relations. My childhood was probably not that much different to many others yet still very distinctive to me. As a child I can always remember getting on well with my sibling yet that does not mean we did not argue, as I believe all children argue with their brothers and sisters . . . My mother believed that a house was to be lived in and so we were always allowed to do pretty much what we wanted. She also believed that a child should not be sat in a corner in case it got dirty so we always made mud pies and dug up the garden.

I only have one brother, who is older than me. As children we would continuously argue over little things. Since I was born up to the age of about 3 or 4 years old, I remember living with my parents, grand-parents, brother, aunt, uncle and two cousins. I never got on really well with my youngest cousin because I can remember constantly arguing with her; even the smallest things that she would do really annoyed me. My cousins were staying with us because their parents went out to work, while my mum was at home taking care of them as well as my brother and myself. My cousins got a lot of attention from my grandmother but she did not pay attention to me. I always got the feeling she did not like me because she never showed any affection towards me. She was always taking good care of my brother and my cousins but she never took any interest in anything I did. I never really got on with my grandmother as a child, even to this day I do not get on with her. The reason for this is partly because my parents would tell me a story about the way she treated me as a child. When I was a baby, I would be lying on the floor, crying and instead of picking me up, my grandmother would push me out of the way by using her leg. I think the reason for this was partly because there were too many girls in my grandmother's family.

Coming from a Sikh family, I found that I did not have a strict upbringing although both of my parents were from religious, strict upbringings. As a child I can remember playing with my neighbours children who were from Jamaica. This never affected my family in any way. My parents would often invite our opposite neighbour, who was an English family, for dinner; they would come to our birthday parties and any religious events. My parents would often go to the temple and pray and would also take part in helping the temple, to make food and to take it in turns to read the holy book. Although religion was not imposed on me as a child, there were times when I had to dress up in a traditional outfit for any religious events that were taking place in our local temple. This was to show respect towards the holy man and the temple and religion.

My three brothers' names were Ray, Gary and Mark. Ray and Mark were children from my mother's first marriage and Gary was from my father's first marriage. My three brothers shared a bedroom. Two in bunk beds, and Ray, the eldest of my brothers, slept in a separate bed. I spent most of my time playing inside as I wasn't allowed to play outside until the age of 8. I attended the WPA nursery. The one thing I remember most about the nursery is the glass of orange squash and the pink wafer biscuits we used to be given at break time. My favourite toy was Noah's ark. As a result my parents took us all to Windsor Safari Park when I was 4 years old. I really enjoyed it. The animals were not in cages but were roaming free in the park. It was like walking through the African jungle.

It was my nan who I have most memories of. She was a very warm and caring person; she lived down our road so she was someone I saw a lot. Every day in fact, she would take my sisters to school or pick us up. She was always on the go and loved cooking, especially fairy cakes. No one could cook cakes like my nan . . . My nan always came shopping with us on Saturday morning. We would walk to Green Street and back again. I remember once when we were on our way home a couple asked the way to a place not far from where we were. Nan was explaining to one of them how to get there, mum was busy sorting one of us out (my sisters and I were always arguing) and the other person stole my mum's purse from the top of her bag. My nan was fuming; you should have heard her! She didn't swear that much normally, but she did that day.

Both of my parents worked, my dad worked at Rolls-Royce and my mum is a nurse. We lived in a two-bedroom house with no bathroom but we did have an outside toilet. I used to visit my aunt twice a week to have a bath and a hairwash . . . All my friends' family worked in the factories, it was not just the men who worked there, you would find that their mums and daughters would be working in the typing pool. It was a close-knit community, as well as whole families working together, all social/fundraising events were to do with the factory, and even at Christmas time you would always have parties or pantomimes to go to. Everybody knew you and all your business. There was also a large military connection with the likes of grandparents who served in the war . . . When I was young there were no fears of main roads or what sort of people were about. I played out in the middle of the road with my sisters and friends without any fear. Nobody played in the back gardens, it was the norm to play in the street and later on everyone had bikes and would go to the parks; you only came home when it was getting dark.

I was raised in a town called Abeokuta. I grew up in a big compound. Compound according to the dictionary simply means an enclosure round a house or factory. Therefore we have a set of people living in a compound and we are relatives. For example, my grandmums, sisters, stepfather, stepmother, stepsisters, great-great-grandchildren, and so on. At my grandmother's there were only 15 children living together as a family. We played together, we ate together from one bowl. We only ate separately when we wanted to eat rice. We also showered in an open bathroom. We slept together on a mat in the big front room . . .

We respect people that are older than us and we found it easy to live with people. If we want to greet an adult that is older than us, girls should lean down while boys should prostrate with their chest on the floor.

I have lived in a beautiful villa with a swimming pool. Thanks to God, my parents were able to afford to buy me all what a child wishes to have. The one thing my parents did not want to get me and this was a dog. In my religion, dogs are considered to be dirty animals and if they are indoors, angels do not enter. But when my father explained to me, I was convinced and I forgot about having a puppy.

When my sister Zineb was born I really enjoyed having a baby sister, but as she started getting older, I started to regret I had a younger sister. When we were both children, Zineb used to imitate all what I did and this really irritated me. My mother told me to take care of her and take her with me wherever I went. For example, whenever I was invited to a birthday party, my mother used to tell me to let my sister come with me, and if I said no, she would not let me go . . . I hated it and I used to cry and cry and shout, 'Why were you born!' My brother was born when I was 9 years old. My sister used to spend time playing with him so I felt that I started getting my freedom back. I never had any problems with my brother since he was a lot younger than me. Now that he is 10 years old, I feel that I am his mother. I have seen him grow each year and I believe that Hadj will never grow up in my eyes. He will always be the baby I used to take care of and kissed him on the lips.

There are recurrent themes in these accounts: significant adults; sparring with brothers, sisters, other relatives and friends; places and spaces; food; animals and possessions. In these memories the students try to locate themselves, define their freedoms and restrictions. There is a sense of boundedness, of the circumscribed limits of most young children's experiences. But reading these accounts the overall impression is the extraordinary diversity and vividness of the memories. One of the questions which runs through this book is, can we do such diversity and self-insight justice in our understandings of early childhood? Does knowing about 'ages and stages of development' illuminate what these students thought or felt?

Because most of the research literature in child development records attempts to establish what is common in young children's behaviour, the issue of what is not common has been of less interest. Moreover, young children's autonomy, competence, interdependence and resistance have been continually underestimated or disregarded, since within the paradigm of child development, children are mostly regarded as immature adults, many steps and stages away from the meaningful, decision-making maturity of adulthood.

Summary

Child development, then, although it uniquely focuses on childhood, has lots of yawning gaps as a subject. It is a near-impossible task to separate out what factors may be universal and apply to all children and what factors are local and particular, and then to find foolproof methods of investigating them. It is difficult to reconcile subjectivity and objectivity, what you feel with what you observe in others. Keep in mind the question of why and how child development is relevant to working with children. Discussion about the methodologies and explanatory frameworks used to try to understand young children crop up in every chapter in this book.

The aim of this book is to explore different ways of investigating, writing about and understanding early childhood. It questions simple assumptions about early childhood as 'the foundation' for later life. It does not try to minimize the importance of early childhood, or the insights that have been gained in the field of child development. But it does try to step back and take a broad view of many of the assertions and assumptions about what children are and what they can do. There is an extraordinary wealth of material to draw upon, as some of the examples in this and following chapters suggest.

Main messages from this chapter

1   Read about childhood. Literature has a lot to say about it.
2   Don't deny your own experiences. They are relevant to the way in which you think about childhood.
3   You need to be an all-rounder to understand childhood. Child development is necessary but nowhere near sufficient as a basis for working with children.

What to read next

Read one of the autobiographical stories of childhood mentioned in this chapter.

2 Researching Reality

The nature of research

When I first began to do research, after many years as a practitioner and policy-maker, I thought research was a way of getting more detailed information about a subject, and relaying it to others as objectively as possible. The word 'research' is commonly used in this way. Journalists 'research' articles for the newspaper; students 'research' essays; planners 'research' an application to use a piece of land for building; MPs' assistants 'research' important political questions. Increasingly, the word 'research' is used to mean checking something out on the web. Research in this sense means obtaining a collection of facts that may be useful in order to present a particular point of view.

But research which is part of scientific activity is, unfortunately, not so straightforward. It is a problematic activity. It is tied to understandings about truth and bias, reality and resources. In the social sciences, especially, dealing with complex human activities, 'facts' are elusive. The famous American novelist William Faulkner wrote at the end of his life:

> Truth – that long clean clear simple undeviable unchallengeable straight shining line, on one side of which black is black and on the other white is white, has become an angle, a point of view.
>
> (1965: 32)

A sense of certainty about what is right is often confused with 'truth'. We cannot invent 'facts' but we can certainly report them wrongly, or interpret them wrongly. Often, people interpret and respond to events unpredictably. Good research has somehow to find the best way of examining an event, in order to try to explain it and suggest under what conditions it might occur again. But if an event is complex to understand, then more time and more care are needed to investigate it thoroughly and unravel what is happening. And that usually – but not always – means more resources to carry out the investigation. Sometimes the words 'scholarly research' are used to indicate that a piece of research has been carried out with great care, and all the possible resources and references have been double-checked before coming to a conclusion.

The theories behind research

Facts and research cannot be separated from theory. Theories are the organizing ideas that bring a number of facts together, and suggest which facts are relevant and should be included and which are irrelevant and should be left out. 'Theory' is used in many senses, from a hypothesis or explanation about a limited set of data, to meta-theories or 'meta-narratives' which try to explain a whole range of events.

We also all hold many 'common-sense' theories about why events turn out the way they do. These common-sense theories are sometimes popularized versions of scientific theories. For example, one of the most powerful theories in child development in recent times has been the idea that very young children are exclusively or almost exclusively dependent on their mothers. I have an old poster of a mother rocking a cot, with the caption 'the hand that rocks the cradle rules the world'. This poster expresses the common-sense theory that mothers, above all, shape the way their children learn and behave. This theory, like most common-sense theories, has some truth in it but at certain times it has proved convenient to exaggerate it. After the Second World War, when society needed to reorganize and find jobs for men returning from the armed forces and provide for evacuated children and war orphans, it became politically expedient for policy-makers to stress how important mothering was. They seized on John Bowlby's theories of attachment and popularized them in many official publications (see Chapter 3).

Many programmes of research were set up to find out if children behaved better or worse, or learnt more or less, depending on the kind of maternal care they received. Much of this research appeared to suggest that children were better off at home with their mothers than in any other form of care. The theory behind these programmes of research was called 'attachment theory' and it gave a scientific voice to many people's worries about the position of women and children after the war. In turn, the theory was popularized through radio broadcasts and popular books and manuals. Many practitioners such as nursery nurses, teachers and social workers, felt, or came to believe, that the research backed up their own deeply felt ideas about what was best for young children. There were even programmes of research to find out why some women defied or denied their maternal instinct and left their children in order to go out to work.

It is only more recently, since the mid-1970s, as society has changed yet again and there has been more insistence on women's rights and equality, that this theory about maternal attachment has been subject to review. Re-examining the research on mothering and daycare with the benefit of hind-sight, much of it now seems to be narrow or biased, particularly in relation to gender or in relation to the variety of family and kinship arrangements across the world. As theories are replaced or modified, the 'facts' change along with them. So research and facts cannot easily be separated from the theories behind them, especially when the theories are implicit. An implicit theory is like a common-sense theory: one that is so widely known and shared that no one considers it necessary to explain or examine it.

Theories are at the heart of practice, planning and research. All thinking involves theories and it is not necessary to use academic texts about theories before using them. A mother may choose to stay at home and bring up her child without reading a single academic text on the matter. But because theo-ries powerfully influence what the 'facts' are and how evidence is collected, analysed and used and understood, it is important to examine them. Theories that are implicit and taken for granted may not only confuse but they may also obscure new insights because they work unnoticed.

In the next chapter, I discuss some of the theories, including attachment theory, which have been a powerful influence in early childhood. These theor-ies are explicit theories about child development, and all have large bodies of research behind them. I use the remainder of this chapter to examine other kinds of theories about how knowledge is produced. Scientific researchers also hold theories, implicit as well as explicit, about how best to do their research and obtain the information they are seeking. They hold theories about the nature of reality and how scientists can describe and explain it. This chapter discusses the main types of theorizing about what constitutes facts and reality.

Theories about theorizing: positivism

Positivism is a view of scientific knowledge and research which can be described as follows:

- One view of the truth: indisputable, scientifically established evidence.
- Precise measurement using sophisticated technology.
- Logical, deductive reasoning from the evidence.
- A neutral observer/researcher.
- Detached, decontextualized data.
- Cumulative progress towards a better, more technologically advanced world.

Most of the theorizing in the physical sciences is what is called 'positivist'. It aims to discover general laws about relations between phenomena, particularly cause and effect. Then the discoveries are, if possible, put to practical use. Science is about changing the face of the world. Electronics, space travel and keyhole surgery, to name just a few recent scientific revolutions, have come about through scientific experimentation. Scientific knowledge is gained through experimentation and deductive reasoning. Experiments are designed to measure and explain associations and to test whether a law can be shown to hold good in a range of circumstances or whether it is disproved. As the facts are accumulated, so the body of scientific knowledge grows. A positivist approach is one that considers that only scientifically proven knowledge is 'true' and other kinds of knowledge or beliefs are less reliable.

A scientist gazing through a microscope symbolizes a positivist approach. The scientist is a neutral observer, separate from what he is observing; he does not influence it and it does not influence him. He is trying to examine intensely the tiniest part of a phenomenon isolated from its context, and what he sees is visible 'hard' data, which he can measure precisely, and then manipulate – and in today's world, perhaps make money out of it.

But the distinctions between observer and what is observed, detaching or removing a fraction of an object to put under a microscope, cannot work so well when it is other people who are being observed rather than inanimate objects. How do you detach bits of people and examine them? Can bits of a body – skin, eyes, toes – represent a person? Similarly, can bits of a child's behaviour – visually distinguishing between different shapes, recognizing a rhyme, showing attachment – be detached and investigated separately and out of context?

Positivism – examples from medical science

It may be helpful to think of parallel problems in medical science. In medicine, thinking about objectivity and subjectivity, and the relationship between mind and body, is a continuous and problematic issue. Is a positivist approach, which treats people as objects, and investigates specific bodily problems in isolation, the best one to use to cure illness? Such an approach has certainly produced spectacular results, for example, in the field of micro-surgery. The body (or parts of the body) is sometimes treated as if the mind does not exist – what people think and feel and how they behave can be considered irrelevant when a doctor decides on treatment. There are many examples in medicine where various kinds of experimental trials indicate that drug treatment 'works' but the processes that are involved are not really understood. There is also always significant individual variation in response to the treatment. For example, there have been a number of research projects on pregnancy and delivery of babies which have investigated women's feelings of comfort and discomfort in the process, and the kinds of situations which make them feel better. A positivist, mechanical view would focus on technical issues and tend to see a woman as a (not very efficient) machine for giving birth. Of course one wants doctors to be well informed about diseases of pregnancy like eclampsia, and appropriate medical intervention saves lives, but nor should women be left feeling demoralized and dehumanized by the medicalization of childbirth – as many have been.

Another common example is high blood pressure. Doctors know how to measure high blood pressure and what drugs and treatment will lower it. They have found out about drug treatment through carefully controlled experiments using double-blind trials. These trials mean that patients who volunteer for the trial do not know which they are having, treatment drugs or a placebo, and neither do the doctors themselves know until after the trial has finished. Then the differences in blood pressure between those who received the drug and those who did not are measured. If drugs appear to work well in the trials, then they can be used for treatment if there are no adverse effects. Yet despite the careful experimentation, and results which show in general that a drug works, doctors still know very little about what causes high blood pressure in a given individual, what the relationship is between stress and high blood pressure, and why individual patients react very differently to stress and to different kinds of treatment.

Pain is another familiar example of the problem of taking an exclusively positivist approach in medicine. Pain relief drugs have been refined through rigorous experiment and cautious insistence on firm experimental evidence such as double-blind trials. Aspirins, paracetamol, and all their chemical cousins have been carefully tested. Yet pain is a paradox, an intense personal sensation, it provides no direct, reliable evidence for the observer. Positivism's strength in precise observation can be a limitation where pain is being assessed. In order to understand pain better, doctors have to think in non-positivist ways, to accept patients' subjective views about what hurts, and see pain as more than physical. Some people never complain and others complain constantly. Feeling pain, and then describing it, is a complicated – and contextual – business.

The reason that these medical examples are relevant and interesting is that they illustrate the conceptual and practical difficulties of separating the systems of the body that can be investigated by positivist scientific methods – that is, anatomy, physiology, endocrinology, neurochemistry, and so on – with subjective feelings.

Positivism – measurement and measuring instruments

Sometimes positivist approaches are called 'quantitative' because they frequently (but not always) rely on large numbers of measurements in order to arrive at a conclusion. The historian Theodor Porter has written a history of quantification called *Trust in Numbers*. He argues that measurement is a kind of artificial language, a means of simplifying communication. Quantification is a means of simplifying and rearranging everyday realities into neutral, abstract terms, so the observer can (try to) be a neutral scientist:

> Quantification is a technology of distance . . . Most crucially reliance on numbers and quantitative manipulation minimizes the need for intimate knowledge and personal trust.
>
> (Porter 1995: viii)

Paradoxically, in highly specialized sciences such as nuclear physics, the progress of science *is* based on knowledge and trust between experts; whereas newer sciences – such as developmental psychology – may feel obliged to stress quantification and measurement:

> In fields dominated by a relatively secure community, much of what we normally associate with a scientific mentality – such as insistence on objectivity, on the written word, on rigorous quantification – is to a surprising degree missing. Scientific knowledge is most likely to display conspicuously the trappings of science in fields with insecure borders, communities with persistent boundary problems.
>
> (Porter 1995: 230)

As pointed out in the previous chapter, Erica Burman suggests that developmental psychology has been driven by technological measurement. As well as all the observation and testing materials, researchers use increasingly sophisticated machinery. Young children's behaviour is very ambiguous, so it needs to be particularly carefully tracked to try to make sense of it, for example, by using frame-by-frame analysis of video footage of young children's responses to particular stimuli which can then be computerized and compared across the sample and the slightest differences calibrated. Scanning machines to measure brain imaging are the latest in very complex technology to try to measure children's responses and assess their capabilities. (See Chapter 4.)

Sophisticated technology can in turn lead to new avenues of investigation. Another historian, Lisa Jardine, in her book *Ingenious Pursuits* (1999) has shown how many of the important technological inventions in the seventeenth century grew out of, and in turn helped to develop, scientific thinking. Measurement and sophisticated measuring instruments are usually part of a positivist viewpoint. Closer and extremely detailed examination of a phenomenon, and very detailed measurements on instruments or measurement scales constructed especially for the purpose of quantifying the information, give more detailed and accurate results. Such technological progress has undoubtedly been essential to the progress of the hard sciences, and has led in turn to important new scientific discoveries. The question is whether it has been a similar spur to progress in the social sciences, or whether, as some writers claim, it has distorted understanding.

Positivism in child development

Much developmental psychology nowadays uses positivist methodologies. Almost all the leading academic journals in the field insist on the use of empirical scientific methods. Many psychologists consider that positivist scientific methods are essential to progress, and progress can only be judged by evidence gathered in this way. Hypotheses about minutiae of behaviour are put forward. These hypotheses are tested on children by measuring their behaviour in detail. If the data supports the hypothesis and the results are statistically significant, then the hypothesis holds good. Even psychologists such as Urie Bronfenbrenner (1979) who are known for their holistic approach to understanding young children, couch their arguments as a series of positivistic propositions which can be measured and must be proved or disproved.

Up to the 1980s, a scientific approach usually meant laboratory-based investigations of children's learning and behaviour. Children came to a psychology laboratory and were presented with different kinds of stimuli, or asked to perform certain sorts of tasks, and their behaviour or responses were closely measured. More recently, journals have become more tolerant of investigations which take place in 'natural' surroundings such as home or school rather than in the laboratory, but these investigations must still meet standard positivist criteria. Often this is done by using standardized measurement scales, such as the Early Childhood Environment Rating Scale (ECERS), which the investigator can apply *in situ*.

Positivistic medical and biological assumptions underpin much of the thinking about young children. A lot is known about children's biological growth patterns. There is an entire branch of medical science – paediatrics – which deals with children's growth and what affects it. Children mature biologically in predefined sequences that can be broken down into stages (even that is subject to considerable variation). It is commonly assumed that a child's behaviour also follows such patterns and sequences. Some psychologists consider that advances in fields such as genetics, biochemistry, physiology, neurosciences and evolutionary psychology will illustrate even more clearly how learning, brain and body are linked. These advances hold out the promise of being able to describe normal behaviour more accurately and to measure the deviance from it. These claims are explained further in Chapter 4.

Other psychologists, however, consider that it is a big – and unjustifiable – leap to assume that the development of a child's learning and other behaviours unrolls in parallel sequences to biological development. In this book, I argue that it does not. Social and intellectual development appear to be of a different order from biological development, involving social interactions and inter-pretations of cultural life. Using exclusively positivist methods may not be the best way to investigate these differences.

Positivism is both a *way* of doing things – relying on experimental manipulation, deductive reasoning, quantitative approaches, high-tech meas-urements and neutral investigators – and a *belief* that by using such methods, we advance unequivocally and cumulatively towards understanding and truth.

Theories about theorizing: social constructionism/naturalism

The difficulties of using positivist theories and methods in everyday life have led social scientists to try to find alternatives that do more justice to complexity and diversity. Naturalist or social constructionist theories contrast with positivist approaches in the following ways:

- Many views of the truth; knowledge not necessarily cumulative.
- Narratives or stories as a way of making meaning clearer, rather than more precise measurements.
- Differences of approach rather than cumulative knowledge.
- Contextualized data.
- Scepticism about progress.

A contrasting view to positivism is to believe that there is not an unequi-vocal view or truth, and that a range of views can be valid in different ways. Instead of being 'hard facts', phenomena are seen as more like parts of an ocean affected by winds, tides and currents, shifting lights and opaque depths. The novelist Isaac Bashevis Singer has provided a striking metaphor to describe truth. In his short story, *A Crown of Feathers* (1977), he ends by saying, 'Truth is as intricate and hidden as a crown of feathers.'

If you take a social constructionist approach, there is no neutral, objective perspective, no scientist looking down the microscope or sitting behind the one-way screen in a laboratory. Instead, the observer/researcher takes the view of a questioning outsider. He also recognizes that he himself might have views and his views might colour what he sees; and that the people he investigates might in turn influence him.

Social constructionists believe the human world is different from the non-human world, and consider that positivist models reduce very complicated things and try to measure the immeasurable. Instead, social constructionists emphasize the meanings which govern how people live and behave. People construct evidence through their own experience. What people say and think and feel, their reported intentions and motives, and the situations they find themselves in, are relevant to understanding their behaviour. Perceptions and emotions influence behaviour.

The social world cannot be understood in terms of cause and effect, or universal laws, or the stimulus–response models of positivism. Instead of trying to predict responses by external causes, social researchers examine the meanings and motives that guide people's behaviour, gradually seeking to describe and construct accounts of particular societies and the complexities of everyday life.

Roughly speaking, there are two kinds of naturalist or social construction theories: postmodernism and critical theory.

Postmodernism

Postmodernism is an extreme anti-positivist viewpoint. Postmodernists are sceptical about what truth is, what counts as knowledge, and who can determine the validity or worth of any enterprise. Postmodernists consider that there are many different kinds of voices, many kinds of styles, and take care not to value or 'privilege' one set of values over another. Postmodernists argue that positivism has produced 'regimes of truth', that is dominant ideas that are held by powerful people, and these are particularly difficult to challenge. Instead, postmodernists are more flexible and more critical of accepted knowledge and theory, and more willing to draw ideas from a wide range of sources. Postmodernism has become fashionable. In architecture, for instance, a postmodern building is one that may include many different styles of architecture from different periods in history – Egyptian statues, Greek columns, Victorian windows and 'smart' high-tech security.

Although postmodernism has become an important theory in very diverse fields – philosophy, geography and architecture – it has so far had only a small (but increasing) influence in the field of child development. It implies paying particularly careful attention to the 'other', to someone who is different from yourself, in order to fully appreciate their point of view. There is a group of psychologists who call themselves 'the reconceptualizers'. One of the leaders of this group is Joseph Tobin, who first made his name with the publication of a study comparing nursery children in China, Japan and the USA. He pointed out that nursery workers and policy-makers in each country had very different expectations of what children could or should be doing, of what was normal and what was 'off the wall'. Tobin came to the conclusion that:

> early childhood educational research should be about the cutting edge of the emerging fields of gender studies, queer studies, postcolonialism and cultural studies. Suddenly the most avant garde of theorists are enthralled with the raw gender and power issues that are

the everyday stuff of our work with young children. Shouldn't we be joining in with the exploration of these issues?

(1995: 232)

Critics of postmodernism argue that the philosophy is too relative, that 'anything goes'. Because postmodernists are so concerned about every voice being heard, they are unable or unwilling to compare viewpoints or approaches or to say that one is better than another. Some approaches are more rigorous than others, some questions are more acute, and some answers rely more heavily on evidence than others. Given that most social policy, for instance, is about change and development, then it is important that Governments ground their policies on good evidence, rather than on speculative values. Critics of postmodernism such as Ann Oakley claim that 'the whole project of desiring to know in order to understand, predict, control and even change is dismissed' (2000: 120).

When there are abuses of power, or gross unfairness, as is the case with the many millions of children who die unnecessarily in the developing world, postmodernism has difficulty in developing a critique or standpoint from which power or abuse can be judged (see Chapter 5 for a further discussion). As a postmodernist, can you say definitely that a particular situation is wrong? This is where psychology strays over the border into philosophy. The distinguished American philosopher Richard Rorty, in his book *Contingency, Irony and Solidarity* (1989), argues that in any situation there will be different points of view and understandings, but that you have to discuss them and reach a consensus, and consensus is perhaps the best you can hope for.

Critical theory

Critical theory is similar to postmodernism in that it attempts to show how people make different but valid sense of their particular experiences. However, critical theory, which developed from sociology, sees society as a collection of many factions competing for power and resources. Instead of seeing deviants as a minority of outsiders, critical theorists show how large groups of people are constructed as inadequate or disabled through their circumstances, such as poverty, instead of through their own failings. Critical theory verges on postmodernism, but postmodernism does not share its radical politics.

In critical theory, science is sometimes defined as a social practice in which knowledge is produced. Those who produce knowledge also control how and when the knowledge is used – 'knowledge is power'. Scientists are a type of elite who have privileged access to information and may abuse their privileges to gain wealth or power.

This kind of critique may be useful in highlighting some of the limitations of conventional child development theory and practices. For example, critical theorists might argue that attachment theory had a political usefulness in keeping women at home when it was expedient to the economy to have them do so. Similarly, Jerome Kagan, the eminent Harvard psychologist, has argued that many of the targeted early intervention programmes in the USA (which, like the Sure Start programme in the UK, aim to help parents from poor areas to bring up their children better) are ways of avoiding confronting the inequalities of society:

> So many people believe in infant determinism [because] it ignores the power of social class membership. Though a child's social class is the best predictor of future vocation, academic accomplishments and psychiatric health, Americans wish to believe that their society is open, egalitarian, without rigid class boundaries. To acknowledge the power of class is to question this ethical canon.
>
> (1998: 147)

Many students write in their essays, when they want to prove a point, 'research says that . . .'. As this section has tried to show, research is not neutral. It, too, has to be weighed up and located. Researchers have different ideas about what to investigate and how to go about it. The integrity of research cannot be taken for granted.

Quantitative and qualitative approaches

These differences among the different kinds of theories to acquiring knowledge are sometimes called quantitative and qualitative methods. Quantitative methods are mostly positivistic; qualitative methods are mostly social constructionist or non-positivistic. In practice, there is usually some overlap, and some borrowing.

Designing research

Michael Cole describes psychologists as having 'a toolkit of techniques' rather as doctors have medicine bags. In his view, the skill of a psychologist, like the skill of a doctor, is in selecting the most appropriate tools to investigate the job with which he or she is faced. Students need to understand what these 'tools' are, and many undergraduate courses on research try to do just that – introduce students to questionnaires, interviews, controlled experiments, and so on. It is indeed useful to understand the repertoire of techniques that psychologists use to investigate and illuminate particular events in the lives of young children and how the children respond to them, and there are many textbooks which do so.

To an extent, everyone has to be pragmatic. It makes sense to know about a range of measuring scales, longitudinal studies, questionnaire techniques, experimental designs and statistical methods. All researchers have to select the most convenient tools and to operate within the time and money resources available. Yet as we have suggested, research involves much more than the selection of appropriate techniques of investigation. How can we take a tiny slice of someone else's reality and make sure we have truly represented their opinions or actions? How do we know if what we have discovered is true not only of the person(s) we have been investigating, but more generally? What checks and balances are there to make sure the research really does what it sets out to do?

As Stephen Gorard and Chris Taylor (2004) point out, many people are wary of quantitative methods simply because they cannot do the maths. Good research, whether large-scale and predominantly quantitative, or small-scale and predominantly qualitative, usually relies on a good grasp of mathematics in order to undertake a thorough analysis of the data. These authors argue that the distinction between quantitative and qualitative is over-sold, and that they are more complementary than in opposition to one another. Qualitative research is sometimes regarded as easier; but in order to be rigorous, it requires as careful a justification and as transparent an analysis as any other kind of research.

Nevertheless, there are differences of approach between researchers who emphasize quantitative over qualitative approaches. Table 2.1 suggests how qualitative and quantitative approaches might affect how research interviews are carried out.

The four well-known and overlapping criteria for assessing research are usually summarized as follows:

- *Validity*. Questions about validity concern the accuracy of the research. Questions about validity might be: How carefully and accurately have the data been collected, analysed and reported? How closely do the findings represent the reality that was observed or experienced or recounted? Have the research methods influenced and altered people's observed behaviour or their accounts?
- *Reliability*. Questions about reliability concern the logic and transparency of the research. Is the analysis of the data logical, or does it contain any contradictions? Can other researchers understand how the research has been carried out and check the results? Does the interpretation of the data accord with common sense, or a 'reality check'?
- *Representativeness*. Questions about representativeness concern the typicality of the sample. Is it just an exceptional or unusual group of children who are being investigated or are they typical of all children? How well is the selection of the sample explained and justified?

Table 2.1 Comparison of quantitative and qualitative approaches

Research aspect	Quantitative	Qualitative
Analytic categories treated differently	Categories are isolated and defined as precisely as possible before the research is undertaken. The research tests predetermined hypotheses	Categories are isolated and identified during the research, i.e. hypotheses come from the data
Different methods of data collection	E.g. predetermined series of questions asked in exactly the same way to each person, because of concerns about generalizability and reliability	E.g. in-depth interviews, more like a conversation. Interest in the insights into a person's views of the world
Sample size and design	More is better. Sample size and design are rigid and pre-decided. Sample constructed to be of the necessary type and size to be able to generalize to a wider population. Possible to take subgroup analysis	Less is more; 15 is an adequate sample size. Sample design is flexible and usually evolves as the research progresses. Aims to work longer and in greater depth with a few key informants, in order to understand how they view the world, what categories and meanings they have. Research concerned with insights, not numbers
Issues about the researcher	Attempts to minimize or even eradicate researcher interference	Recognizes that the research process can never be neutral. The researcher is a crucial part of the research process – an instrument in data collection. The interviewer cannot fulfil qualitative research objectives without using a broad range of own experience/imagination/ intellect. Recognizes the complexity of the relationship between the researcher and the informant and the potential power issues which may affect the interview

- *Generalizability.* Questions about generalizability concern the way in which the findings can be generalized to other groups and contexts. For example, the famous Head Start programme in the USA is concerned mainly with very poor black and Latino children. There are doubts about the extent to which the findings from studies about Head Start have any relevance in other countries where the gap between rich and poor is less extreme than in the unequal USA.

All these questions about validity, reliability, representativeness and generalizability can be further explored. While they are a useful rule of thumb for judging research, they beg the wider questions of what is acceptable science, and whether developmental psychology is amenable to the positivistic scientific methods of traditional hard sciences.

Evidence-based policy and practice

> If social science is something different from science, how can we be sure about its difference from fiction.
>
> (Oakley 2000: 120)

All government policy is an intervention in the lives of its citizens. Politicians believe that certain courses of action will lead to certain positive results (and to their re-election). In the UK, the government has introduced literacy and numeracy hours in schools, child tax credits, regular inspections, NVQs, Sure Start – a string of reforms that it believes will bring about 'better' early education and care. How do we know any of these work in the very basic sense that they do more good than harm? Do we take politicians' words for granted? How do we know that any apparent effects of these interventions are not just due to chance? How should the interventions be judged?

This raises two issues. First, the government itself values research findings. All the major childcare initiatives launched by the Labour Government in England have been evaluated. The Sure Start programme, the Children's Fund, the Neighbourhood Nurseries, and many others, have all been evaluated by large teams of researchers who have won contracts to undertake the research. The National Centre for Social Research carries out regular reviews of childcare take-up and parent preferences for the DfES. However, the pressure to come up with positive results could jeopardize the independence of researchers. The government own the research, and may ask for it to be presented in the best possible light, even when the findings are inconclusive, as with the national evaluation of the Sure Start programme (Rutter 2006). The research, although commissioned from prestigious teams of researchers, might still present problems of methodology – as indeed the Sure Start programme does (Clarke 2006; Rutter 2006). As well as directly commissioned government research, there are a number of independent bodies that undertake research and evaluation. The National Audit Office (2004, 2006) has published two major reports on early years in England. The Institute of Fiscal Studies has examined the economic effectiveness of Government early years policies (Brewer and Shaw 2004; Brewer and Sheperd 2004; Brewer et al. 2005). Almost every week there is another report on early years provision, some of it recycled from one advocacy organization to another.

This gives rise to the second issue concerning evidence-based policy. Since the year 2000, the amount of research which has become freely available on governmental and university websites, and through university databases, has transformed ease of access to research information. The difficulty is no longer in accessing research findings, but in evaluating them. Given the glut of research information, the problem more than ever is to be discriminating, and *NOT* to accept research findings unconditionally because they are published on the web, or carry an official endorsement. Research training now necessarily involves teaching students to be open-mindedly critical about what they read. Because the findings are up on screen, it does not mean that they are 'true'.

One solution to this glut of research has been to carry out meta reviews of the available evidence. There are now procedures for carrying out meta reviews, called systematic reviews. A systematic review carefully compares methods, analysis and findings in a given area, and suggests which evidence is the strongest, and at every stage of the review, the procedure is transparent and logged on the web. These have been adopted in medicine (Cochrane Reviews) and social sciences (Campbell Collaboration). The Department for Education and Skills (DfES)[1] in England has now funded an attempt to develop a systematic review technique for education. It is based at the Social Science Research Unit at the London Institute of Education and called the Evidence-based Policy and Practice Information Centre (EPPI) (Research Evidence in Education Library www.eppi.ioe.ac.uk).

Evidence-based policy is a controversial area, because its critics say that it values positivistic, quantitative research over qualitative research. This is necessarily true in medicine, but is less so in education. The EPPI reviews are deliberately trying to compare qualitative small-scale studies alongside more large-scale, quantitative studies. The 'gold standard', that is the most convincing research evidence, is said to be randomized controlled trials (RCTs). It is worth considering randomized trials in more detail, because they have such a high reputation as a research method in evidence-based policy.

Randomized controlled trials

In medicine, because the risk of so many interventions is a life or death risk, it is vital to know how well drugs or operations or any other medical intervention works. The most rigorous method for testing a medical intervention (or cure) is called a randomized controlled trial (RCT). A group of people are *randomly* divided into two smaller groups; one group gets the treatment – for example, a tablet containing the new medication – the other group gets a placebo, a tablet which looks like medicine but is harmless. The groups are more or less the same – they have been selected randomly – so if those in the group taking the real medicine become healthier than those taking the placebo, the difference is almost certainly due to the medical intervention. If, however, the groups are still the same after the experiment, and no one group is healthier than the other, then the medicine is ineffective. Usually these RCTs are carried out with very large samples.

Some researchers have tried to use RCTs to measure the effectiveness of childcare. Most of these experiments have been carried out in the USA. One famous RCT, known as the Abecedarian project, was carried out in North Carolina. Two groups of children were randomly selected. One group received full-time childcare and the other received only home visiting. At age 6, the cognitive and social development of the children who received full-time childcare was compared with that of the group that got only home visiting. In this RCT, the children who got full-time childcare did better than those who got only home visiting. The children were followed up into adulthood, to see if there was any long-lasting difference between the groups that could be explained by the initial childcare intervention, but the effects petered out (Ramey and Campbell 1991). Other longitudinal RCTs, however, have come up with different results. The interpretation of these findings is discussed further in Chapter 8, because economists have made so much use of them, in pronouncing on social policy issues.

Research, like most other things, has its fashions. At the time of writing, the concept of evidence-based policy and evidence-informed practice is a popular idea, and one subscribed to by governments in the UK, the USA and elsewhere. Research in early years nowadays is closely linked with government, for good and for bad. But blue skies research still goes on. If researchers come up with good ideas – and even better, have rigorous methods for investigating their ideas – then there are still options for funding. What we need most, besides critical researchers, are critical readers.

Summary

This chapter has explored some ideas about research. It has looked at some of the assumptions that underpin research. There are lots of ways to investigate a topic and the methods that researchers choose to reflect their theoretical approach. But the methods themselves have also to be well thought out and carefully described. The mere fact of doing research is not enough; it has to be good research: valid, reliable, representative and generalizable.

Main messages from this chapter

1   If you do not want to drive your tutor up the wall, do *not* call looking things up on the web 'research'. Research is a complicated process of testing out ideas in a systematic way.
2   Never take research for granted, or think that it is beyond reproach. Never say 'research says'. Researchers use different methods to test out their ideas. Researchers are not always good at reporting what they have done. Find out what their method has been, and see if you agree with it. Be critical in how you describe research.
3   Methodology is (surprisingly) exciting. The methods researchers use can make all the difference to what they want to find out. Good questions can be spoilt by bad methods. Clever ways of investigating are worth knowing about.
4   Keep reading. It is important to be up to date about research.

What to read next

Oakley, A. (2000) *Experiments in Knowing: Gender and Method in the Social Sciences*. Cambridge: Polity.
Roberts-Holmes, G. (2005) *Doing Your Early Years Research Project: A Step by Step Guide*. London: Paul Chapman.

Note

1   Now renamed the Department for Children, Schools and Families (DfCSF).

3 Not Piaget Again

This chapter takes an overview of theories in child development. A number of recent books and articles have expressed concern about the idea of development itself.

First of all, development is assumed to be holistic in the sense that physical, cognitive, emotional and social development are all interrelated and interact with one another. They undoubtedly do. But these categories are themselves artefacts. They are ways of conceptually carving up the changes that take place as young children grow. These categories are being challenged, not least by psychologists and others working outside of Europe and America.

Second, development is taken to imply a steady, predictable progress from babyhood to adulthood, with recognizable milestones on the way. But development is characterized by considerable plasticity. There is an enormous margin of adaptation and adjustment to life experiences. Although age is an important variable in understanding growth and development, the changes that come with age are more typically uneven and patchy in any individual, than absolutely regular and predictable.

Third, development is assumed to be continual and cumulative. Early experiences lay the ground for later ones. Again this is clearly partly true. There are critical periods – for example, in the womb or in early infancy – when good nutrition is extremely important for later development. Language acquisition appears to be critically timed, although then potential for such acquisition in the case of bilingual and multi-lingual speakers may be considerably underrated.

But early experience may be overemphasized. Good schooling may make an enormous difference; so might a good income for someone who has hitherto been very poor. Just because children – people – are so very adaptable, change is possible in all kinds of ways at all ages. In fact, there is an enormous self-help industry which proclaims just that – it is never too late to change.

Fourth, the pace, extent and recognition of the changes of growth and development depend partly on where you grow up. Development cannot be understood outside of a historical and cultural context. Being poor in Mali, or even in Britain, is a different life experience from being rich in America. Most of the children who have been studied by psychologists live in North America or Europe. So studies in other parts of the world that explore children's development, and, more importantly, the ideas that are used to describe and explain development, are very important to right this imbalance.

'Development' is sometimes taken to mean that children are worth less than adults, and their views and concerns are of less importance. Development is synonymous with being a minor. But children, even very young children, demonstrate enormous competences and strong feelings. Relationships between adults and children are invariably unequal; adults are more powerful. Sociologists of childhood such as Berry Mayall, Alan Prout and Alison James have been arguing that these power relationships require more analysis. Indeed, a major governmental research programme in the UK, led by the Economic and Social Research Council (ESRC), called the ESRC Children from 5 to 15 Programme, has been devoted to exploring them.

All these positions are explored in other chapters in the book, as well as in this chapter. They are summarized here as a backdrop and as a reminder of both what child development aims to do and how it falls short.

On the whole, practitioners and policy-makers have extracted from and simplified the diverse field of child development to suit their own needs (and without taking much account of the different research perspectives). Yet child development obviously contains some important insights because it is a branch of psychology that focuses on children. A large section of it is concerned with very young children, because that is where the greatest puzzles are. The transformation of babies into children who have sophisticated repertoires of language and behaviour is an everyday miracle. Tracking the miracle gives rise to all kinds of philosophical and ethical issues. Some of the chapters in this book have tried to discuss those issues, but this chapter is more pragmatic. It gives a very brief description of major theorists or schools or theoretical groupings in child development. It also discusses the work of some researchers who have not produced grand theories, but whose work has been important in refocusing ideas in child development.

In child development, ideas change, sometimes rapidly. As in any science, ideas stack up and then get overturned. The ideas that seemed to be lost may return later, slightly changed or disguised. Psychological theories borrow from one another and at the same time psychologists disagree with one another; or they may work in 'silos'; that is they work so separately from one another that they never take account of what is happening outside of their own speciality.

In human sciences, for the reasons discussed in the previous two chapters, it is difficult – or impossible – to provide a coherent theory that deals with all the psychological aspects of human life. No theory has yet managed to get anywhere near the rich mixture of psychological attributes that make up human life – feelings and memories; physical energy and sensual responses to the natural world; learning and creativity; sociability, conviviality and talk. Child development research has provided great insights into the lives of young children, but its findings are not fixed, and it has many subdivisions. It does not offer a magic potion which we have only to swallow in order to understand children. It is more like a large indigestible lump with lots of gristle.

There is also a time-lag factor. It often takes a long time for theories to become popularized, and by the time they become well known, science has moved on. Practitioners and policy-makers used to find it hard to keep up with academic knowledge; the books and journals they needed were not readily available. It is much easier now for those with access to the web to become familiar with the debates, disputes and changes that are taking place. But access to the web is exaggerated, and in poorer countries it is fairly limited. Consequently, many practitioners who have studied child development are stuck in the time-warp of their initial training. It has been hard to do otherwise.

The theories of child development offer signposts to different routes to understanding young children. This chapter gives a brief account of some of the signposts. One route goes in the direction of children as learners and thinkers. Another route leads to feelings; how children try – with or without adult help – to tame their powerful emotions. A third route is socio-cultural; how children are shaped or socialized by the community or society in which they grow up. A fourth concerns language, the most complex and important skill that we acquire.

There are so many contradictions and paradoxes that, for all the signposts, you end up in a maze. It prompted one famous psychologist, Jerome Kagan (1984) to say that children were like nothing so much as a rubber band, stretching into any shape. For instance, children are 'meaning-makers' but they can only take their meanings from or test them on other people. Children are highly individualistic (at least in some societies) but they must learn to live with and through others. Children are highly creative and expressive, but they have to learn to express their creativity – in music, dancing, storytelling, painting or whatever – by consistent practice. The paradoxes are many.

The chapter is divided into four sections: learning and thinking; learning in context; emotions and feelings; and language. Child development as a discipline is about much more than this, of course. The chapter is intended to provide a short introduction to some of the main debates about understanding young children.

Learning and thinking

Jean Piaget

A generation of practitioners was educated on the psychology of the Swiss psychologist Jean Piaget. His ideas now permeate a lot of basic practitioner training in early childhood. To learn about child development is to learn about Piaget. Most students at university who have come through a vocational route have been given a watered-down version of his theories. Piaget now belongs to history; his ideas have been superseded, and the classroom practices which arose out of his theories have largely vanished. But his theories represent the time-warp in which so many people are stuck.

Piaget focused on how children acquire knowledge. He considered that the most sophisticated form of thinking and understanding was scientific thinking; that is, testing out ideas, learning about quantification, reasoning logically, and arriving at new solutions. He tried to understand how children changed the way they think. Babies show intense reactions to the stimuli around them. How do they end up being able to reason deductively or logically? How do they learn to cope with mathematics, which is one of the most abstract ways of thinking? What happens in between?

Piaget suggested that there were various stages on the way to becoming a logical thinker. He based his ideas on close observation of his own children, from babyhood onwards. He suggested that children gradually learn to understand the properties of the objects they played with – whether they are hard or soft, or big or small; whether they have a wrong way and a right way up; whether their shape changes or stays the same; whether they taste or smell good, and so on. Babies have to learn to use and control their eyes and hands. Everything has to be learnt through seeing and touching. There are so many objects that learning how to manipulate them and what properties they have takes a lot of time and effort.

At the same time, children are learning words, and to give names to the objects they are manipulating. Gradually, they can use gestures, and then words to fix the objects in time and space; a teddy is furry and soft and has a snub nose and still is a teddy whether you hold him by an arm or a leg. Words are symbols, they are a short-cut to understanding.

Gradually children become more deliberate in their manipulations and deliberately and systematically experiment with objects; until finally they can do 'thought experiments', that is, work things out inside their heads without the need for any props. When children can solve problems in the abstract, and by reasoning establish cause and effect – *if* I drop the teddy in the bath it will become saturated with water and sink; I wonder how much water it will absorb before it sinks? – then they are thinking in a sophisticated way. (They are also no longer children but adolescents or adults playing with their younger sibling's teddy.) Mathematical reasoning is the pinnacle of thinking. Then the absorption capacity of the teddy can be expressed as a mathematical equation!

Piaget tried to categorize these stages of thinking, to *theorize* about them. He suggested that there were four main stages, each with a number of subsets. The first stage, *sensorimotor*, referred to babies coordinating what they see and hear and feel, and linking these sensory perceptions to their own actions, for example, getting hold of an object and moving it about. In the next stage, *preoperational*, children can begin to use words and gestures to signify what they mean. But they are still fixed on surface appearances, what things look like rather than what they are. In the third stage, *concrete operational*, children can begin to systematically combine, separate, reorder and transform objects – to understand that water, for example, takes the shape of its container but remains the same. And, finally, at the stage of *formal operations* children (by now adolescents) can think logically and are interested in abstract ideas.

I have skimmed through these ideas (which fill many books), partly because they are already so well known. But I include them also because, looking back, it is possible to see how important they were, and yet how narrow a perspective they offer. When Piaget was developing his theory, in the 1930s, school was a place where children were taught the three 'R's: reading, writing and arithmetic. Teaching was didactic. The teachers made children read in groups from set readers (*Janet and John* was the most well known), memorize poems, practise their handwriting, learn to do times tables in their head, and copy sums from the blackboard. Teachers had to fill children up with knowledge. Piaget turned the tables. He argued that children had to find things out for themselves. They had to develop their own ways of thinking. They had to experiment, to take the lead themselves. It was the teacher's job to provide a well-resourced classroom, where children could have lots of opportunities to learn for themselves how things worked, with guidance and suggestions from the teacher.

These ideas chimed in with nursery school traditions of play. Children had always been allowed to play in nursery school. Piaget provided a theoretical legitimation of 'learning through play'. His ideas were especially popular with those working with young children.

Not only was Piaget a prolific writer, but his work inspired many other psychologists to test out his ideas. Academic journals and books reflected the interest in his theories. One of the most famous of these attempts was carried out by Margaret Donaldson, who tried to repeat some of Piaget's experiments in order to replicate aspects of his findings. However, she suggested that children could reason better if the task was familiar to them, and they understood the motives behind what they were being asked to do. In other words, context and relationships were also important in learning. Piaget underemphasized them; or rather he was interested primarily in *epistemology*, that is, how things come to be known, rather than in individual children's understanding of objects and events.

Piaget's ideas influenced education in a number of countries. In 1967, in the UK, the Central Advisory Council for Education published its major review of primary and nursery education, known as the Plowden Report. The members of the review board were impressed with Piaget's ideas and suggested that schooling should be radically changed to reflect his theories. Instead of children being taught from the front, by the teacher, there should be lots of workstations or corners, with many different kinds of resources, where children could experiment and try out different activities for themselves. Many nursery classes may have adopted these approaches, but it is unlikely that primary schools ever went overboard about them. But whether they did or not, there has been a backlash. Successive governments have condemned this 'child-centred' approach. They have demanded that education goes 'back to basics'. Teachers stand in front of the class again, children have to read and write in the literacy hour, times tables have to be memorized. The wheel has come full circle in England – while paradoxically, in many other countries, Piaget is still being introduced as offering a 'new' way of doing things.

Lev Vygotsky

'If Vygotsky didn't exist, someone would have to invent him.' This is the standard joke about Vygotsky. Piaget's theories relegated adults to unobtrusive helpers. Vygotsky put them centre-stage again. Teachers help learners learn. They are indispensable.

Lev Vygotsky was a brilliant Russian psychologist, working at a time when the Soviet Union was in revolutionary turmoil in the 1920s and 1930s. In Central Asia in particular, literacy levels were very low, and people were not used to education. Vygotsky tried to find ways of learning and teaching that drew on people's experiences, yet at the same time encouraged them to go further. Put in a nutshell, Vygotsky believed that learning should build on what the learner already knows, but that the teacher should demonstrate the next steps, and encourage the learner to move on. He coined the phrase 'zone of proximal development' to describe the intellectual space between the learner and the teacher. Children depend on adults to fill in the gaps for them, to tell them about the rules of any social encounter and to fill in missing information.

Piaget regarded play as a kind of scientific rehearsal, and thought that children would grow out of it once they had mastered abstract thinking. Vygotsky defined play differently, as a kind of mental support system which allows children to represent their everyday social reality. Play enables children to think and act in more complex ways, to invent their own rules and narratives. 'Let's pretend' gives children an opportunity to renegotiate reality. A small girl organizing a tea party in the home corner, for example, would not be able to organize a tea party at home, boil the kettle, make the tea and so on without help; a small boy mending a toy sink with a hammer is not likely to be able to repair the sink at home. Vygotsky wrote: 'In play a child is always above his average age, above his daily behaviour; in play it is as though he were a head taller than himself' (1978: 102).

Vygotsky emphasized the social nature of development, the way in which most cues for learning are social. Piaget's child is a bit of a loner; by contrast, Vygotsky's child is context dependent. Children respond to the reality they see and experience around them, and what they learn reflects this reality. This is one reason why the Soviet state created a near-universal kindergarten system, in order to give children an orderly upbringing, in contrast to the sometimes chaotic life around them. Even in remote parts of Central Asia, there were very good kindergartens where great attention was paid to the daily detail of children's lives – although since transition, in 1990, the kindergarten regimes have ossified for want of resources and interest (Penn 2005).

Vygotsky's ideas took even longer than those of Piaget to become popularized. Although he was also working in the 1920s and 1930s it was not until the 1970s that his work became known in translation, when Piaget was already well known. Like Piaget, Vygotsky's ideas spawned many experiments and sub-theories. There is a vast literature on these ideas.

Vygotsky was regarded as a 'social constructionist'. He supported the idea that children construct or create themselves out of the repertoire of behaviours and ideas available to them in their particular environment. Piaget could also be described in this way, but Piaget emphasized the importance of the material world in providing the cues for growth and development, whereas Vygotsky emphasized the cultural cues.

Vygotsky's importance today cannot be underestimated. His ideas spawned new thinking in many areas of psychology – for instance, ideas about communities of practice and activity theory (see below).

Jerome Bruner

Bruner describes himself as a polymath, a person whose interests range across many fields. He began by exploring some of Piaget's ideas about children's learning. Then, like so many others, he discovered Vygotsky. Inspired by the notion of the zone of proximal development, he popularized the idea of 'scaffolding' to describe how adults help children learn:

> If the teacher were to have a motto . . . it would surely be 'where before there was a spectator, let there now be a participant.' One sets the game, provides a scaffold to assure the child's ineptitudes can be

rescued by appropriate intervention, and removes the scaffold part by part as the reciprocal structure stands on its own.

(1960: 33)

Bruner thought that schools could do a great deal to teach children, and that the teacher's role in fostering cognitive development is crucial. He suggested early on that 'any subject can be taught to any child of any age in an honest way'. Moreover, 'the task of teaching a subject to a child of any particular age is one of representing the structure of that subject in terms of the child's way of viewing things' (1960: 33).

By the 1990s, Bruner was describing himself as a cultural psychologist, although he had few connections with the group of cultural psychologists described in the next section (he was in another silo). He considered that psychology should be 'meaning free', by which he meant that societies create their own meanings and systems of values. 'The very people and cultures that are its subject are governed by shared meanings and values' (1990: 20).

Bruner has been an intelligent mirror of the changes in theorizing about child development. He has moved from Piaget, through Vygotsky and Chomsky, to a view that to learn is to create meanings from the stream of events and activities within one's own society. Most recently he has become interested in narrative and the construction of identity. In an introduction to a book that stresses the relativity of child-rearing practices he writes 'child-rearing practices and beliefs reflect local conceptions of how the world is and how the child should be readied for living in it' (Bruner 2000: xi).

Learning in context

Learning and thinking have increasingly come to be seen as a social activity. The contexts of learning, and the part played by communities and societies in shaping the context in which learning takes place, have been the focus of much theoretical work in the past two decades.

Urie Bronfenbrenner

Urie Bronfenbrenner was an American psychologist who visited Russia and China in the 1950s and 1960s. He was always concerned about the circumstances in which children grew up, but the visits crystallized his thinking. He was impressed with the kindergarten systems in those countries. They offered full integrated daycare and education and they were very well equipped. Children were well fed (even when food was scarce in the Soviet winters), and they had lots of opportunity for exercise and rest. It seemed to indicate that children and childhood was being taken very seriously by society. His book

Two Worlds of Childhood (1965) contrasts Russian emphasis on childhood with the way children were treated in the USA. Whatever else communism did or did not do, Bronfenbrenner was impressed by the support given to young children. (Some people consider that Bronfenbrenner was fooled and only taken to the best places. But my own experience of kindergarten systems in Soviet Central Asia in the 1990s, after the fall of communism, confirms the picture that he gave.)

There is an African proverb, 'it takes a village to bring up a child'. Bronfenbrenner developed a theory, which he called the ecological theory of development, in which he tried to outline the different layers of influence on children growing up. Children were influenced first of all by the *microsystem* in which they grow up; that is, their home environment, their parents, siblings and friends. The next layer is the *mesosystem*, the neighbourhood, the school and other community influences. The third layer is the *exosystem*, the local government, local industry, the way in which life is formally organized at a local level. Finally, there is the *macrosystem*, what the government does (or does not do), the beliefs and traditions of the wider society.

Two Worlds of Childhood is a very readable book, much more so than his later book *The Ecology of Human Development* (1979) in which he puts forward his ecological theory. Bronfenbrenner, despite his broad attitudes, was a positivist through and through, and this book is expressed as a series of theorems. He made many 'scientific' predictions and hoped they would inspire other scientists to test them out as rigorously as possible. But his theory was too wide and operated at too many levels to be testable. It was an important signpost; it reminded people that governments and local communities can have an influence on how children develop. We know the converse is true, that poverty harms children; it is harder to 'prove' the other way around. For although Bronfenbrenner wanted strict scientific enquiry, it is more or less impossible to set up large-scale experiments to see what happens when the government changes its policies, if indeed it does – in the USA, childcare provision was a mess in the 1960s and is still a mess today.[1] There is no overall system of state-funded early education and care, as in most other developed countries. Instead there is heavy reliance on voluntary organizations and parental contributions; a private market with a bit extra for the very poor. Rosemberg has shown in Brazil how this patchwork model is implicitly adopted by the World Bank and other international donors and applied to poor countries. Bronfenbrenner tried to show how this wider political and policy environment affects what is provided on the ground for children.

Bronfenbrenner has been very influential, as much in psychology as in social work and family studies. He is well known (and much quoted) for saying that every child needs an adult who is crazy about him (or her) in order to grow up.

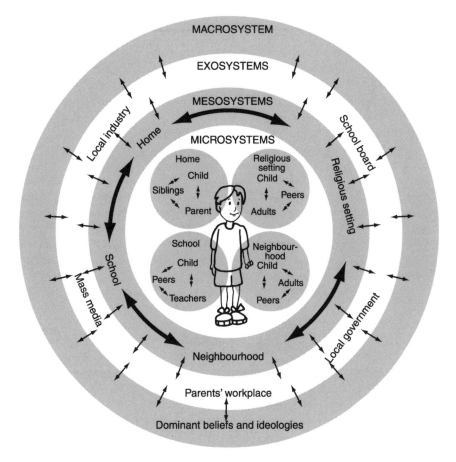

Figure 3.1 The ecological approach, which hypothesizes the layers of influence on a young child's development.

Barbara Rogoff

Barbara Rogoff was inspired by Vygotsky. She was interested in exactly how adults shaped and guided children's learning and thinking, and she wanted to know if these processes were influenced by the community or society of which the adults were members. She carried out her most well-known studies in Mayan peasant communities in the mountains of Guatemala in South America. She systematically observed young children and noted how they took part in the same activities as everyone else, gardening, childcare, food preparation. They did not have childhoods apart from adults, as in North America.

In the Mayan communities, there is a tradition among the women of

Figure 3.2 Bronfenbrenner's representation of ecological influences is schematized and orderly. In reality, life is likely to be much more complex, and a more realistic diagram would be like this scrawl from Mothibi.

weaving. Every household has a loom. Rogoff wanted to know how young girls learnt to weave. Weaving is a complicated process that requires a great deal of skill. Rogoff concluded that young children joined in the task gradually over days and months; they watched, then they were allowed to do a tiny bit, then a bit more, until they themselves became competent weavers. Rogoff called this process *guided participation* and explored it as a model of learning for children.

In her book *Apprenticeship in Thinking* (1990), Rogoff argued that children do not think in isolation. Thinking is an everyday, social activity. The activities that take place, and the goals that underlie them, are culturally determined, and different in different communities or societies. She defines thinking as 'people's attempts to negotiate the stream of life'. Guided participation is the way in which adults help children to negotiate everyday life. Her position can be summarized as follows:

- Events and activities are inherently dynamic. Life is always changing.
- Events and activities are organized as goals – people only do things when they see the point of doing them (or are told to do them).
- Meaning and purpose cannot be separated out from their everyday context.
- Mental processes are part of this process of meaningful action and interaction.
- In order to understand actions and activities you have to look at the daily detail of what is happening.
- There is infinite variability in events, nothing ever repeats itself exactly. So there can be no single universal goal of development.

Barbara Rogoff's work has also been very influential. Although she did important fieldwork in Guatemala and other countries, she is based in California and now concentrates on trying to improve local learning and schooling. She is part of a wider group of psychologists, loosely called cultural psychologists because of their belief that all learning is social and negotiated with others – a far cry from Piaget.

Michael Cole

Michael Cole is the most well known of the cultural psychology group. Like his colleagues in the group, he carried out his early work abroad, first in Liberia, among a group of people called the Kpelle. In Liberia, he worked with Jean Lave (perhaps the most radical member of the group) exploring how children learnt to read and count using an unusual alphabetical and numerical system. In Russia, where he went next, he translated Vygotsky and first introduced his ideas in English.

He argues that ideas about development, about how the mind works and how children learn, are in a state of flux. 'We seem to be living in a period when orthodoxies no longer retain their holding power and new possibilities abound' (1996: 3). Like Rogoff, he considers that 'the mind' emerges through the joint mediated activity and co-construction. He argues strongly against the more traditional view of thinking and learning whereby learning is an individual, isolated experience and there are universal laws that can explain it (the Piagetian point of view).

In his key book *Cultural Psychology: A Once and Future Discipline* (1996), he sets out his ideas. He considers that many aspects of developmental psychology are misguided, in particular, the reliance on traditional experimental methods. His book is partly a discussion about the methodologies that cultural psychologists can adopt. He raises the question of whether the entire enterprise of scientific psychology is deeply flawed at its foundation. If culture takes so many different forms, if people are so different, and the places they live in so dissimilar, can developmental psychology deal with this variety of events and activities?

He thinks it can. But he is still wedded to the idea of a positivist science. (He named his research centre in California the Laboratory of Human Cognition.) He concludes that while methods must become more adaptable to the variety of human conditions, rigorous research is inescapable as a way of finding out about learning, thinking and behaviour. He concludes that it is necessary 'to create a methodology, a systematic way of relating theory to data that draws both upon the natural sciences and the cultural sciences, as befits its hybrid object, human beings' (1996: 330). He suggests that psychologists should get more involved in everyday activities, as participant observers, and work out what processes are involved, and then try to investigate them through carefully controlled interventions. He and his colleagues, for instance, worked on an out-of-school computer project for children with learning difficulties, to try to understand the learning tactics children and adults use in this situation. He does not underestimate the difficulties of trying to understand and record reality: as he concludes at the end of his book, inevitably 'the failures are sure to outnumber the successes'.

Yet another development of these ideas is what is called 'activity theory'. Cole worked with a Finnish psychologist, Yrjo Engestrom (who in turn drew on Russian theory derived from Vygotsky) to develop ideas about how learning takes place in organizations. Activity theory and distributed learning postulate that new learning takes place from the negotiation of different points of view within an organization. Open-ended organizations are most likely to produce new learning. These ideas have been taken up in the UK by Anne Edwards et al. (2006), for instance, and used in the DfES National Evaluation of the Children's Fund in the UK, in order to explain how professionals can most effectively work together to promote children's interests – a theory of inter-agency working.

Jean Lave

Lave is a colleague of Rogoff and Cole. She took the same ideas about thinking and learning as a co-mediated activity in a slightly different direction. She was not a theorist of early childhood, as were most of the other people included in this chapter. But she was interested in describing the contexts in which learning takes place. Her catchphrases are 'situated learning' and 'communities of practice'. She thought learning in any situation was not only about the specific content of what was being learnt or taught, but also about the entire social situation in which that learning took place. So if there was a seminar for early childhood students about the work of Jean Lave, students would not only be learning about her work, but also what the lecturer thought about her, what fellow students thought about her, how those ideas fitted into other ideas being taught on the course, and how it fitted in with the experiences of practice the students already possessed. And so on. Nothing is learnt in isolation. She argued that 'learning is a process that takes place in a participatory framework, not in an individual mind. This means, amongst other things, it is mediated by differences of perspective amongst co-participants' (Lave and Wenger 1992: 15).

She studied a number of 'communities of practice'. She investigated, for instance, how supermarket butchers learnt their trade; and how people learnt to keep off alcohol. She argued that learning was a 'trajectory of participation'. As people joined the group or community of practice, they are apprentice learners. They copy some of the practices they see, but it is not until they have a comprehensive understanding of the processes in which they are involved, and they can perform their tasks without thinking, that they become full members of the community of practice. The community or group itself changes as new members join and old-timers retire. In modern management-speak, this might be called an organizational culture. New members of the organization tend to be regarded with caution, but gradually come to be accepted, and might eventually be in a position to make changes. Lave argued that it is only possible to understand the culture of an organization or a group by exploring their everyday practices in detail, that is, by *deconstructing* what they do and why they do it.

These views are so far away from those of Piaget that some developmental psychologists have found them hard to accept – or regard them as irrelevant. This perspective does not appear to allow for any differences in the way children learn from the way adults learn. Others have considered that Lave's ideas provide an interesting example into the way that, for example, schools work (or do not work) as places of learning.

These difficulties about incorporating ideas about culture into psychology, and overlaps with anthropology and psychology, are discussed further in Chapter 5.

Emotion and feelings

The great Viennese psychoanalyst Sigmund Freud, working in the first half of the twentieth century, claimed that emotional life and feeling were the core of human existence. Men and women might deny their emotions, or suppress them, but they inevitably shape our lives. The two most important emotions are love and hate; they are biological drives that we experience as feelings. Mostly these feelings are buried deep in our unconscious (the *id*). Most of us have developed an internal watchdog, our conscience, or in Freudian terms, the *superego*, to monitor our feelings and prevent them from breaking out and causing havoc. The rational, everyday self Freud calls the *ego*.

Freud was a psychiatrist. He developed his own case study method. This was a systematic way to explore people's feelings, even if they are long buried, by enabling them to explore their dreams and fantasies in a safe environment with a trained listener – a psychoanalyst.

Freud has inspired more followers and more interest in his theory of psychoanalysis than any other theorist, and in the middle of the last century most psychology drew heavily on his ideas. Susan Isaacs, for example, the British child development expert who founded one of the first departments of child development at a university (at the Institute of Education in London) eventually left her teaching and writing on child development to become a psychotherapist herself.

One of the most influential British psychotherapists was Melanie Klein (with whom Isaacs trained). Klein's view was that mother–infant relationships were very strong and powerful. Mothers had to tame the aggressive all-consuming passion of their infants. (Melanie Klein did not manage it herself, and her relationship with her daughter was always badly strained.) During the war, it became a common view – a common-sense theory – that aggression was a natural instinct which had to be controlled. The *British Medical Journal* declared in an editorial in 1944 that 'Destructive impulses let loose in war may serve to fan the flame of aggression natural to the nursery age' (cited in Riley 1983: 1).

Practitioners who learnt about child development, were, for a period, learning how children's emotions could best be channelled. For a long period in the 1970s and 1980s, psychology journals contained many studies of aggression, and whether daycare, in particular, made it worse. The history of childcare is discussed in Chapter 6, but in this section we consider the theme of emotionality and how it has been dealt with by child development theorists.

Wilfrid Bion

One of Melanie Klein's colleagues (and, famously, psychoanalyst to the playwright Samuel Beckett) was Wilfrid Bion. Although relatively little known outside of psychoanalytic circles, he has had a substantial influence, in the UK at least, in thinking about mothers and babies. His own experience of deep pain and distress in the First World War led him to hypothesize that infants experienced violent and ungovernable pain and despair. Mothers or carers act as a kind of container, soothingly, even absent-mindedly in a kind of 'reverie', containing their infants' acute anxiety and violent emotions until they run their course; and thus demonstrating to the infant that they are safe and nothing will happen to them. This acceptance and understanding of the depths of the infant's anxiety and emotional distress function as a kind of emotional regulation, enabling infants to gradually recognize and deal with their own emotions (Bion 1962). The training of psychotherapists working with disturbed children has been influenced by Bion's theories, and the journal *Infant Observation* features articles written within this psychoanalytic tradition.

Some psychoanalytically orientated feminists have criticized Bion and psychoanalytic theorists more generally for their emphasis on the role of mothers, and for pathologizing mother–infant relationships. Burman (2007), for example, offers a critique of the way in which the future emotional life of the infant is assumed to exclusively hinge on the 'well-balanced' mother's or carer's 'sensitivity'. Whether derived from Bion, or Bowlby – see below – it is certainly a widespread view in the literature on childcare, that childcarer sensitivity in a one-to-one relationship is a mark of 'quality' and a predictor of good outcomes (Belsky 2006). Burman and others have questioned this view as culturally specific. Apart from anything else, it reduces fathers, siblings and all other people to ciphers in the emotional life of the infant, a perspective certainly not borne out by anthropological studies, and contradicted to an extent by the work of Judy Dunn (see below) and others.

John Bowlby

John Bowlby was much better known than Bion, although perhaps less highly regarded in psychoanalytic circles. He was a psychiatrist based at the Tavistock Clinic in London. He was familiar with and influenced by Melanie Klein. Working for the World Health Organization after the war, he visited children in hospitals, nurseries and orphanages who had been separated from their parents, and was shocked by the fear, apathy and unhappiness of many of the refugee children he saw. As well as Melanie Klein, he had also been influenced by evolutionary biology and ideas about young animals needing the protection of their parents until old enough to fend for themselves. He concluded that a child was necessarily attached to a caregiver. It was a biologically based behaviour for self-protection. He put forward his theory of attachment – that children needed a warm continuous relationship with a mother figure and without it they would be emotionally damaged. Lack of mother love was likely to lead to children, boys especially, turning to aggression and delinquency in adolescence.

Bowlby's theory of attachment struck a chord in the public mind. After the disruption of the war years, traditional family life appealed to many people. His theory was widely (mis)interpreted to mean that mothers should stay at home with their young children. If they worked, they ran the risk of causing their children harm.

Bowlby's theory was more sophisticated than this. He argued that attachments went through several stages. First of all in pre-attachment phase, children just needed a caregiver to attend to their needs. They do not seem to notice or be concerned if the caregiver is unfamiliar. Gradually they begin to discriminate, and then, from about 6–8 months until about 18–24 months, they become firmly attached to one or two people and experience considerable anxiety when that person departs. Eventually mother and child establish a warm reciprocal relationship, where there is give and take.

Mary Ainsworth, a psychologist, systematically investigated the theory of attachment. She devised a test known as the strange situation test. A child plays with her mother in a strange room. Then the mother leaves and a stranger comes in. The child's reaction to the return of her mother is measured. There are three categories of reaction. An *anxious/avoidant* child does not take much notice of the stranger or of the mother when she returns. A *securely attached* child reacts positively to the stranger at first, but then cries and is upset when the mother leaves, and finally is comforted when she returns. An *anxious/resistant* child clings to her mother, is very upset when she leaves, and is not calmed when she returns. This test has been carried out with children in a number of countries. In some countries, for example, Guatemala, far fewer babies show separation anxiety, although researchers claim that the overall pattern is the same. Separation anxiety is at its most acute when the child is 10–12 months old; it then drops off. Separation anxiety is most extreme in those westernized countries where nuclear families are the norm. In more communal or collective societies it is far less acute.

This test would now be regarded as unethical. Any procedure which deliberately causes children distress should be avoided. Bowlby's theory is still a prominent one in some psychoanalytic circles, for example, at the Tavistock Clinic, but attention has switched to trying to understand the cognitive processes involved in babyhood, as the child learns to recognize her mother and gradually gains a sense of her own identity.

Sociobiologists (people who study social behaviour in animals) are also interested in attachment theory, as Bowlby originally was. Hrdy (1995) suggests that while Bowlby did an important job in stressing the vulnerability and dependency of very young infants, he was mistaken in supposing attachment was dyadic. There are many kinds of co-operative arrangements, or alloparenting, among primates. As Chapter 5 also shows, there are many kinds of childcare arrangements among humans.

Judy Dunn

Judy Dunn is an English psychologist who carried out a landmark study of very young children growing up in their families. She was interested in what happened when siblings came along. Would children get jealous? How would they respond? She observed the children within families and followed them up over a period of years. She concluded that even very young children were capable of sophisticated emotional responses and emotional manipulation. Young children's relationships were rich, complex and varied, and even those of siblings might differ markedly. There were marked and poignant differences between children: 'one child is happily a member of a circle of close companions; another has just one intense and close friendship; another is without friends' (Dunn 1993: 1).

In her book *Young Children's Close Relationships* (1993), in a series called 'Beyond Attachment', she suggests that theorizing about emotions and relationships has many gaps. Attachment theory was clearly inadequate. She suggested first of all that children are highly responsive to the quality of relationships and emotional exchanges within the family. They pick up tension, for example, or confidence or caution. They know when things are going wrong, even if they cannot voice their worries. Second, social competence is not general but person-specific. She argues that we should move away from a simple notion of a 'competent' or 'incompetent' child. Instead we should realize that competence depends on the company and the circumstances. Children behave differently towards different people, or even at different times towards the same people.

Methods for investigating children's emotionality and social relationships had to be devised *in situ*. These aspects of children's daily life could not be systematically investigated in a laboratory. But it is ethically problematical to be an observer in a family situation, and confidentiality is an issue. Dunn relied on controlled observations and interviews with parents for her data, explaining to them as she went along what she was doing and why.

She concluded that friendships are vital to children, not only for fun but also for fundamental social skills. Friendships can offer warmth and security, perspective taking, conflict resolution, moral understanding and a sense of self. Some young children have considerable powers of understanding, sensitivity and intimacy. Friends may quarrel more, but life with friends is more distinctive and more exciting.

> Friends can create a world of great involvement and high adventure, and they can do it at the tender age of 3 or 4. They must co-ordinate

their efforts with all the virtuosity of an accomplished jazz quartet, and they must manage the amount of conflict between them. These things require enormous social skills.

(1993: 3)

This does not sound at all like Piaget's egocentric child, who has to learn to share with others. Instead, Dunn concludes, children are emotionally aware, and understand the feelings of others:

Most children recognize and respond to the feelings of others and behave practically to improve or worsen other people's emotional state. They understand the connections between other's beliefs and desires and their behaviour. They have some grasp of what is appropriate moral behaviour for different relationships. Such sophistication means that even young children can be supportive, concerned, intimate and humorous with others – or they can be manipulative, devious, and teasing and deliberately upset others.

(1993: 109)

Other psychologists have studied children's friendships outside the family, in nurseries and schools. They have also concluded friendships are important. However, Dunn's point is that family is an incubator of emotions. Within the family, between parents and children, and between siblings, emotions are likely to be heightened. Social and emotional understanding (like the thinking and learning described by the cultural psychologists) is interactive. It does not lie within the individual; it is a product of the way in which people come together. Dunn and her colleagues, however, were investigating nuclear families, a Euro-American model of the family which is far from universal.

Her work is small-scale. It does not claim to offer a grand theory or to make predictions – but it is widely cited. Both the methodology and the conclusions have stimulated discussion about young children's capacities.

Howard Gardner

Howard Gardner is an American academic who has been concerned primarily with theories of intelligence. I include him in this section because he has developed the idea that some people have an aptitude to be sensitive to the feelings of others. They are emotionally gifted.

He theorized that instead of there being one kind of intelligence, usually defined as being able to do well at school, there were multiple intelligences. These are:

- *Linguistic intelligence* – being clever with words, finding just the right phrase to express yourself, quick to understand new meanings.
- *Musical intelligence* – sensitivity to pitch, tone and rhythm, able to play instruments or sing easily.
- *Logico-mathematical intelligence* – ability to engage in abstract reasoning and to do maths (Piaget's intelligence).
- *Spatial intelligence* – to see, remember and create visual images; to have a sense of space, distance and proportions.
- *Bodily–kinesthetic intelligence* – to move gracefully, to use your body expressively in dance or mime.
- *Personal intelligence* – to have an accurate sense of yourself, to be able to understand your own feelings and motives (sometimes called wisdom).
- *Social intelligence* – to understand the feelings and motives of other people.

Gardner has criticized schooling heavily because it has taken so little notice of psychological findings – including his own:

> Put 20 or more children of roughly the same age in a little room, confine them to desks, make them wait in line, make them behave. It is as if a secret committee, now lost to history, had made a study of children and, having figured out what the greatest number were least disposed to do, declared that all of them should do it.
>
> (Gardner 1993: 138)

His different kinds of intelligence are only schematized, although he does make various predictions and considers brain research will eventually substantiate the gist of his theory (but he may be over-optimistic – see Chapter 4). In reality, there is likely to be much more of a mixture of these aptitudes. They are a way of highlighting the great variety of human behaviour and the different values people hold. It is clear that in different societies or communities, different kinds of intelligence are valued. Euro-American societies (over)value linguistic and logico-mathematical intelligence. Other societies, for instance, some communities in northern India or West Africa, may value musical and kinaesthetic intelligence very highly, for example, the praise singers of Mali and Senegal. Robert Serpell has suggested that intelligence is defined in some African communities as learning how to be helpful to others; stupidity is being unhelpful. Pastoralist communities, who are constantly on the move, have a very finely tuned spatial intelligence. Young Inuit children in northern Canada, for example, can draw extremely accurate maps (Marshall 1940).

There have been some efforts by neurologists and psychologists to find which part of the brain, if any, can be linked to these different kinds of intelligence. The psychologist Daniel Goleman has written a popular book entitled *Emotional Intelligence* (1996). Getting on with other people, liking and being liked, are extremely important skills in almost every job. He considers that children can be taught to be more sensitive to others, but he also believes that the basis of emotionality is physiological. Joseph LeDoux, a neurologist, suggests that there is a part of our brain, deep inside the cortex, that regulates emotions. These claims for brain research are considered in Chapter 4.

Language

Language is what differentiates mankind from all other species. It is an extraordinary system of communication, making use of symbols – words – and a complex range of sounds. Societies have evolved many different languages. Each language uses a different set of symbols, stringing them together in different ways (grammar), and using different sound ranges (speech) and, for languages that are not oral, different signs on paper (writing).

If you compare the way people talk, even people who speak the same language and have the same accent, you can hear all kinds of variations. Speakers use different pitch, volume, tone quality, stress and patterns of breathing. Every language identifies a small number of distinctions in sound called *phonemes*. Some languages have as few as a dozen, none has more than 90. English has about 40 phonemes. The phonemes used for one language may be quite different in another, with little overlap. Some of the sounds we hear in English do not have a counterpart in, say, Chinese, which relies much more on tones and pitch. At birth, babies can respond to the entire range of phonemes, but fairly soon they learn to hear and reproduce only those of their own language. This is what makes second or third language learning so remarkable. Young children can learn two or more sets of phonemes, and never confuse them; and then match them to the vocabulary and grammar of the appropriate language.

Some languages have a high status. English is at the top of the pile. If you speak English, you can get by in most places in the world. It is an international language, the language of trade, diplomacy and academia. Other world languages are Arabic, Spanish, French, Portuguese, Chinese and Hindi. Other languages are at the bottom of the pile. For example, of the 50-plus languages spoken by the indigenous Indian peoples of Canada (now known as First Nations peoples), only two are expected to survive another generation – Ojibway and Cree (Abley 2003).

English speakers are under little pressure to learn other languages because they can get by in so many places. Other language speakers have as their starting point the need to recognize and speak several languages. In many ex-colonial countries, for example, children routinely speak three languages:

their mother tongue (that is, that of their village or community), the regional language they need when they move out of their village or small community, and the colonial language, which is the language of schooling. In Tanzania, for example, a child who comes from the Kilimanjaro area will first of all speak Chewa, the village language; then Swahili, the language of East Africa; and finally English. In ex-colonial countries, and in many European countries, most children are bilingual or trilingual.

As one Latin American writer put it, 'el monolingualismo es curable' – monolingualism is curable (cited in Burman 2007). It is worth bearing this in mind since much of the debate about language learning concerns English speakers, and assumes that they are monolingual. There are also relatively few studies of children who speak both high status and low status languages. It seems likely that the latter will almost always lose out.

Even though most studies of language learning have looked at an atypical group – monolingual English speakers – the phenomenon of language acquisition is startling. In a matter of a few years children acquire a remarkable number of words, and even more remarkably, know the rules for putting the words together – the grammar of the language. This is a skill of early childhood. Native speakers rarely get the pronunciation or the grammar of their language wrong. Yet adults learning a language, unless they are very talented or are used to learning languages, invariably make mistakes. How can children learn so much in such a short time, and why can adults not learn in the same way?

Children do not just learn a vocabulary. They learn that words are *symbols*. The word 'hot', for example, can refer to many different objects – a radiator, a saucepan, chips, water in the bath – and yet young children can grasp the concept of 'hotness'. Words refer to objects or to properties of objects, even when the object is not there. So the questions for language learning are, how do children discover what words mean?; how do they learn to arrange words and parts of words in a way that has meaning to others (grammar)?; and how do they do this twice or three times over, if they are bilingual or trilingual? These problems of language have not been solved. But as ever, there are many theories, and even more experiments and investigations into the minute details of language learning.

Behaviourism

Behaviourism, also known as *operant conditioning*, was a popular approach in the first half of the twentieth century. Its major theorists, John Watson and B.F. Skinner, believed that all behaviour is the result of instruction and imitation for which the learner gets systematically rewarded or punished. In other words, parents and other teachers are very clear indeed about what they consider to be good or useful behaviour and what they consider to be poor or pointless behaviour; they reward the good behaviour and correct the bad.

Most developmental psychologists now favour more interactionist approaches to understanding young children – as discussed in the previous sections. But behaviourist approaches are still used in some circumstances, for instance, in dealing with problematic behaviour in children. A major parenting programme in widespread use today, for example, is based on the idea that parents should consistently reward good behaviour with praise and consistently ignore bad behaviour, so that the child learns which behaviour is most appropriate (Webster-Stratton 2007).

Behaviourists considered that even the most complex activities, such as learning a language, could be explained by imitation and conditioning. So babies learn to talk by continually being talked to, and having their mistakes corrected. Like most theories, this one recognizes a partial truth: mothers usually do spend a lot of time with their children coaxing them to talk and structuring what they say. But children's language learning is so rapid that no one could ever talk to them enough to account for all the words and grammar they use. Experiments have shown that parents do not usually systematically correct their child's language; instead it is as if the language gradually slots into place. Children do not just learn to speak, they learn to generate language.

Noam Chomsky

Noam Chomsky is an American linguist. (He has a parallel life as a radical political theorist, for which he is still more widely known and respected.) He argued that language is so complex that it cannot be explained psychologically. Children do obviously acquire some of their verbal and non-verbal behaviour by casual observation and imitation of other adults and children, but their speech goes way beyond imitation. They produce sentences that nobody has heard before.

Chomsky argued that the capacity to understand and generate language is different from other behaviour. It cannot simply be learnt. The brain must be preprogrammed for language. Chomsky proposed that every child is born with a language decoder, what he called a *language acquisition device*, or LAD. This decoder enables children to recognize the underlying structure or grammar of any language they hear, no matter what the language. The experience of hearing a particular language triggers the decoder into action.

Chomsky's work has been to study *generative grammar*, that is, the rules that govern the way in which language is used:

> There must be some set of principles that we are capable of applying in novel situations – without limit . . . These principles have to be part of our nature, because there is no way to acquire them from experience . . . It also follows that they must be uniform.

> (Chomsky 2003: 41)

Chomsky has tried to describe the rules, but he did not go further than that. 'It is pretty abstract, because when you deal with anything as complex as human beings, you're always on the surface (2003: 41). Nevertheless his theory, like that of Gardner, has given rise to neurological and genetic research. Can LAD be discovered? Neurological studies seem to indicate that language ability is located in the left hemisphere of the brain. This is discussed more in the next chapter.

Interactionist views of language development

Neither the behaviourist nor the LAD explanation for language acquisition is entirely satisfactory. One is impossible (children learn from the examples in their environment) and the other is miraculous (our brains are wired up for language). Interactionists try to find a third way.

Bruner, for example, proposed, in a much quoted article, that language was neither

> the virtuoso cracking of a linguistic code, or the spinoff of ordinary cognitive development, [n]or the gradual take-over of adult's speech by the child through some impossible inductive tour de force. It is, rather, a subtle process by which adults artificially arrange the world so that the child can succeed culturally by doing what comes naturally, and with others similarly inclined.
>
> (1982: 15)

There are many interactionist perspectives. Most acknowledge that the brain has some sort of language decoder – although it is yet to be found – but are interested in the ways in which the environment influences language development. Interactionist research includes studies of deaf children; how teachers can shape language development; and, increasingly, bilingualism.

Summary

Child development is a sprawling discipline. It relies on a variety of methodologies and approaches. There are important theorists who have tried to redirect or rethink how we investigate young children and, as adults, relate to them. These theories have produced shifts in our understanding. But it is misleading to rely on them too much, or to foreground them in teaching. The bulk of the work in psychology is carried out by thousands of researchers beavering away at thousands of small (and not so small) experiments and observations to investigate young children's capacities, their behaviour and, increasingly, their views and opinions. Most of this work is written up in academic journals. It is an extremely complex field. This chapter has offered a few signposts.

Main messages from this chapter

1 Piaget was important but he has been superseded.
2 Learning is not a lonely activity but is inescapably social.
3 Feelings and attitudes are making a comeback; they may profoundly influence learning.
4 Language is at the heart of learning.

What to read next

Cole, M., Cole, S. and Lightfoot, C. (2006) *The Development of Children*, 5th edition. New York: W. H. Freeman.

Note

1 For a recent description of early education and care in the USA, see OECD (2000a).

4 Genes, Neurons and Ancestors

> The brain with which you are understanding my words is an array of some ten million kiloneurons. Many of these nerve cells have each more than a thousand 'electric wires' connecting them to other neurons. Moreover at the molecular genetic level, every single one of more than a trillion cells in the body contains about a thousand times as much precisely coded information as an entire computer.
>
> (Dawkins 1988: xiii)

The workings of human bodies – and almost all living creatures – are extraordinarily intricate and complex. We know a great deal about bodily processes and how the body develops, grows and ages. We know that it is possible to regulate and control those processes, with drugs and surgery and through the provision of more healthy and hygienic living and working arrangements. In the UK, there is an entire public service – the National Health Service – dedicated to these ends. And yet we do not understand even very basic biological processes of the human body. Despite recent progress in genetics and the neurosciences, there are still immense gaps in our knowledge. In addition, we do not understand, and do not conceptualize very well, the relationship between consciousness and the body. What is happening inside us and what is happening outside of us, and how are they connected? In particular, the brain is a great mystery. What is the relationship between the physical substance of the brain and the mental processes it supports?

Growth and maturation are influenced by diet, lifestyle and disease. The study of growth and maturation has been given new dimensions by recent medical research – for instance, embryology or molecular biology.

Biological maturational processes are uneven. Different systems of the body run on different timescales. When we speak of biological maturation we refer to a composite account of intricately related molecular machinery. Norms of maturation have to be continually updated as circumstances change, and new facts are discovered. For instance, children in rich countries are bigger than children in poor countries. Obesity in children is a major health problem. Bodily changes reflect nutritional environments. The body gets accustomed to different kinds of food, and then cannot cope easily with changes in diet. For example, nomadic groups in very cold countries such as northern Canada and Mongolia have fat-saturated diets that would kill people elsewhere. In Mongolia, nomads claim that they can tell where an animal came from the taste of its fat. An Inuit woman described to me how raw whale blubber is 'soul-food'. I tasted the rubbery fat but to me it was so nasty that it was impossible to imagine it as comfort food! Diet leads to distinctive and measurable changes in physique and well-being, but it is highly contextual.

The spread of new diseases such as HIV/AIDS affects morbidity rates (the death rates of the population). In some countries life expectancy has been reduced to 40 years or less. Similarly, changes in drug use seem to be leading to new reactive patterns to illness and disease. The emphasis on hygiene in the care of young children, and overuse of antibiotics and painkilling drugs, have probably resulted in children with less effective immune response systems and less resilience. A recent survey of mothers of 15-month-old children undertaken in London asked the question, 'Was your child on any kind of drugs last week?' It revealed that 50 per cent of the sample were given painkillers and 10 per cent were on antibiotics (Wiggins 2001, personal communication). In some other European countries – for example, France – reliance on pills and prescriptions is even higher.

Certain kinds of cells – embryonic stem cells – seem to be what drive biological change. They have unique regenerative functions – they can repair and refresh. Stem cell biology is prophesied to hold the key to ageing. Stem cells are those which appear to operate the triggers or controls for the growth, development and possibly the regeneration of different bodily systems. This process is at its most dramatic when babies are growing inside the womb. Embryology – the study of the way a foetus develops in the womb – is an important area of research. Study of embryonic growth may tell us why certain bodily organs can repair themselves or regrow after damage.

Molecular biologists are attempting to chart the extraordinary interactions between nano-particles of bodily proteins. Too tiny to investigate without sophisticated equipment, body proteins – the chemicals of which the body is made up – seem to combine and recombine in unique ways in each of us. The uniqueness of the way each body is constructed – and wears out – suggests that medical interventions need to be highly targeted. Each ill person may need a different combination of drugs and diet to deal with malfunctioning body parts. This is the next medical revolution.

Speaking of ages and stages in terms of biological maturation is to make crude assumptions about rates, sequences, sites and constancy of development. Charts of normal growth and development skip over or minimize enormous complexities and variations. Statistical norms constructed from large population samples may be useful for mapping gross abnormalities, but they do not tell us much more than this. Nevertheless, it may be helpful, in treatment terms, to know about certain abnormalities in given populations, for example, defects of vision or hearing or thyroid deficiencies. Children's growth and bodily development are matched against population percentiles in order to decide whether those who lie outside the range of what is normal need medical treatment. About 6 per cent of children are likely to have some kind of problem. Clinical check-ups or follow-ups for young children are a good idea in case there are conditions that can be picked up and treated. But not all abnormalities can be treated or corrected, and, as the biologist Steven Jay Gould (2000) has pointed out, there are always inherent problems in trying to define what is normal. Definitions of normality easily slip over into racist eugenics.

In any case, an overview of these biological maturation processes would still beg the question of whether or not what happens in the body can ever explain or predict behaviour. On the one hand, certain psychological theories, such as those of Gardner and Chomsky, seem to beg the question about neurological underpinning. On the other hand, many psychologists are wary of using biological growth as a metaphor to explain the development of learning and behaviour in children. This is not only because of the inherent difficulties in understanding biology, but also because of the value judgements implicit in describing behaviour. As the psychologist Jerome Kagan put it: 'All societies invent categories that simultaneously describe and explain the 10–20% of children whose profile of behavioural accomplishments is least pleasing (1998: 13).

This chapter focuses on how information from the biological sciences is sifted and used to explain or justify ways of understanding and working with young children. The field of cognitive psychology, for example, is increasingly predicated on the neurosciences and understandings about brain functioning. Genetics is used to describe behaviour, for example, as an explanation of why people are obese (a genetic predisposition to eat too much). Evolutionary psychology speculates about the operation of genetic inheritance and its modifications. These relatively new areas of work, genetics, neurosciences and evolutionary psychology, and what we claim they teach us, are discussed here.

Genes

DNA

Genes are made up of microscopic amounts of four chemicals, adenine, cytosine, guanine and thymine (coded A, C, G and T), which appear in long and varying sequences of several hundred repeated patterns in each gene. There are approximately 30,000 genes in the human body, arranged into 23 pairs of chromosomes held together on a chain of sugar and phosphate. The genes and the chain on which they are distributed are called collectively the DNA. The DNA was referred to by its discoverers as the double helix, because it formed a chain which appeared to loop back on itself.

Most cells in the human body contain DNA in their nucleus. Each DNA forms a unique pattern. This uniqueness, coded in the cells of the body, has enabled forensic scientists, for example, to track down criminals on the basis of a scrap of skin tissue or a strand of hair.

The DNA is reformed with each new individual. The mother's and father's DNA combine at conception. Some of the genes which are inherited from parents are dominant, and manifest themselves in the new individual; others are recessive and are not apparent. Although recessive genes stay on in the DNA, they do not get activated unless two individuals with the same recessive genes conceive. In this case, because there is no dominant gene, their child may display the recessive gene. Some well-known conditions, such as haemophilia, are carried on recessive genes. These genetic inheritance patterns were discovered by the scientist Gregor Mendel in the nineteenth century, but it is only very recently that the importance of his findings about genetic inheritance has been understood.

Cells replace themselves continuously – no part of your body is older than ten years. The DNA contains genetic instructions for replication, so that each new cell that is created will contain the same genetic information – although as we age there is wear and tear on the DNA. The genetic information may become distorted and variations or mistakes occur. Some genes appear to act as housekeepers. These repair and maintenance genes switch on chemicals designed to correct, compensate for, or eliminate mistakes. With age, as the DNA becomes slightly more unstable, the 'housekeeper' genes are busier and may themselves fail to work. Cancer is an indication that the housekeeper genes are not working properly at their job of clearing the body of damage. Where there is a malformation in a particular gene, the instructions to replicate itself may be damaged, so it reproduces more damaged genes. (Genetic damage could, of course, be environmentally caused, for instance, by a virus or radiation.)

Gene malformation may have all sorts of knock-on effects on other genes. It should trigger the housekeeper genes, provided they too have not retired. For example, some work on cancer is now focusing on one such housekeeper gene, called Tp53, on chromosome 17, which appears to deliver a chemical 'suicide pill' to cells which have mutated. If Tp53 is itself damaged, then the mutated cells continue to develop, that is, the cancer grows. The HIV/AIDs virus is an example of an environmental cause that appears to target the housekeeper genes.

Genetic engineering or manipulation relies on the repair and maintenance functions of genes. In 1968, scientists investigating bacteria discovered

Figure 4.1 The double helix, a diagram of the structure of human genetic inheritance. From Dennis and Gallagher (2001).

'restriction enzymes'. The job of these enzymes is to cut out strands of DNA when they encounter particular sequences of the chemical letters that signify that some damage has occurred. But there is also an enzyme, called ligase, which mends or stitches together loose or damaged bits of DNA. These mechanisms, restriction enzymes and ligase, are, very roughly, the basis of genetic engineering. Scientists use the restriction enzymes to cut out bits of the DNA, and then use ligase to splice them together again.

Genetic engineering raises all kinds of ethical problems (not least the huge profits which biotechnology companies might make if gene therapy proved effective). Most countries have strict ethical guidelines concerning genetic research with humans. The limited application to humans in the treatment of certain genetic diseases has not yet proved very successful, partly because of the enormous complexity of the human body. But there have been experiments with genetically modified animals, for example, mice and monkeys, resulting in the creation of 'transgenic' animals. Techniques for genetically modifying plants are commonplace because plants are much easier to reproduce. According to the campaigning organization Genewatch UK, 60 per cent of all seeds sold commercially are now genetically modified.

The Genome Project

Most of the work on genes has been done on fruit flies and other creatures that reproduce very quickly. Some of it has been done on the great apes, with whom we share 98 per cent of our genes. For obvious ethical reasons, less has been done on humans. But the new techniques for extracting and analysing DNA, developed in the course of work on bacteria, fruit flies, and other plants and animals, have meant that it has become possible to isolate human genes and analyse them in greater detail. The Genome Project, described very well by the scientific journalist Matt Ridley (1999), is an attempt to map all the genes on the human body, to identify them and show where they are located on the chromosomes. This project was completed in 2000, but it raises more mysteries than it solves. It has been described as being like a list of all the parts for a Boeing 747, down to the nuts, bolts and washers, with no idea about how the parts fit together and no understanding of the principles of flight.

The genome blueprint, then, does not tell us much. Some genes seem to have no obvious purpose. The precise function of most genes, and even more importantly how the genes interrelate with one another and with the environment, are not really understood. Genes operate digitally; they switch on and off, and trigger other genes to do the same, in immensely complex and little-understood patterns. There is a great deal of apparent overlap and redundancy and what appears to be junk information or spam.

Some people have argued that in order to understand the genome, it is necessary to take an evolutionary approach. Charles Darwin, the nineteenth-century scientist, in his book *The Origin of the Species*, suggests that evolution occurs through the slow adaptation of species to their environment over hundreds of thousands of years. Stephen Jay Gould coined the phrase 'deep time and endless motion' to describe the immense timespan and infinitesimal nature of these changes. All the time, species reproduce, and, in reproducing, small variations occur. Change is ceaseless. The most successful new individuals survive, prosper and reproduce. The least successful die out. If there are extraterrestrial events such as a meteoric impact, or even if there are local microclimatic changes, the species which survive are those that best adapt to the new environmental circumstances. Successful individuals then pass on their genes to the next generation. This is popularly called 'natural selection' and 'the survival of the fittest'.

Through this process of slow modification, human beings evolved. Descended from ape-like ancestors, we share a single common ancestor with all other living things on Earth. This common ancestor, the first living thing, lived about 4 billion years ago. It was very simple. About 600 million years ago the first multicellular organisms began to appear in the sea. Then land-dwelling creatures emerged about 500 million years ago. The first primates appeared 55 million years ago.

Figure 4.2 This diagram of the patterning of a human genome shows how complicated it is to decipher or decode genetic information. No one is really sure what these sequences signify. From Dennis and Gallagher (2001: 25) (Sanger Centre/Wellcome Photo Library).

Darwin did not know about genetics, but like Chomsky hypothesizing about language decoders, Darwin speculated that genes must exist. The geneticist Steve Jones (1999) in his book *Almost Like a Whale*, has attempted to use genetic information from the twentieth century to illustrate and elaborate Darwin's theory, which was drawn up in the nineteenth century. Darwin's theory does indeed fit very neatly with twentieth-century genetics. On the one hand, genetics supports Darwin's speculation about the gradual changes in species, and the way in which new variations and species occur through spontaneous variations in the genes and through the recombinations of reproduction. On the other hand, the theory of evolution explains the curious composition of the genome, and the fact that there is so much overlap between the human genome and that of other species. The human genome contains in itself the history of the evolution of the human species:

> DNA provides millions of links to the past some of which have revealed unexpected patterns . . . Man and pig, or man and cow, share

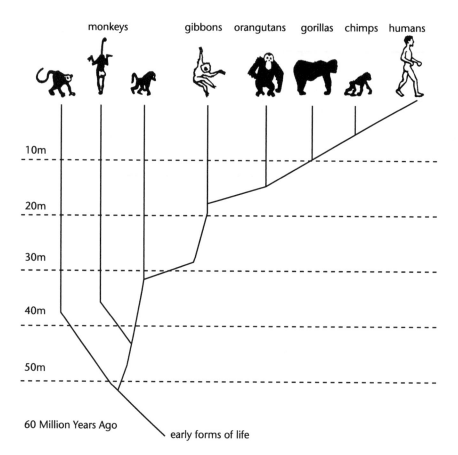

Figure 4.3 This simple evolutionary chart gives an idea of the timescale for human evolution. Evolutionary psychologists are concerned with the last 10 million years of human evolution.

more than fifty long sequences [of DNA] ... The genes of many creatures have been read end to end. They reveal groups within groups beyond the imagination of earlier naturalists. Thirty thousand genes have been located in humans, almost as many in mice. PIG-MAP, the cartography of swine is up to 600 or so ... A tiny nematode worm, the only animal to have had all its DNA letters read, has nineteen thousand and ninety-nine genes altogether ... Several bacteria and single cell parasites have also been deciphered.

Their landscapes have much in common. Whole sections are the same in mice and men, and two thousand human genes have exact homologues in mice. A trudge along the DNA shows more than half of a certain mouse chromosome to be more or less identical in the arrangement of one of our own; and cows are even more like us. Half of all plant genes have a mouse equivalent. The nematode worm shares a fifth of its own heritage with yeast (from which it split a billion years ago) . . . A gene that in humans causes an inherited disorder of the nervous system has an exact match in yeast (which has no nerves at all).

(Jones 1999: 304)

Our genes therefore have accumulated, developed – and survived – over an unimaginable timespan. Some of the common ancestors from which we evolved have left their genetic mark on us, as on other branches of their descendants. And yet, despite knowing so much, we know very little. While much of this genetic information is documented, much remains to be decoded. Are all the junk sequences in the genes, which appear meaningless and which have no obvious purpose, really junk? How do the genes programme the body into action?

The next stage of the Genome Project is called the *proteome* project. This is nano-technology at the frontiers of science. This stage of understanding genetics involves much greater molecular analysis of how genes produce the proteins that make our bodies, the science of 'proteomics'. The aim is to produce miniature machines, on a nano-scale, capable of swimming through our bodies to dispense drugs or perform micro-engineering works on targeted cells. Like atomic physics, this is the stuff of science fiction.

Genetic research consumes an enormous amount of time, energy and money. Some scientists argue that the results are not worth it. They distort our understanding and divert resources away from more practical research on killer illnesses such as malaria. David Horrobin (2003) reviewing the evidence in the *Guardian* newspaper, claims that 'the idea that genomics is going to make a major contribution to human health in the near future is laughable' (*Guardian* Comment: 12 February 2003). So although the tabloids come up with sensational headlines about genetic research – 'gene for obesity discovered', 'aggression – it's all in the genes' – genetics, as yet, does not tell us very much about behaviour.

The big (and unanswered) questions in genetic research could be summarized as follows:

- Where do our genes come from?
- How do genetic blueprints affect everyday bodily processes?
- How do we interpret the effects of apparently redundant genetic material?
- How are genes related to behaviour?
- Should ethical considerations govern gene experimentation and manipulation?

Evolutionary psychology

Genetic research has spawned an industry of sub-disciplines. Sociobiologists explore how genes might predict behaviour. Evolutionary psychology argues the other way around: that certain behaviour patterns have only come about because of natural selection and genetic inheritance. Since these behaviour patterns emerged in response to certain environments, then understanding what environments may have been like in the past can tell us something about the origins and persistence of behaviour patterns now.

John Tooby and Leda Cosmides are two psychologists who are credited with 'inventing' evolutionary psychology. As well as the genetic research and theories of evolution, they drew on some of the findings of the neurosciences and cognitive psychology (see below) to argue that the mind is made up of lots of different systems. Each subsystem evolved in response to certain evolutionary pressures. Cosmides argued, in a now famous analogy, that the mind is like a Swiss Army knife. Like the knife, which has lots of gadgets to deal with lots of different tasks – corkscrew, tin-opener, file, scissors, and so on – the brain has lots of intellectual gadgets which have been added through natural selection. Tooby and Cosmides believe these modular brain functions have evolved in order to deal with specific environmental problems. (cited in Evans and Zarate 1999.)

The two authors hypothesize that the first humans were hunter–gatherers living in small groups in the African savannahs. They argue that these early groups of humans interacted closely with their physical and animal environment. They organized themselves into small and mobile groups of hunter–gatherers. Their dietary and work patterns created ecological and evolutionary characteristics that are still present today. For example, they ate as much as they could when the food was available, and ate very little when it was not. This pattern of eating does not work in today's (rich) world of plenty when food is always available, so that there is a temptation to gorge all the time. Understanding these early origins, Tooby and Cosmides suggest, will help us understand our behaviour in the present.

Cosmides and Tooby claim that ultimately all behaviour will be traced to genetic programming of the brain, and theorizing about such behaviour patterns now will throw new light on genetic research. The evolutionary adaptations they identified in early human communities included dealing with such problems as:

- avoiding predators (learning how to avoid danger, fighting or flight);
- eating the right foods (finding high-fuel foods such as fat and sugar; disgust with rotten foods; eating as much as possible when food was available);

- forming alliances and friendships (living socially and in groups in order to maximize defence against predators);
- reading other people's minds (predicting and controlling behaviour);
- communicating with other people (signalling danger, improving cooperation, using language);
- selecting mates (finding people with good genes, avoiding those with bad genes);
- providing help to children and other relatives (enabling the gene pool to survive, rearing children, parenting).

It is these last two, the emphasis on distinctive, and essentially unchangeable, behaviour patterns for men and women, that have been most controversial. Men and women, the evolutionary psychologists claim, have distinctive adaptive behaviours. Men can spread their sperm (genes) without great effort and their best reproductive strategy is to have as many partners as possible. Female reproduction requires much more time and effort, and it is in women's interest to secure the attention and protective care of one male. Women therefore have had to develop strategies to ensnare men, and to ensure their investment in bringing up children. Women are more cautious than men in consenting to sex, and spend more time on their appearance. They are attracted to older men who have more resources. Men, on the other hand, prefer younger women, who have more reproductive capacity. Women are more likely to be jealous than men, in order to make sure they do not stray. Women's natural abilities will lead them to prefer childcare to work outside the home. And so on. What in other circumstances might be regarded as the most outrageous sexism has found an academic respectability in evolutionary psychology. The sociobiologist Sarah Hrdy (1995, 2005) has fairly neatly provided evidence to dismiss these speculations. In her study of neonates in the great apes species, she suggested that females acting together co-operatively guaranteed an infant's best chance of survival. In the groups she observed, there were always extra females – aunts and grandmas – to help out with childrearing. As she put it '*the window for bonding is fairly open-ended*' (1999: 538). She argues that this co-operative care, or alloparenting (the technical name for it) is not only essential for survival, but can explain the long period of childhood dependency. The notion of male–female pairing is, in this scheme of things, relatively unimportant compared with female cooperation!

Bogin has attempted to summarize the evolution of childhood, that is, the gradual adaptations of genetic inheritance that makes childhood a good strategy for survival of the species. He hypothesizes that the smallness of infants and their relatively slow rate of bodily growth (relative to other mammalian offspring) confer advantages in feeding and babysitting. Children are easier to feed, consume less, and can be looked after by people other than their parents, yet have the long childhood they need to maximize the plasticity of their brains and learn about their environment:

> The five themes of childhood (feeding, nurturing, low cost, babysitting and plasticity) account for much of the evolution of and pattern of growth of our species. Understanding these themes helps resolve the paradox of human growth and evolution: lengthy development and low fertility.
>
> (Bogin 1998: 37)

I have summarized these evolutionary ideas very briefly indeed. Since these ideas are in themselves offered at a broad level of generality, these summaries may appear rather crude. Critics such as Steven and Hilary Rose (2000) consider these evolutionary explanations to be absurd. However, such ideas have been considerably elaborated in many papers and books by evolutionary psychologists and their close ideological cousins, the sociobiologists. The sociobiologists are powerful popularizers. Perhaps the most well known is the American E. O. Wilson, who has written a series of books, including *Consilience: The Unity of Knowledge* (1998). He argues too that human nature and human behaviour are governed by the evolutionary process of natural selection. In his view, all individual and cultural practices are governed by the impulse to get a Darwinian advantage for our genes. Natural selection shapes our behaviour, moral impulses and cultural norms. The way we feel about each other, the basic things we think about each other and say to one another are with us today by virtue of their past contribution to genetic fitness.

Richard Dawkins, the English sociobiologist, took the arguments still further in his book *The Selfish Gene* (1976). His claim is that all life, and all explanations about life, are ultimately about the replication of genes. He and a number of other writers have speculated about cultural units, called 'memes', which mirror the action of the genes. Memes include catchphrases, tunes, clothes fashions, stiletto heels, and so on. Precise predictions about human behaviour will be possible when we know still more about the composition of genes and can link them up with 'memes'. If we know that certain genetic malformations cause well-known diseases such as cystic fibrosis or sickle cell anaemia, then surely it cannot be long before we discover the gene for lying or the gene for flirting.

These reductionist arguments, that everything can in the end be explained by the genes, have also been adopted by some prominent writers in the field of child development. The American psychologist Sandra Scarr argued in her presidential address to the US Child Development Society in 1992 that children's development could only properly be understood in an evolutionary perspective. Genetic inheritance crucially shapes each child's life, and individuality can only be interpreted in terms of the reactions of genes to 'culture'.

Like the evolutionary psychologists, Scarr regards genetics as unproblematical. In her view, the genes clearly determine more than 50 per cent of human behaviour, and it is only a matter of time before we understand the genetics involved. Her view is that we are pussyfooting if we pretend otherwise. (She also regards culture as easily described and assigned, an issue we return to in Chapter 6.)

The implication of saying that 'it's all in the genes' is that the environment in which children are raised is of relatively minor importance. At its most extreme, this argument has been used to justify neo-liberal economics. The poor are born to be poor and will stay poor whatever you do, and the rich are born to be rich and will become rich whatever you do. The economic marketplace is no more than a reflection of the biological survival of the fittest. Scarr's claims are along these lines. She regards most forms of childcare as 'good enough'. She claims that only in extreme cases is childcare likely to have very harmful or very positive effects on children. (In the absence of any systematic state funding for childcare in the USA the only regulated or funded childcare programmes tend to be early intervention programmes targeting very deprived communities – like Sure Start in the UK.) The debate Scarr provoked has focused a great deal on such early intervention programmes. Her critics argue that she is mistaken in relying so heavily on genetic evidence and evolutionary psychology, and even if she has not said so directly, her position supports the view that it is not worth intervening in poor communities with early childhood programmes. (This argument about intervention takes a different twist where neuroscientific evidence is concerned, as we shall see.)

The argument that 'it's all in the genes' does not mean, in the eyes of the sociobiologists and evolutionary psychologists, that we cannot or should not interfere with or manipulate the genes. The biological determinist argument that our genes control us is ironic, since we are also hoping to control our genes with scientific technology. If genes exist for criminality or other anti-social traits, gene therapy might be more effective than any other kind of intervention such as special schooling or prison. It has even been suggested that there is a gene for homosexuality, which has caused great concern among gay and lesbian communities because of the ethical implications of gene therapy.

> On the one hand . . . our biology is our destiny, written in our genes by the shaping forces of human evolution through natural selection and random mutation. This biological fatalism is opposed by Promethean claims that biotechnology, in the form of genetic engineering, can manipulate our genes in such a way as to rescue us from the worst of our fates. It offers to eliminate illness, prolong life, grant our children enhanced intelligence and better looks – a cornucopia of

technological goodies undreamed of even in the science fiction of prior generations.

(Rose and Rose 2000: 4)

Aldous Huxley in his novel *Brave New World* described a society where some people – the alphas – are bred to be clever, and others – the betas and the gammas – are bred to be drones. It may be a long way off, but it is no longer an impossible scenario. Genetic manipulation and modification, and cloning, are *already* taking place. The sociobiologists and evolutionary psychologists argue that genetic evolution could be used to understand, predict and control behaviour. In fact, Leonidas has claimed that, in the future, evolutionary psychology will replace or overtake other forms of psychology. (cited in Evans and Zarate 1999.)

The brazenness of some of these claims, especially those relating to the behaviour of men and women, and to 'memes' or 'cultural units of transmission' have sparked a considerable scientific debate. The arguments against using genetics and evolutionary psychology to explain behaviour can be summarized as follows:

- Genetic information is extremely complex. The biochemical processes involved cannot be translated into behaviour patterns except in the most extreme cases (such as Huntington's chorea, a degeneration of the nervous system that strikes in middle age or earlier).
- Darwin's theory of evolution put forward the survival of the fittest as an important, but not the only, mechanism to explain how humans evolved. Later writers have emphasized the random nature of many genetic changes, and the importance of major changes in the environment in skewing evolution.
- Human beings are so clever and competent that they can largely override their genetic inheritance. Children can, through learning, acquire all sorts of characteristics from their parents and other children and adults, without waiting for the generations-long process of translation into the genes.
- Evolutionary theories are too vague because they are based on speculation about human ancestry for which there is little or no direct evidence.

Ultimately, the argument revolves around scientific understanding and methodology. As we saw in Chapter 2, scientific theories deal with certainties, concrete phenomena that can be isolated and independently investigated, by a neutral scientist. Traditional scientific explanation is regarded as more robust and more predictive than any other type of explanation. Wilson even claims that we are programmed to adopt the scientific, atomistic model of thinking by our genes:

The descent to minutissima, the search for ultimate smallness in entities such as electrons, is a driving impulse of Western natural science. It is a kind of instinct. Human beings are obsessed with building blocks, forever pulling them apart and putting them back together again.

(Wilson 1998: 53)

This traditional model of scientific investigation may need considerable modification when applied to the human sciences. Dawkins' idea of a 'meme' or 'cultural unit of transmission' or 'particles of culture' is an attempt to atomize culture and provide a 'scientific' explanation for it. Mary Midgley (1998), a philosopher who has tried to address the issue of explanatory models in the sciences, argues that thought and behaviour cannot be meaningfully broken down into particles. They are more akin to ocean currents or wind force, where the overall pattern and context offer clues to understanding, rather than the miniscule constituent parts. The arguments about scientific modelling and Darwinism climax with brain research. Trying to understand how the brain works raises all the problems discussed above all over again with added emphasis.

The neurosciences

Neuroscience, that is, the study of how the brain works, is an umbrella word which covers all kinds of disciplines and technologies. There is neuro-anatomy, neurobiology, neurochemistry, neuroendocrinology, neurophysiology, neuro-pharmacology, neuropsychiatry, neurosurgery, and so on. It is clear that there have been remarkable advances in neuroscience in the past two decades and in particular in the past five years. The afterlife of a scientific finding is cynically reckoned to be about seven years; after that, unless it is exceptional, it is out of date. In philosophy, ideas are still worth considering after two thousand years; but in experimental psychology anything over ten years is beginning to look dated, and in brain research, as in computing, if it was published last year it may well have been refuted or overtaken. The USA declared that the 1990s were the decade of the brain. Conventions on neuroscience attract not a mere 400, but 27,000 delegates.

What the brain is made of

The human brain is one of the most complicated structures in the universe. It appears to be organized in sections, and certain parts of the brain seem to be associated with language, seeing, hearing, and so on. But only very approximately! If there is damage to the brain, either at birth or subsequently, other parts of the brain may take over (Johnson 1999). The brain seems to be individually 'sculpted', that is, each person's brain develops in response to what happens in the environment, nutritionally and cognitively. The brain also responds to the maturation of other parts of the body, for example, to the production of hormones. But whatever the processes are, they have proved far too complicated to unravel, and there are those who think that understanding the brain may be beyond the capacity of humankind.

The brain is made up of around 100 billion nerve cells, or neurons, and around the same number of glial cells, which are the supporting and nourishing elements of the brain. About half of the neurons are located in the cerebral cortex, an intricately woven tissue folded into six layers. Neurons vary in appearance. 'There are long thin neurons that send single snaking tendrils to the far reaches of the body; star-shaped ones that reach out in all directions; and ones that bear a dense branching crown like absurdly overgrown antlers' (Carter, quoted in Meade 2001: 4).

The functioning of the brain involves the flow of information through elaborate circuits consisting of networks of neurons. There is a microscopic gap in the junctions between the axon of one neuron and the dendrites of another. Information must cross these gaps via hook-ups called synapses. Each neuron may have between a few thousand and up to 100,000 synaptic connections.

Communication between neurons involves both chemical and electrical signalling. There are other electrical junctions for communication between glia and between neurons and glia. No computer has ever come anywhere near the complexity, precision or speed that characterizes the human brain.

Some of the research on the development of the brain comes from embryology. We know that at the same time as the synapses are being connected up,

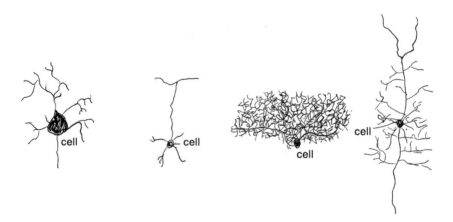

Figure 4.4   There are many different types of neural cells. This is an example of some characteristic shapes.

| 1 month | 3 months | 6 months | 15 months |

Figure 4.5   The connections between neurons develop rapidly after birth. This is a picture drawn from photomicrographs of infant brain tissue. Even so, it is only schematic, and not from one infant.

the axons or connections become protected or myelinated. Myelination is the laying down of a fatty sheath which insulates axons and reduces muddled connections, in order to speed information flows.

During foetal growth, neural cells divide at a phenomenal rate. Neural proliferation continues after birth, but at some point the instruction to proliferate is switched off – sometime in the late teens. At birth, a baby has billions of neurons. Many will be discarded and die off. Nature frequently overprovides and selects out. Redundancy appears to be a protective survival technique.

Each neuron is bathed in a continually changing chemical environment of neurotransmitters, neuromodulators and hormones, called neuroproteins. About 30,000 different proteins affect the neurons. Neurons react differently to these proteins. Some are profoundly changed; others may be washed with a potent sauce of aminoacids and yet be unaltered or unaffected. Some neurotransmitters act extremely fast, as superconductors; others have a modulatory or inhibitory effect. Understanding the effects of drugs on emotions and cognition may provide more information about the chemical architecture of the brain. But the starting point of investigation is that the biochemical processes involved in the brain are unimaginably complex.

Investigating the brain

A major difficulty in investigating the human brain is accessing it. The neuroscientist Steven Rose describes the struggle to *begin* to understand how the brain works. He discusses the methods and experiments needed to find out more about the brain, and the proteins that affect it, in his very readable book *The Making of Memory* (2003). (In this book he also dwells on the difficulties of reconciling subjective individual experience and memory with objective chemical experiments on the brains of chickens.) Genetic inheritance can be investigated without too much damaging bodily intrusion. The brain cannot.

Until relatively recently, neuroscientists were highly dependent on three sources, all of which had grave limitations from the point of view of understanding the relationship between brain and behaviour. First, they were dependent on animal studies – prodding or excising the brain tissues of partially electrocuted rats or kittens or squid or some other vivisected creature. Second, information comes from autopsies, from examination of the brain tissues of the dead. Embryos have been a very useful – but for many, ethically problematical – source for analysing the stages of development of the brain. Third, neuroscientists have relied on studies of brain-damaged patients. But there are also great difficulties inferring brain function from brain-damaged patients – it is like trying to explain how tennis is played from watching the actions of a blind one-legged man.

New non-invasive techniques are being developed which rely on measurements somewhat similar to electroencephalograms (EEGs) that measure electrical activity in the brain. There are surges of activity in the brain as we think or act, which are expressed in metabolic changes. Unlike EEGs, new techniques can measure not merely the level of activity, but also its location within the brain. So, for example, if you recite a poem, you might get one pattern showing up in your brain; if you gobble down a cake you may get another.

There are basically three types of metabolic imaging:

- Regional cerebral blood flow (rCBF), in which an inert radioactive gas dissolved in blood indicates where blood flow has increased.
- Positron emission tomography (PET), where the radioactive analogue of glucose, or sugar, is injected into the blood to measure cumulative metabolism in different brain regions.
- Magnetic resonance imaging (MRI), which uses the response of water molecules within the brain to changes in the level of brain activity.

All these imaging techniques are extremely expensive to use. Such scanning techniques can only be used in laboratory settings, and they usually require subjects to keep very still. New techniques of brain imaging are constantly being tried, and the imaging machinery is rapidly becoming more sophisticated and more widely available. But even so, the information gained is rudimentary. The coloured blobs of the PET scan each represent assemblies of millions of cells or neurons.

Cognitive psychologists are teaming up with neurologists to use and develop these techniques. Systematic testing of children with brain disorders suggests that children use a variety of learning strategies, some of which were of use in circumventing their disability, some not. Studies suggest that infant learning strategies, and the learning which ensues, develop very gradually and in response to environmental stimuli. The brain appears to be very flexible, rather than preprogrammed for modularity as the evolutionary psychologists suggest. However, tests on very young children also raise ethical issues. Ethical guidelines exist but some query whether they are sufficient.

Theories about the brain

Despite all this intense research, the brain is so very complex that our knowledge, despite constant new technologies, is rudimentary and highly conjectural. No one has any kind of overall theory about how the brain works. So it is hardly surprising that, as yet, neuroscience does not add up to a coherent explanation of how we think and become the way we are.

> Studying the brain and its activity is possible at many levels, from that of the output of the entire system to that of isolated receptor proteins . . . yet many of [these] subdisciplines continue to churn out results relatively uninfluenced by . . . those working in adjacent parts of the field . . . We have masses of data and lots of limited theories . . . but we still lack any grand unified conception of what it means to be a brain and how it does what it does.
>
> (Rose 1999: 5)

Brains do many things at a time and with incredible rapidity. Despite Rose's caution about there being no overall theory of brain functioning, some popular writers on the neurosciences have made big theoretical leaps.

For the evolutionary psychologists, the most powerful evidence of the genetic preprogramming of the brain into modules is demonstrated by 'the language instinct'. Steven Pinker takes Chomsky further than he himself wanted to go. In two influential and popular books, *The Language Instinct* and *How the Mind Works*, Pinker (1995, 1998) claims that humans have a language instinct, and are preprogrammed to learn language. Pinker argues that there is no way babies can infer grammar, that is, the rules of language, from the number of words that are spoken to them, yet all babies learn to speak their language grammatically. Therefore, Pinker says, a baby's brain is preprogrammed to learn a language, and once language is learnt, then in some way the preprogramming switches off; it becomes much more difficult to learn a second or third language as we get older. The development of language in very young children is taken as evidence that the first three years are so important.

Computer modelling has been another source of theories about brain functioning. The metaphor of the computer as a brain is a powerful one. Science fiction has always assumed that computers will eventually be programmed to act like humans. Brain modelling has turned out to be more difficult in real life. Deep Blue, the chess computer, is capable of evaluating 200 moves per second, and can beat ordinary chess players, but still gets beaten by the great chess grandmasters, whose human tactics outwit it. (In a legendary and disputed game Deep Blue did once beat the World Chess Champion Gary Kasparov in 1997.) But the most recent research on computer modelling suggests that if one abandons the supposition that human brains are merely extremely powerful data storage and processing machines, but work, for example, like neural nets, sifting and hierarchically ordering and recoding information, then better approximations of human brain activity can be developed.

This theory about neural nets has been developed by the evolutionary neuroscientist Terrence Deacon. Deacon hypothesizes that, as a baby grows, her brain develops a whole series of nets or sieves to sift through incoming information. At first the net is so coarse, it catches only the most obvious features of this information; then quite rapidly the nets get finer and finer. He says that because babies know so little, and have no words, they have to scan the incoming information for landmarks and signs, and grammar offers such landmarks. So if you take the phrase, 'give the cup back to mummy', a baby might take some time to recognize words like 'give' and 'cup' and 'to' and 'mummy' and she will recognize first of all that there is an invariant pattern to the order of these words. It is rather like learning a tune; you can follow the tune before you pick out the individual notes – and the individual notes on their own mean very little without the tune.

Different languages have different grammatical patterns and these are what a baby picks up first of all in learning how to understand what people say to her. Deacon's ideas about language acquisition seem to be borne out by various computer modelling experiments. Computers cannot learn the rules of grammar from simply storing all the data that comes in and trying to analyse it. It is not logically possible. Human learning is simply not cumulative, least of all a baby's learning. But if the computer is programmed differently, as a kind of neural net, to pick up certain patterns, then, with great difficulty, it can learn grammar.

As the neural nets get finer, and the baby begins to sift out words, then this ability to pick up grammar is lost; the signposts are already in place, they form the layout of the next, finer neural net, and the baby's brain will now scan for more detailed information about words and meanings. This theory would explain why young children can learn languages easily and adults cannot. Language is the first and most special example of learning, and the symbols and meanings language gives us enables us, with enormous flexibility, to develop, continue and accelerate these processes – the coding, refining, sifting, comparing, storing, recalling and excluding. With language we can use and call upon a spectacular amount of information about the world.

A key question is the extent to which language is culturally determined. Language is essentially a question of prioritizing and relaying information from the environment: creating ways of interpreting information, deciding what is relevant, what can be coded, what should be stored, what it is necessary to recall, what can be emphasized and embroidered. These decisions are, in the last resort, cultural and value-based. These cultural issues are considered in Chapter 6.

Yet another theory about brain functioning has been put forward by Gerald Edelman (2006), a Nobel Prize winner for his work in medicine. Like most neuroscientists, he too cautions against trying to claim too much in understanding the extreme complexity of the brain, and warns about extrapolating from neural science to behaviour. He suggests we know next to nothing about the neural underpinning of language development, or if indeed the concept of 'neural underpinning' makes any kind of logical sense. His theory tries to take account of experience (which he defines as bodily experience not just 'mental' action), the extraordinary plasticity, and the unique patterning of each brain. The term he coins is 'neural Darwinism'. He suggests that the development of neuronal circuits in the brain leads to enormous microscopic anatomical variation that is a result of continual selection. Overlapping circuitry routes are selected and reinforced through adaptation to external signals. These circuitry routes link with the release of neurotransmitters such as dopamine and serotonin, which in turn reinforce and amplify them. Slightly tongue in cheek (one hopes), Edelman calls this brain feedback, selectivity and adaptability a 'generator of diversity' or GOD for short!

Ideas about bodily, and in particular visceral, responses, and their influence on brain functioning, have been put forward by Joseph LeDoux in his book *The Emotional Brain* (1998). He suggests that although we conventionally conceptualize thinking and feeling, the intellectual and emotional, as separate activities, in the brain they are not separate at all, they appear to be so interconnected as to make our conceptual distinction between them a dubious one. Other neuroscientists have commented on the effects of stress, and the way in which our perceptions of events influence bodily reactions. It is well established that certain kinds of drugs, such as cocaine or amphetamine, affect the way we feel, although exactly what is going on in the brain even the neuropharmacologists have difficulties in explaining.

A further important development in these arguments is put forward by Bennett and Hacker (2003). A neurophysiologist and a philosopher working together, they argue that the concept of 'mind' cannot be mapped onto studies of the brain. The processes of consciousness and learning require a different order of definition and explanation from the descriptions and depictions of the various neurosciences. In their view, correlations and comparisons are logically meaningless. Like Edelman (2006), they also question whether the brain is the important organ we take it to be, in that other bodily events are also crucially important in shaping our sensations, from digestion to breathing to blood flow. The body functions as an integral unit, and studies which conceptually dismantle the brain and isolate it, are problematic. Whatever the strengths of their arguments, they have not been sufficient to deter popular science magazines like *Scientific American* from running regular articles on the (potential) power of the brain.

Theories about brain functioning revolve around a number of key (and unresolved) issues:

- How does the brain develop? What kinds of cell division are taking place and with what rapidity?
- Are brain functions segmented or modularized, according to genetic preprogramming? Or is the brain preprogrammed only to be very flexible?
- How significant is the number of neural connections in brain functioning?
- Are there critical periods when neural connections and pathways are established? Or can neural connections and pathways continue to develop throughout life?
- Do certain kinds of environments enhance brain development?
- How does brain functioning respond to the many kinds of bio-chemical/hormonal influences to which it is subject, either naturally or artificially through drugs?

What kind of scientific explanation?

Even if we were clearer about the answer to these questions, would they lead to a greater understanding of behaviour in general, and of child development in particular? Pinker concludes his book *How the Mind Works* with a chapter entitled 'The Meaning of Life'. He thinks we should reduce what we can to atomistic, scientific explanation and accept that we are not programmed to deal with the rest:

> Consciousness is activity in layer 4 of the cortex or the contents of short-term memory. Free will is in the anterior cingulate sulcus or the executive sub-routine. Morality is kin selection and reciprocal altruism.
>
> . . . Maybe philosophical problems are hard not because they are divine or irreducible or meaningless or workaday science, but because the mind of Homo sapiens lacks the cognitive equipment to deal with

them. We are organisms, not angels, and our minds are organs, not pipelines to the truth. Our minds evolved by natural selection to solve problems that were life and death matters to our ancestors, not to commune with correctness or to answer any question we are capable of asking.

(Pinker 1998: 561)

The attraction of scientific explanations, however incomplete, is that, as 'hard' evidence they promise greater predictive power than do psychology and human sciences. They also offer an enormous potential for social control. As Rose comments:

Science is about both knowledge and power. The new neuroscience is not merely about understanding but also about changing the world ... Anxiety, depression, anger at social injustice are all now potentially to be explained in terms of disordered biochemistry, itself more often than not the result of disordered genes ... The technological thrust to generate a psycho-civilized society by brain manipulation, from psycho-surgery to tailored drugs is very strong.

(1999: 17)

It is partly this enormous prestige, and potential for manipulation, that makes the neurosciences so seductive a resource for early childhood.

The next section explores how the early childhood literature has drawn on neuroscientific evidence to support its own, more tentative conclusions.

What lessons are there for early childhood from the neurosciences?

What do the neurosciences tell us about early childhood? In his book *The Myth of the First Three Years*, Bruer (1999) explores the limitations of the neuroscientific evidence. His answer to this question about what neuroscience tells us is 'absolutely nothing'. His exasperation is understandable. There are frequent claims that neurosciences 'prove' that intervention in early childhood is justified by scientific research on the brain. Some of these claims are explored in more detail below. It has become a common (mis)understanding, put forward in many books and articles, and stated confidently from many conference platforms, that, although there is virtually no direct evidence, brain research offers us clues about how to promote the development of children.

Despite Bruer's cautions and despite the sceptical views of many neuroscientists themselves about the limitations of what they know; despite the near impossibility of providing an explanatory framework which relates the incredibly complex physiological and chemical processes of the brain to behaviour and consciousness, the early years community has latched onto 'brain research'. Such research seems to prove that early childhood is a valuable time and that investment in early childhood is a social, economic and even moral necessity. (Can we allow young children's brains to shrivel because we don't intervene!) It appears to be such a good campaigning argument that its fallacies are overlooked.

One of the most well known of those who say that brain research justifies investment in early childhood is an elderly retired Canadian physician called Fraser Mustard, whose work has been hugely influential with the World Bank. In a rather grandly titled paper, 'Early Child Development and Experience-based Brain Development – the Scientific Underpinnings of the Importance of Early Child Development in a Globalized World' which was presented first at a World Bank conference in 2005, and written up for a policy think tank in 2006, he reviewed the evidence on brain research. The paper itself, and the references, contain a hotch-potch of information including neuropsychiatric studies of small-scale drug interventions; studies of animals who have had brain surgery, such as kittens whose neural eye connections have been excised; studies of severely malnourished or maltreated children, and cost–benefit studies of early childhood interventions (see Chapter 8). There are no studies which relate a particular kind of early childhood experience, other than gross abuse, to brain development, in fact, no discussion at all about what constitutes a good regime for young children. (Nor is there any discussion of what is meant by 'a globalized world'.)

Essentially the arguments about the relevance of brain research to early childhood rely on three main assumptions.

- brain connectivity – the development of synaptic connections – equals greater learning;
- critical periods, after which it becomes harder to establish such synaptic connections;
- an enriched environment can promote faster and denser neural connections.

Synaptic connections

As discussed above, brain research is extraordinarily complex, multifaceted and fragmented. Almost all of it has been carried out on animals. Human tissue is available only from autopsies or from brain-damaged patients where intervention appears justifiable. Counting synaptic connections, given the density of the cortex, is scientific work at the borderline of the possible. Bruer recounts a series of studies by Pasko Rakic and colleagues on brain development in rhesus monkeys. This relied on electron microscopes to enlarge tissue samples by 14,000 times. They then counted the synapses in each of at least four specimens from dozens of animals. They counted over 500,000 synapses in 25,000 electron micrographs. Each micrograph required very careful analysis in order to distinguish synaptic densities from all the other brain information contained in the micrograph – the variety of neuronal cells, non-neuronal cells, sheathing, blood vessels. Bruer quotes one of the researchers as saying to him, 'This is a sparsely populated field. In fact one might say that the study of postnatal brain development is so sparsely populated that it does not really exist as a field of scientific enquiry at all (Bruer 1999: 72). Tracing the development of synaptic connectivity in a given human individual has not so far been undertaken. Indeed, even in rhesus monkeys, the cortical interference involved in operating on the monkey and obtaining brain tissue is likely to skew any subsequent results obtained from the subject.

Critical periods

The evidence on critical periods is equally hard to prove using neuroscientific studies. The evidence that does exist comes partly from behavioural studies on learning and attachment in a variety of species, and partly from studies of language development. There is evidence from animal studies that there are critical periods in learning. Young children appear to learn languages effortlessly, but as adults find it much more difficult. As the next chapter demonstrates, attachment of young children to their mothers or carers exists but is a much more flexible process than previously thought. So there is certainly evidence that at certain times learning is easier than at others; but we are unclear from a behavioural, let alone a neuroscientific point of view, about the dimensions of critical periods. We also know that the brain can recover from trauma, and that if part of the brain is damaged, other parts can sometimes take over. It is possible to say very generally indeed that young children are vulnerable, and their mental and physical health and well-being are important. But it is a big step from this very general statement to argue for particular interventions to spur children's development.

Enriched environments

Our understanding of the effects of enriched environments on brain development is also drawn mainly from animal studies. However, even with animal studies, there is a problem about defining a 'good' or 'enriched' environment. Generally, the word used is 'complex', but complexity only in relation to the normal environment of a laboratory animal, not in any absolute sense. Most of the work on the effects on the brain of living in a complex environment has been in relation to rats. There is fairly clear neurological evidence that rats' brains do develop, in fairly circumscribed areas, mainly visual, in relation to certain kinds of complex environments, but this development also appears to take place in rats of all ages.

As discussed above, other information about the plasticity of the brain comes from brain-damaged patients who are able, to an extent, to learn new skills and develop compensatory mechanisms in different parts of their brain. This hardly amounts to neurological evidence about the importance of enriched environments for young children. There are behavioural studies about enriched environments, which suggest that in behavioural terms they may be important, but the evidence about neurological mechanisms which mirror behavioural development is conjectural.

Information about neuronal patterning in children is very limited. PET scans, for example, involve the use of radioactive materials and cannot be given to young children unless there are substantial reasons for intervention. Yet one of the most frequently cited research findings, quoted, for instance, by NAEYC (National Association for the Education of Young Children) as evidence for their manual on developmentally appropriate practice (see Chapter 9) is that of Chugani et al. on brain development. The study reported the results of PET scans on 29 epileptic children, ranging in age from 5 days to 15 years, many of whom had been medicated since infancy and some of whom were medicated on the day they were scanned. Their results were compared with those of seven normal adults ranging from age 19 to 30. This study indicates that, based on PET analyses of brain glucose metabolisms, the brain does show some maturational patterns. The interpretation of these glucose uptake patterns is very tentative indeed, and there is only indirect evidence that they are related to neuronal growth and the development of synaptic connections. Despite this very limited and atypical sample, this work is continually cited. As Bruer remarks:

> Chugani's 1987 PET study is ... possibly one of the most over-interpreted scientific papers of the last twenty five years ... It is taken as the paradigmatic example of how neuroscience is providing 'hard data' about the first three years of life.
>
> (1999: 72)

Why rely on brain research to justify practice in early childhood?

Why, then, has there been such a furore over brain research underpinning child development? To use the word 'furore' is not to exaggerate. The following extracts are from the mass-market magazines *Time* and *Newsweek*.

Experience in the first years of life lays the basis for networks of neurons that enable us to be smart, creative and adaptable in all the years that follow.

(*Time magazine*, 13 Feb. 1997)

Every lullaby, every giggle and peek-a-boo, triggers a crackling along his neural pathways, laying the groundwork for what could someday be a love of art or a talent for soccer or a gift for making and keeping friends.

(Begley, *Newsweek*, 19 Feb. 1996)

You hold your newborn so his sky-blue eyes are just inches away from brightly patterned wallpaper. ZZZt: a neuron from his retina makes an electrical connection with one in his brain's visual cortex. You gently touch his hand with a clothespin; he grasps it, drops it, and you return it to him with soft words and a smile. Crackle: neurons from his hand strengthen their connection to those in his sensory-motor cortex.

(Begley, *Newsweek*, 19 Feb. 1996)

Others using more sober language make very similar points. Anne Meade, in *Promoting Evidence Based Practice in Early Childhood Education*, summarizes neurological research, and while admitting there is little or no mention of play in the neuroscientific literature, goes on to claim: 'brain research contains considerable implications for the role of play in early childhood education . . . Is this type of play where children use all modalities – the senses, physical activity, emotion and representations – particularly conducive to synaptic growth? (2001: 22).

Mary Eming Young, senior adviser for the World Bank's $1,000 million loan programme to develop early childhood programmes in 29 countries, claims, at some length and citing Chugani, that brain research justifies the bank's investment in early childhood. Another recent publication from the World Bank *Efficient Learning for the Poor: Insights from the Frontiers of Cognitive Neuroscience* (Abadzi 2006), encapsulates in its title the sheer silliness of those wishing to extrapolate from neuroscientific evidence. Abazdi has useful things to say about adult learning, but also has recourse to 'brain architecture' to justify her conclusions, and in order to support particular World Bank programmes. For neo-liberals, neuroscientific arguments which focus on individual change are more acceptable than the alternative, which is to admit the need for radical socio-economic intervention to change the circumstances of poverty. Mustard's paper also includes claims that ECD is necessary to achieve 'high quality populations' and that 'without ECD many societies risk slipping into chaos with the negative effects on our initiatives on globalization' (2006: 2), remarks that contain so many unexplored and probably unwarranted assumptions, that his reputation as a guru almost defies belief.

Jerome Kagan has been the most persistent psychological critic of the view that intervention in the first three years matters. He also argues that the evidence about brain research is used in a very cavalier way. He also raises the question at the heart of the debate about the relevance of brain research, that is whether intervention should be on the level of the individual (an enriched environment) or at the level of society:

> Psychological determinists have assumed that every kiss, every lullaby, or scolding alters a child's brain in ways that will influence his future. But if slight changes in synapses, like some amino acid substitions, are without functional consequences, then every smile at an infant is not to be viewed as a bank deposit accumulating psychological dividends.
>
> (1998: 20)

Kagan calls this popular emphasis on the developing brain capacity of infants the myth of infant determinism. The reason that such explanations are so popular, he claims, is that intervention protects the myth of equality in a society that, like that in the USA, is profoundly unequal. Instead, he argues that social class (and cultural context – see Chapter 6) are the most powerful predictors of future performance.

Arguing for the funding and provision of services for young children has been, at least in the USA, an uphill struggle, where children have been a very low political priority and levels of poverty are extremely high. The brain research arguments appear to offer extra ammunition. In particular, they appear to offer a solution to childhood poverty and inequality that can be addressed on an individual level – enriched environments for targeted populations – rather than on a societal level – redistribution of resources. They also appear to offer the possibility to individual parents to enhance their child's development, to hurry it along, hence the enormous popular interest in the *Time* and *Newsweek* articles quoted above, and the rush of popular books, like that of Kotulak. His book *Inside the Brain: Revolutionary Discoveries of How the Mind Works* won a Pulitzer prize.

> For millions of American children, the world they encounter is relentlessly menacing and hostile. So with astounding speed and efficiency, their brains adapt and prepare for battle. Cells form trillions of new connections that create the chemical pathways of aggression; some chemicals are produced in over-abundance, some are repressed . . . What research can now tell us with increasing certainty is just how the brain adapts physically to this threatening environment – how

abuse, poverty, neglect or sensory deprivation can reset the brain's chemistry in ways that makes some genetically vulnerable children more prone to violence.

(1996: ix–x)

Underlying these claims about the importance of brain research is our (by now) familiar debate about scientific method. Although they also involve speculation and conjecture, universally agreed scientific methods have been extremely successful in revealing the physical world. The discoveries of science have gone hand in hand with rapid technological developments, from computers and radar to bombs. Human sciences can boast no such successes. The fields of genetics and neuroscience are extremely important and mesmerizing areas of research in their own right, but their great attraction to the field of human sciences is that they appear to offer an incontrovertible underpinning to behavioural and social events. A new branch of psychology, evolutionary psychology, rests on the exploration of such claims.

Meanwhile, philosophers doggedly persevere trying to explain the nature of explanation:

How can there be an objective world of money, property, marriage, governments, elections, football games, cocktail parties and law-courts in a world that consists entirely of physical particles in fields of force, and in which some of these particles are organized into systems that are conscious biological beasts such as ourselves.

(Searle, cited in Midgley 1998: 247)

Mary Midgley, in a series of papers and articles, sensibly suggests that there are many different ways of knowing and explaining the world and many ways of being in it. Our contribution is to be alert, well informed and critical – no mean task given the inevitable scientific dogfights about the status of new knowledge in ground-breaking biosciences such as genetics and the neurosciences. Midgley argues that we should be concerned to justify our practices not only in terms of what we know but also in terms of what we value. Ethics, values and social commentary have their place in all methodological enquiries.

Summary

This chapter considered the arguments that the understanding of behaviour can be enriched by brain research and genetics. It also briefly explored evolutionary psychology, which claims to be based on genetics. These are very popular topics for discussion and are frequently aired in the press. But the evidence that brain research and genetics can help us understand young children is at a very early stage, and might mislead us more than it helps us.

Main messages from this chapter

1   Genes are extremely complicated and, despite many recent findings, we know relatively little about how they work.
2   The brain is still more complicated, supremely so, and it is foolish to make predictions about young children's behaviour using current findings from the field of brain research.
3   You need to keep up with ideas about scientific research in the fields of genetics and the neurosciences, but do not be seduced by them.

What to read next

Dennis, C. and Gallagher, R. (eds) (2001) *The Human Genome*. Hampshire: Palgrave/ Nature Publishing Group.

Rose, S. (ed.) (1999) *From Brains to Consciousness? Essays on the New Sciences of the Mind*. London: Penguin.

5 On the other side of the world

The previous chapter was about the extraordinary developments in genetics and neurosciences. It also suggested that those working in the field of early childhood have overreacted to and overinterpreted those findings. This chapter explores the other end of the continuum. In what ways do wider cultural and socio-economic circumstances shape how children grow and learn? What sort of notice do we take of those circumstances?

Anthropology

Anthropology is about the study of culture. Like all the other disciplines discussed in this book, there are no right approaches or right answers. There are certain major themes that crop up in the study of anthropology – self, identity, interpretation, meaning – but there are many perspectives in dealing with them. The doggerel verse sums it up: 'Two men look out from the selfsame bars; One sees mud, the other sees stars.'

Anthropology is above all about 'culture'. But culture is a very slippery concept. The classic 1871 definition is that

> culture . . . taken in its wide ethnographic sense is that complex whole which includes knowledge, belief, art, morals, law, custom and any other capabilities and habits acquired by man as a member of society.
> (Tylor 1871, cited in Peacock 1986: 6)

This is a long list and more or less impossible for anyone to investigate or describe. For instance, is culture what goes on in people's heads, their attitudes and understandings? Or is it what they actually do, the way they behave in certain circumstances?

A culture is taken for granted by those who belong to it. We think about what we ourselves do as (mostly) rational and self-chosen, but in fact we may be drawing on very traditional cultural ideas. Peacock, who wrote a useful textbook for beginners on anthropology (Peacock 1986), uses the example of time. In Europe and America we tend to think of time as a line stretching between the past and the future, divided into centuries, years, months, weeks, days, hours, minutes and seconds. Every event we unhesitatingly classify along the timeline – births, marriages and deaths, jobs, any important event. The future is movement on the timeline. This notion of time is embedded in the English language (for example, English has several past tenses – some languages have no past tense). Our understanding of work, 'getting ahead', 'careers', and so on, is time bound. Time so ties us down that there are even those who protest against its demands. The 'slow food movement' is a (leisurely) campaign that makes the point that the quality of what we eat is more important than the time it takes to produce it – a movement that started in Italy, where good food traditions are very strong. There is now the 'hurried child' syndrome, a young child who is pushed to accomplish learning more quickly, by starting school early. But in other parts of the world, time is not such an obsession. In Buddhist tradition, time is circular, and comes around again. In parts of Africa it is rude not to come to a consensus in a discussion, however long it takes. Peacock, somewhat tongue-in-cheek, cites a Pacific Island society where 'time was not so much a line along which one moved as it was a puddle in which one sat, splashed or wallowed' (1986: 5).

Another example is the concept of self. In Anglo-American societies, the individual is the elementary unit of human experience. The individual is the building block of society. 'Each child is an individual and must be treated as such', is a basic tenet for many early childhood practitioners. Yet in other societies a person is known not by their own individual name, but by a name that links them to other people. In some Moslem societies, a person is known by the name of his father or tribe. In some African societies people are called by the name of their children. When I visit some of my African friends I am called 'Mama Loveday' after the name of my eldest daughter. Many traditional societies are collectivist, and members of the society consider that 'fitting in' with others is far more important than doing anything by yourself. For all the emphasis on individualism in Euro-American societies, the individual is, paradoxically, a product of the group. What we term 'individual' is a cultural construct. Without belonging to a society or a culture, without speaking the language of the society or the culture, we would have no existence in it.

We take time and self for granted in Euro-American societies, yet to an outsider (and to some insiders), these aspects of 'culture' are rigid and ritualistic, and probably irritating. For example, we asked my African son-in-law, visiting England for the first time, what he noticed most. 'People do not greet me in the street or on the buses', he said.

The anthropologist from outside tries to uncover habits and traditions that are so ingrained that people do not know they possess them. In one sense of the word, culture is a name that anthropologists give to the taken-for-granted but powerfully influential understandings and codes that are learnt and shared by members of a group, but seem mysterious to those outside of it. This is popularly known in anthropology as 'making the strange familiar and the familiar strange'.

'Culture' is also a shorthand word for describing a conglomeration of different, and sometimes incompatible, views and understandings in a given society or community. Within a 'culture', people hold different views about what that culture means, what it involves and how it should be upheld. There are arguments about 'British' culture, for example. Does it include Scotland, Wales and Northern Ireland? Has it been changed by immigration patterns over the twentieth century? Is the royal family still important or is it irrelevant? Are cricket and warm beer an essential part of British culture? There are many questions to ask about 'British culture' and the answers might differ radically according to who is giving their opinion. Anyone reading the *Guardian* newspaper, for example, might suppose the monarchy is obsolete and is now a joke; whereas tourists watching the changing of the guard at Buckingham Palace might consider that Britain is still a land of pageantry and ancient rituals.

Anthropologists have often chosen to carry out their work in parts of the world that are different from those where they usually reside. This encounter with other 'cultures' has the effect of sharpening up one's own cultural identity. By thinking about how other people do things, you become more aware of how you do them yourself – in something as minor as food preparation or as major as religion. As Peacock comments: 'A major mission and contribution of anthropology has long been, and continues to be, to enhance our awareness of the power and reality of culture in our existence' (1986: 7).

The method anthropologists commonly use is called *ethnography*. This is a kind of participant observation, living the life of the people you are trying to understand, noting down as much as you can about it, as systematically as possible. Clifford Geertz (1973), a well-known anthropologist, argues that anthropology is about interpretation of meaning. In his book *The Interpretation of Cultures*, he defines culture as 'a web of significance'. The anthropologist can never fully understand a culture outside of his own, but he can learn how to describe it and analyse the meanings or significance of events very carefully indeed. This method of describing he calls ethnography, or 'thick description'.

'Thick description' is a useful way of documenting and understanding events from the perspectives of other people, but as other anthropologists have pointed out, it too is problematical. It is what we might call the glass bubble problem. Cultures are regarded as static and self-contained, inside a glass bubble and the anthropologist is a peeper, trying to write down or photograph what he sees. James Clifford and George Marcus, in a well-known book called *Writing Culture* (1984), argued that anthropologists, in telling the story of their travels, exaggerate them and make them more romantic than they are. Bronislaw Malinowski, one of the earliest and most renowned of anthropologists, kept a diary during his trips to New Guinea and North Melanesia. It was a shock when it was posthumously published because it illustrated all too clearly how he stood apart from the societies he was investigating and was sometimes contemptuous of them. (Malinowski 1967)

The contribution of anthropology to understanding childhood

Anthropologists, until recently, have not spent much time investigating childhood – with a few notable exceptions. Margaret Mead and a group of like-minded colleagues, working in the 1920s and 1930s, wanted to investigate whether parenting was the same everywhere. She worked in a number of countries, including, most famously, Samoa in the Pacific Islands and in New Guinea. She demonstrated how different communities held very different views about childrearing and about sex roles in relation to parenting. In one of the tribes she studied, the Arapesh, men seemed to be very gentle and did most of the childrearing. In another, everyone was a bit rough with the children. Her accounts are very readable, even today, and like the best of anthropological accounts, make you reflect on the culture you are living in as well as the one she is describing. She has been criticized for exaggeration by male anthropologists who went back to the same place and, using the same ethnographic methods, came to different conclusions. Then she was exonerated again, by female anthropologists who argued that the sex of the anthropologist gave them different insights. Women anthropologists used women informants; whereas male anthropologists listened more to men. Mead and her colleagues were especially concerned with proving or disproving various aspects of psychoanalytic and personality theory. Psychoanalysis and personality theory no longer have the hold on psychology that they once had, so Mead's work may now appear dated.

Jahoda and Lewis (1987) have summarized work on the anthropology of childhood. They argued not only that psychologists had been unable to deal with cultural difference but also that these differences were so powerful and pervasive that it was nonsense to talk about universal norms of behaviour. They gave some remarkable examples of childrearing traditions. One contributor to their book describes musical games for children in a community in South Africa. The best musical results were obtained when all participants combined the maximum of individual skill and fellow-feeling in the realization and elaboration of a basic musical pattern. 'Pleasing others and pleasing oneself in musical performance were two interrelated aspects of the same activity' (1987: 110). (This tradition was probably translated to the USA and re-emerged as jazz.) But it is at odds with the view in Anglo-American countries that children should be encouraged to be creative individuals, but they cannot be creative as part of a group; you can stress one or the other but not both together.

Montagu (1978), who was concerned about arms build-up and political aggression, questioned whether aggression was innate. He claimed that there were communities who were almost entirely non-aggressive. In his book *Learning Non-aggression*, he collected anthropological accounts of communities where aggression in children was almost unknown. One such account describes learning among pygmy communities in Zaire. Children learn in turn security, dependence, independence, interdependence, coordination and cooperation. For instance, one game taught to younger children by older peers is swinging from ropes in trees. The game is to coordinate the swinging, so that everyone can take part and it becomes 'a perfect ballet' in which all children learn to demonstrate mutual coordination and agility. He describes games like this as 'the essence of co-operative communal life, to which competition is the antithesis' (1978: 184). Montagu concludes that, 'whilst potentialities for aggression exist in all human beings at birth, such potentialities will remain nothing more unless they are organized by experience to function as aggressive behaviour' (1978: 7).

Nancy Scheper Hughes, an American anthropologist, has focused on child-rearing conditions that seem to damage children. She has written a brilliant and widely acclaimed 20-year account of the everyday life of women and children in a shanty town of Alto do Cruzeiro in the north-east of Brazil, *Death Without Weeping* (1993). She tries to understand the neglect women appear to show their young children, and the apparent casualness and indifference with which they react to frequent infant death. This is behaviour which would appear to be abusive by conventional North American or European standards. She concludes that the way the women respond is not a matter of poor 'cultural' parenting practices that need correction, but a mirror image of the way in which the shanty women themselves are treated by their wider society as being worthless and of no account. Being able to accommodate and to accept and even joke about the unrelenting grimness and misery of their everyday life enables them to survive. They are often resilient in the face of tremendous odds. She writes that:

> The problem is of course, how to articulate a standard or divergent standards, for the beginnings of a moral and an ethical reflection on cultural practices that takes into account but does not privilege our own cultural presuppositions.
>
> (1993: 21)

Robert LeVine has described anthropology as a 'gadfly' to developmental psychology. He and his colleagues at Harvard University carried out a series of studies in Africa on childcare and schooling. He concluded that many of the assumptions that are commonly made about the need to stimulate young children and the need to talk to them in order to help them learn are more a reflection of concerns of Euro-Americans than hard fact:

> The leap from factors to optimize school skills [in the USA] to universal prerequisites of cognitive, language and emotional development is misguided . . . Children whose early environments lack these factors . . . acquired different skills, virtues and preferences in accordance with their own goals for human development. If these findings seem surprising in the context of existing theories of child development, then it indicates how far we have to go in integrating evidence from other cultures into our conceptions of what is possible during childhood.
>
> (1994: 274)

More recently, there has been a recurrence of interest by anthropologists in the study of childhood. Alma Gottleib, a Chicago anthropologist, has argued strongly that early childhood is a legitimate and useful focus of study for anthropology. She writes in the Preface to her study of infancy in West Africa that:

> My major aim has been to challenge the assumption of an Everybaby that somehow exists outside of culture. Such an assumption implicitly underlies the two thousand or so parenting manuals now sold in bookstors and the myriad parenting advice columns dotting newspapers and magazines, so popular in many Western countries. In challenging the basic operating model behind the fact of such widely consumed folk models passing as neutral expertise, I hope to present an alternate model of a baby that is deeply constructed by culture.
>
> (2004: xvi)

Her study of the lack of importance of attachment in the community she studied raises many questions about normality and understanding of childhood. She and a colleague Judy DeLoache followed this up with a witty book *A World of Babies: Imagined Childcare Guides for Seven Societies* (2004) which is the strongly recommended further reading for this chapter.

Increasingly in their studies of childhood, anthropologists are trying to use children as informants. Children often have wise views about their own position, and where they fit into their community. Sam Punch (2001), for example, interviewed children in Bolivia about what they thought about being made to do household tasks. (They were ambivalent.) There are many more such studies appearing in the literature, although almost all with older children.

Anthropologists have indicated some of the ways in which dearly held assumptions about childhood in the UK and USA do not seem to be borne out by anthropological studies. Their views link up with those of the cultural psychologists discussed in Chapter 3. But both anthropologists and cultural psychologists have to come to terms with the issues raised by Sharon Stephens and Nancy Scheper Hughes. First, 'culture' is contested, it is not straightforward and whatever it is, it is constantly changing. Second, poverty and injustice cut across 'culture'.

Cultural change and globalization

Some writers have gone on to question vigorously the notion of culture. Renato Rosaldo, for instance, argues that people are misled if they think that culture is ever fixed or final. In all cultures there is a continual ebb and flow and reshaping of ideas, as the example of Britain shows us. Tolerance and understanding of culture are not merely about trying to understand and make allowances for someone different from ourselves. Culture, he says, is almost always fought over, it is 'a field of contention' in which the key words are 'change, experience, conflict and struggle' (Rosaldo 1993: 105). The cultural historian and anthropologist Eric Wolf also argues that 'culture' has for ever been 'assembled, dismantled, and reassembled' (1990: 391).

Ideas about culture have also become entwined with those of globalization and knowledge transfer. Globalization theory is sometimes interpreted to mean that everyone is getting sucked up into the powerful ways of operating and thinking of the world's richest consumer cultures. Globalization suggests ideas and values from the North (developed countries) have been heavily superimposed on those of the South (less developed countries). But that underestimates the importance of local understandings. There have been nuanced studies of knowledge transfer between North and South which illustrate the very particular way in which global ideas are articulated, contextualized and reapplied in local circumstances. Local adaptations may be creative, and may involve considerable resilience, reworking or resistance, but in no way can recipients in the South be regarded as passive vehicles for change. Rosaldo and Xavier (2002) describe the shifts in understanding between North and South, from South to North, and from South to South, as people struggle to come to terms with new ideas and make sense of them in their own, often very different circumstances.

Jan Nederveen Pieterse explores these ideas of what he calls 'global melange' in his book *Globalization and Culture* (2004). He argues that there are two sets of assumptions about culture and locality. The first set of assumptions present culture as territorial and static; the second presents culture as translocal and fluid. Traditionally we have viewed culture as something which is place-bound, language-bound and community-bound and mostly enduring and unchanging. Pieterse argues, on the contrary, that cultures are always hybrid, translocal and often multi-lingual. 'Border crossing' is a normal human condition not an exception. He is taking the long view, and over centuries, as Wolf also argues, this might be a useful interpretation. The question is whether is a useful way to conceptualize culture as gradations of hybridity in the short term.

Majid Rahnema, an Iranian, has edited a collection of essays, mostly from authors in the South, called *The Post-development Reader* (1997). This has now become a standard text critiquing ideas of development and globalization. He argues that ideas about development are the economic equivalent of the AIDS virus, in that they are so pernicious and have spread so rapidly. Traditional societies operate in a holistic and multidimensional way, minimizing risk to members. Ecologically, they are more likely to respect their environment, and regard it as a god-given source of life without which it would be unimaginable for anyone to live:

> Most activities have a multi-purpose aspect and are an opportunity for everyone to learn from others. Life organized around them often becomes the space for collective apprenticeship where the younger and the elder each in their own way, learn from each other. Children may not be sent to institutions specializing in education, but they are much less infantilized than their urban peers, whose world is reduced mostly to schools. Similarly 'technologies' are never just a collection of tools or imported 'gadgets'. They are organically incorporated into people's way of life. And they often require the co-operation of ever-widening human groups, beginning with members of the household. Far from leading to new forms of dependency they are tools that correspond to a profound need to be autonomous; not only an extension of people's hand and brain, but also a constant reminder of their need for conviviality.
>
> (1997: 115)

This is the world of self-sufficient interdependent small communities that, in Rahnema's view, is being fatally infected by ideas of economic development and market capitalism. While this may be a romantic view, nevertheless he amasses a good deal of evidence from the South that 'global' ideas about progress from the North have been used oppressively and have done more harm than good.

Sharon Stephens, an anthropologist particularly concerned with children's experiences and understandings, has pointed out the difficulties about investigating or upholding cultural traditions when they conflict with each other or with what we think is good for children:

What sort of social visions and notions of culture underlie assertions within international rights discourses that every child has a right to cultural identity? To what extent is this identity conceived of as singular and exclusive, and what sorts of priorities are asserted in cases where various forms of cultural identity – regional, national, ethnic minority or indigenous – come up against one another?

(1995: 3)

Whether through globalization, or other means, 'culture' is for ever being amalgamated and reshaped as people from different communities come into contact with one another. In certain places at certain times – as in most capital cities in the twentieth century – these cultural encounters are accelerated and intensified. The populations of major cities are swollen by refugees, immigrants and economic migrants. The issue then becomes one of *identity*. Should the newcomers try to keep to their familiar ways and traditions? Or should they drop them and try to become like everyone else – except, of course, everyone else is not the same. What kind of British person should a refugee to Britain become? A royalist? A cricket player?

And what about the people who were there before the latest wave of refugees arrived? How do they view the identity of the refugees and incomers? To settled populations in North America and Europe, it is *other* people, usually distinguished by the colour of their skin, who have these quaint blocks of irrational, or sometimes destructive, beliefs and practices; funny colourful clothes; strange, strong foods; and idiomatic or incomprehensible speech patterns. 'They' have 'a culture' which is sometimes tolerated and sometimes resented. Long-term residents of that country, especially if they are white, feel less need to question or comment on their own culture.

People newly arrived from poor or war-torn countries, especially children, often feel bad about their identity. The pressures are intense to conform, to adapt and to change. In his autobiography *Out of Place*, Edward Said, originally a Palestinian, describes his life-long struggle to fit in, to become American. As a child sent to a holiday camp he felt horribly peculiar. 'So beginning in America I resolved to live as if I were a simple, transparent soul and not to speak of my family or origins except as required, and then very sparingly. To become, in other words, like the others, as anonymous as possible' (Said 1999: 137).

George Lamming, the Caribbean writer, describing his childhood after coming to England, wrote: 'No black boy wanted to be white but no black boy liked the idea of being black. When you asked Boy Blue why he was so black he would answer, "Just as I wus going to be born the light went out" ' (Lamming 1979: 1).

Identity is even more of an issue in ex-colonial countries. Geographical borders of countries in Africa or Asia or South America reflect the past efforts of colonial administrators to rule, rather than sensible borders based on ethnic, linguistic, religious or class or even geographical boundaries. In Nigeria, for example, there are many different and competing traditions and histories, including long-standing religious, linguistic and ethnic divides. It does not make sense to talk about children coming from 'Nigerian' culture, especially when their families settle in the UK. Yet, as Brian Street points out, that is what all too often happens:

> Even though the concept of culture appears not to be rooted in biology (race) it is in fact very often premised on assumptions about fixity and permanence: the idea that somebody, for instance, might come from Nigeria and settle in England, somehow bringing along a bag with Nigerian culture in it, with which he or she is then stuck . . . A person belongs to a given culture, that is how they are, they must think that way and behave that way.
>
> (Street 1999: 54)

How galling, then, to be labelled as Nigerian, when Nigeria itself is made up of so many groups, many of whom are at odds with one another. The children of these 'Nigerians' may themselves have very ambivalent attitudes to assimilation, as Edward Said did in the USA.

Anthropologists then deal with a range of questions to do with culture. The word 'culture' is used by anthropologists as a useful abstraction to describe a holistic view of how a group of people, a community, or a society. But it is full of pitfalls as a workable concept. So much so that some anthropologists now focus more narrowly on concepts such as *identity*, or *beliefs* or *meanings*. They also no longer focus their research exclusively on far-away or exotic places, but find it equally challenging to use ethnographic methods to examine the everyday world where they live.

The circumstances of 80 per cent of the world's children

The situation of most of the world's children is very different from those we conventionally study in North America and Europe. It is these Euro-American children who are taken as the norm in child development. In describing and analysing the situation of poor children from the other end of the world, we are faced not just with differing cultural descriptions but also with a global socio-economic system which, as some argue, always favours the rich over the poor, both across and within countries. The financial and ideological power of the developed world – from here on called the North – is undisputed. It is the North, and in particular the USA, that calls the shots. The recent war in Iraq is a clear example.

Children from the South are profoundly affected by this wider global economic context, over and above any cultural differences. The global statistics on children are appalling. An unacceptable number die at birth or soon after. The campaigning group Jubilee 2000 estimated that more than 7 million children die unnecessarily each year. Many of those children that survive have limited and falling access to education and healthcare, particularly girls in poor Asian countries. Many of the goods used and consumed on a daily basis in the North, such as food, flowers and clothing, are produced using cheap child labour in poor countries. Almost all cities have growing populations of street children. There has been a resurgence of endemic diseases once under control, such as tuberculosis, and a failure to deal with new ones such as AIDS – an estimated one in four children in Sub-Saharan Africa is affected by AIDS. Many millions of children are refugees fleeing from wars and natural disasters.

Every year UNICEF publishes a booklet entitled *The State of the World's Children*. This gives statistics concerning the position in countries in the South. In 2002, there were more than 100 million children without access to basic education, 60 million of them girls. Well over 4 million children have died of HIV/AIDS, and more than 13 million children under 13 have been orphaned. Two million children have been slaughtered (UNICEF's vocabulary), 6 million children injured and 12 million left homeless because of conflict.

Disease in poor countries has always been a problem, not least because of the unavailability of medicines. Drugs companies, for example, are reluctant to finance research into malaria, which is one of the biggest killers of children. This is because there is no money to be made in developing drugs for poor countries – people simply cannot afford them. The worst epidemic is now HIV/AIDS. The *British Medical Journal* has run a special edition on HIV/AIDS. Among the many problems caused by the HIV/AIDS epidemic is the number of children who have been orphaned:

> AIDS has devasted the social and economic fabric of African societies and made orphans of a whole generation of children. Although donor agencies initially viewed the plight of orphans as a short-term humanitarian disaster, they now acknowledge the long-term social consequences of African children growing up without parental love and guidance. The potential of these children to form a large group of dysfunctional adults which could further destabilize societies already weakened by AIDS has increased the urgency of finding an effective solution to the orphan crisis. Africa is home to 95% of the world's 13 million children orphaned as a result of AIDS. The numbers will rise until at least 2010, by which time a third of African children will be orphaned.
>
> (*BMJ*, 26 Jan. 2002: 185)

The most extreme condition that children experience, apart from HIV/

AIDS, is war. It turns daily life inside out, and leads to terrible suffering. War, unfortunately, is not a rare exception. There has been a long-running war in Afghanistan, another in Palestine. There are other, less well-reported wars that have been going for many years in Sudan, Angola, the Congo, Liberia, Sierra Leone, Colombia, Sri Lanka and Indonesia, Chechnya and Kashmir. There are countries where wars have been fought and finished, leaving a dreadful unhealed legacy of bitterness – for instance, Iraq, Iran, Bosnia, Rwanda, Tajikistan. Women and children are the vulnerable victims of such wars. The world's population of refugees is at least 60 million, but the number of those affected by war and its aftermath is still greater. Mary Kaldor has argued that war itself has changed. 'Old wars' were fought between soldiers; 9 out of 10 people killed in wars used to be soldiers. Now the position is reversed: 9 out of 10 people killed are civilians, many of them children. 'New wars' involve organized crime (violence undertaken by privately organized groups, warlords, paramilitary units and so on for private purposes, usually financial gain) and involve large-scale violations of human rights. Such wars are often fought for precious minerals valued in the North such as diamonds or oil. These wars are aided by advances in technology – landmines, powerful small arms, cellular phones and computer links.

Graca Machel has edited for UNICEF a book about war entitled *The Impact of War on Children* (2001). She details the terrible circumstances of many children affected by war. Among the children she describes are child soldiers. Rootless and orphan children, themselves victims of war and economic disaster, are drawn into war – or warlord armies – because it offers at least the short-term possibility of food and survival. The Polish journalist Ryszard Kapuscinski also describes child soldiers:

> I sometimes read stories about a child in America or Europe shooting another child. A child killing one of his contemporaries, or an adult. Such news is usually accompanied by expressions of horror and outrage. In Africa children kill children in enormous numbers, and have been doing so for years. In fact, modern wars on this continent have been, and still are, largely wars of children.
>
> (Kapucinski 2001: 185)

One of the reasons that this picture is so shocking is that in the North we believe that young children will be nurtured and cared for. They should be free to be childish, and free to play. Child development assumes a benign environment. Child psychology is built on the assumption that adults should be protective towards children, or, as the journalist Madeleine Bunting expressed it, 'a parent's primary role is to convey . . . the reassurance that the world is a predictable, trustworthy, safe place' (*The Guardian*, 31 Dec. 2001: 14). Much, indeed most, of the work undertaken in the field of child development tries to investigate the ways in which adults can create a benign environment in which children grow up and learn. However, *most* of the world's children grow up in environments that are far from benign. They grow up in circumstances of extreme poverty, pollution, danger and exploitation. Developmental psychology claims to be a universal science, but as yet has had very little to say about the extent or the effects of these circumstances.

Are situations like this inevitable? Could anything be done about AIDS, child soldiers and child poverty in the South? There are two opposing views about such child poverty. The first is that it is caused by the current economic system – sometimes called neo-liberal economics, or the global market – which inevitably leads to exploitation and inequalities, and makes the gap between rich and poor greater, breeding misery and discontent. The other view is that the global market is an economic fact of life. Poor countries are still developing, and they have to learn to cope with the global market. They need help to catch up to the education and health standards of the North, but in the future they will be economically better off. The best way to deal with illness, child poverty and warfare is to encourage more economic development and more democracy.

At the centre of these arguments are the World Bank and the World Trade Organization. The brief of the World Bank (and its sister organization, the International Monetary Fund or IMF) was originally to assist in the redevelopment and reconstruction of broken economies after the Second World War. It now acts as banker to all the world's poorest countries. It loans them money, at heavy repayment rates. Most poor countries are now heavily in debt to the World Bank. The money that was lent to poor countries to help them invest in production and develop their economies has been conditional on the adoption of neo-liberal market philosophies and 'structural adjustment' policies (see Chapter 8). The idea behind such policies is that competition is good, individualism and individual gain are the motors of development, and everyone should have an opportunity to become wealthy. State control, state interests and state regulation, where possible, should be minimized.

The World Trade Organization (WTO) is a body set up to regulate international trade. Although many people consider that it is important to have such a regulatory body (just as it is important to have international laws, and an international justice system which can bring dictators to trial), there has been a great deal of concern about how the WTO operates. Like the World Bank, it is accused of favouring big corporations over the needs of the poor. The example usually quoted concerns patents for drugs or genetic research. Should big drugs companies, for example, be able to fix the prices of life-saving drugs or take a patent out on a commonly used tropical plant? Or be able to charge prices for AIDS drugs that are out of reach of most people in the South?

The UK charity ActionAid tried to launch an advertising campaign against patents. They tried to patent salted chips, as an example of the absurdity of claims for intellectual property that the WTO support. ActionAid has 'invented' a ready-salted chip, and have filed for a patent on it. If successful, we would have legal rights over the Action-Aid Chip, and any chips that have salt added to them. So we could demand that chip shop owners throughout the UK pay for a licence to add salt to their chips. With 300 million servings of chips sold each year, we could stand to make millions.

Why can we do this? New patent rules allow companies to get exclusive rights over basic foods and even nature itself, simply by adding something to it or modifying it in a way that has not been done before.

Why has ActionAid done it? To draw attention to the threat that the patenting of staple crops by big companies is posing to poor farmers in the developing world.

(www.actionaid.com)

These arguments about the role of the World Bank and debt relief may seem a long way from the concerns of early childhood practitioners. But as the Inter-Church Coalition on Africa suggests, the well-being of many millions of young children, that is about 80 per cent of the world's children, depends on these wider economic, political and cultural assumptions and how they are put into practice. It matters even more because the World Bank and a number of other international donors have decided to invest in child development. They argue that such an investment would bring economic returns. This is where we return to the ideas about child development discussed in Chapters 1 and 8.

Child development interventions in the South

There has been a dramatic expansion in early childhood provision in most of the world's cities. There are nurseries and childcare settings in every city throughout the world. A recent review of early childhood programmes in the South was carried out by Robert Myers for the 1999 World Education Forum Conference at Dakar, Senegal. Mostly, he suggested, these programmes are private businesses for the children of the better off, geared towards preparation for school. Ex-communist countries tended to have widespread and high-quality early childhood services, but UNICEF has shown that these are decreasing dramatically post transition to a market economy.

Myers commented on the understandings of children and models of services that have fuelled this expansion. He argued that ideas about childhood from the North have a near monopoly, and this makes for considerable tension.

> Frameworks and knowledge . . . continue to originate, for the most part in the Minority World. Accordingly a tension often arises between 'received truth' linked to Minority World knowledge base and values guiding an agency, and local knowledge linked to another set of values rooted in some part of the majority world. These may overlap, but are different.
>
> (Myers 2000: 25)

This chapter has discussed anthropological perspectives. These perspectives suggest that ideas about self-identity and culture are problematical. It is also hard to detach them from ideas about race and power. There are strong reasons to believe that there is tremendous variation in the way in which people construe their identity. But on top of issues of identity, there are pressing issues of poverty and the dreadful lives many children lead. Yet, on the whole, the view persists in child development that there is 'developmentally appropriate practice' that can be applied irrespective of time and place, and despite or in ignorance of these conditions. There are universal and essential truths about young children and how to care for and educate them. These are said to apply everywhere in the world, with minor cultural variations. The overriding assumption, which appears in the literature on early childhood practice, is that the ages and stages children go through, and the familial contexts in which learning takes place, are similar everywhere. Leading American educators have claimed that 'children are pretty much the same everywhere and the people teaching them have pretty much the same ideas' (NAEYC International Seminar: Toronto 1999). International agencies promoting child development have also made the same claims and appeals to universal standards. This is not too different from the UK government's view. This statement on early childhood comes from a DfES website in 2003:

> Given the right opportunities and the right learning environment children will develop in similar ways whatever their background. Culture may affect, and sometimes even determine, the topics, methodologies and techniques we use, but there is an underlying universality. As long as we keep in mind that everything we do is concerned with the development of the whole child, we are all doing the same sorts of things for the same sorts of reasons.

The World Bank also holds that child development programmes can be lifted up and applied wherever necessary (Penn 2002). Mary Eming Young is a senior public health specialist at the World Bank. She argues for a targeted intervention approach for poor children. Using evidence exclusively from the USA, she argues that

> Evidence suggests that [ECD] programs are effective in addressing
> such vital human development issues as malnutrition among chil-
> dren under five, stunted cognitive development and unpreparedness
> for primary education . . . Early childhood interventions can increase
> the efficiency of primary and secondary education, contribute to
> further productivity and income, and reduce the cost of health care
> and public services . . . Deficits in individuals caused by early mal-
> nutrition and inadequate care can affect labour productivity and
> economic development throughout society. Properly designed and
> implemented interventions in the early childhood years can have
> multi-dimensional benefits.
>
> (Young 1998: 209–10)

The World Bank in particular funds early childhood programmes in poor
countries, based on assumptions about better parenting and improved life
chances from early childhood education. This view that targeted early childhood interventions to poor children will improve their life chances, irrespective of inequalities or cultural traditions of the society in which they grow up, is
a powerful one. It is a very common approach towards poor children, in rich
countries as well as poor.

Why is it that those programmes for poor children ignore socio-economic
conditions? One of the reasons is that child development as a discipline
works at a micro level. It focuses on individual circumstances and individual
learning. Many studies detail the effect of certain kinds of education or care
programmes on young children. The underlying assumption is that it is
not the job of researchers or teachers to change the socio-economic circumstances of children. That is more properly seen as the job of politicians.
The only change that can be brought about at the micro level of child development is to influence the individual actions of children, their carers and
teachers.

How does child development take account of
socio-cultural and economic conditions?

Psychology has, for most of its history, been a positivist science that claims to
seek universal truths and to uncover universal patterns. Developmental psychologists largely believed that psychological processes can be investigated
through the study of the individual behaviour and learning of children; and
by aggregating the findings from many children and from many studies universal norms or laws can be established. Children are assumed to pass through
the same stages and to show the same age-related characteristics whether they
live in remote parts of Nepal or in Chicago. This view is changing rapidly. Here

I consider some of the criticisms from within child development, besides those of the cultural psychologists.

Critics of child development argue that psychology cannot be the same as biology, and the society or community a child grows up in makes a critical difference to the way he learns and feels. Child development, in seeking universal norms, has been based on too narrow a sample to be able to establish any norms satisfactorily, even if it were possible to do so. Robert LeVine, an anthropologist concerned primarily with childhood, has surveyed psychological handbooks over a period of 50 years in order to explore the extent to which environmental issues and cultural impact are taken into account. Although there have been substantial changes in developmental psychology in that time, for example, in awareness of infant capacities, the narrow sample base of psychology has, in his view, always been a problem. He points to the language studies of Ochs and Schieffelin as an example of the misperceptions of developmental psychology.

> To most middle-class Western readers, the description of verbal and non-verbal behaviour of middle-class caregivers with their children seem very familiar, desirable and even natural . . . The characteristics of care-giver speech [e.g. baby-talk] and comportment [the way babies are held] that have been specified [by psychologists] are highly valued by members of white middle-class society, including researchers, readers and subjects of the studies. [But] the general pattern of white middle-class caregiving that has been described in the literature are characteristic neither of all societies nor of all social groups.
>
> (Ochs and Schieffelin 1984: 283)

Cross-cultural psychology is a rapidly developing field. It recognizes the narrow sample base of psychology, but considers it can be addressed by investigating the behaviour or learning styles of children and their parents from different cultures or communities by systematically comparing them. But cross-cultural psychology itself begs the question of scientific methodology. Can behaviour and culture be broken down into little sections and compared? Paul Eldering and Lotte Leseman (1999) argue that research studies on 'culture' fall along an axis. One end is behavioural universalism. Behavioural universalism is the view that the same behaviour traits and patterns appear in children wherever they are, perhaps with minor variations according to culture. These minor variations can be charted accurately through cross-cultural surveys. This view accepts the positivist approach: cultural behaviour patterns can be broken down and compared.

The other end of the axis is cultural relativism. From this perspective 'cultures' cannot be usefully compared. Each community or society generates its own meanings and ways of behaving and, in any case, these are themselves continually changing. So no comparison could be straightforward. Many cross-cultural studies operate somewhere between these extremes. For instance, the well-known study by Tobin compared children in nurseries in China, Japan and the USA. He and his colleagues filmed the children in the nurseries in each country and talked to the staff. Then he showed the films to staff in the other countries, and asked them to discuss what they saw. This method revealed the assumptions held by the workers in each country, but also gave them a forum to comment on their own beliefs in the light of what they saw.

Many of the socio-cultural psychologists discussed in Chapter 3 have steered clear of any wider analysis of culture. They have avoided the anthropological and socio-economic debates raised in this chapter. They have focused more narrowly on specific groups. They have used the phrase a 'community of practice' to describe a particular set of circumstances entered into in a particular place at a particular time. Culture in this sense is not synonymous with nationality or ethnicity.

Jerome Bruner concedes that culture is nuanced and conflictual. He argues that culture 'rarely conforms to anything resembling a cookbook of recipes or formulas for it is a universal of all cultures that they contain factional or institutional interests' (Bruner 1996: 14). But not even he acknowledges the socio-economic circumstances that affect so many children. Is this blindness, or lack of concern with the circumstances of so many children, displayed by the early childhood community excusable or inevitable?

The ethics of childhood

There is some common sense in the traditional micro approach of child development that emphasizes that children and their parents must learn to cope with bad circumstances and change them from within. But increasingly this approach is being challenged. One of the grounds for doing so is that it is *unethical* to stand by and see so many children suffer. We certainly consider that we have obligations to protect children within the UK and have many mechanisms in place to do just this. On an international basis, the UN Convention on the Rights of the Child lays an obligation on all signatories to the Convention to ensure 'protection, participation and provision' for all children. Whilst this obligation is open to many interpretations (see Chapter 7), it is clear from the above discussion that the rights of children to grow up in safe environments are not being met.

The sociologist Zygmunt Bauman argues that through the media of television and telecommunications, those who live in rich countries see and read about those who live in poor countries. And with such knowledge comes guilt and obligation.

We live in a globalizing world. That means all of us, consciously or not, depend on each other. Whatever we do or refrain from doing affects the lives of people who live in places we'll never visit. And whatever those distant people do or desist from doing has its impact on the conditions in which we, each one of us separately and together, conduct our lives. Living in a globalizing world means being aware of the pain, misery and suffering of countless people who we will never meet in person . . . Our world, whatever else it might be, is also a producer of horror and atrocity . . . [There is] an abysmal gap between the suffering we see and our ability to help the sufferers.

('Quality and Inequality', *Guardian*, 29 Jan. 2001)

John Rawls, the American philospher, argued in his weighty and landmark book *A Theory of Justice* (1999), that justice is most required when life is brief and there is a struggle for scarce resources. He argued, in effect, for the old maxim 'do as you would be done by'. To apply his argument, if you were reincarnated as a female child orphan in Tanzania, or a child soldier in Sierra Leone, would you receive just treatment? If not, should you do something about it?

There are not only empirical issues, but unavoidable ethical and moral issues as well in trying to confront and intervene in the practices of others. Neither developmental psychology nor neuroscientific and genetic research can, by themselves, produce answers to such very difficult questions. But nor can we afford to disengage from such moral difficulties, if only because so many children suffer.

Summary

This chapter considered how the differences in attitudes and behaviour between groups and communities of people have been investigated, and how significant those differences might be in terms of understanding children. Anthropology has been an important discipline in carrying out such studies. These differences are usually summed up as 'culture'. The chapter concludes that the word 'culture' is used in such a blanket way as to be misleading. The chapter also points to the inequalities in life chances between children who live in prosperous countries such as the UK and the USA, and those who live in poor countries. Being poor in a poor country also shapes how young children grow and what they learn.

Main messages from this chapter

1   Beware of using the term 'culture'. It raises more problems than it solves.
2   Poverty and injustice cut across 'culture' and make life very difficult for young children wherever they are growing up.
3   When children die in their millions, this raises profound ethical and practical considerations for everyone.

What to read next

DeLoache, J. and Gottleib, A. (2000) *A World of Babies: Imagined Childcare Guides for Seven Societies*. Cambridge: Cambridge University Press.

6 Past, Present and Future

Everyone has a past, a history of life events that has made them into what they are now. In Chapter 1, I considered how we personally remember the past and how it affects us. But in a similar way, all ideas and practices have a past. The actions we take now, the policies that shape our actions, the places we work in, have a history. Is it worth knowing about the past? Many people would argue that it is not; the past is gone, done and dusted. Henry Ford, who founded the Ford Motor Company, is famous for saying 'History is bunk'. Some cynics say that the only thing you can learn from history is that you can learn nothing from history; its messages are always ignored. The argument put forward in this chapter is that history *is* important. The past helps us understand the present, and, contrary to the cynical view, even helps us shape the future. Studying history is a means of exploring the past, of understanding the continuities, the discontinuities, and the wider contexts of what we do and how we behave. History is also a useful discipline in studying early childhood.

Science is about establishing general rules, and making general predictions. History, like anthropology, is concerned with understanding the uniqueness of situations, the special features that make a person or a place, or a time, different from any other. History is also concerned with the play of power. Who pulls the ropes behind the scenes? Isaiah Berlin sums up the particularity of history very well:

> Historians, whose business it is to tell us what actually happened in the world [consequently] fight shy of rigid theoretical patterns into which the facts may sometimes have to be fitted with a good deal of awkwardness and artificiality. And this instinct is a sound one. The proper aim of the sciences is to note the number of similarities in the behaviour of objects and to construct propositions of the greatest degree of generality from which the largest number of such uniformities can logically be deduced. In history our purpose is the opposite. When we wish to describe a particular revolution – what actually took

place – the last thing we wish to do is to concentrate solely upon those characteristics of it which it has in common with as many other revolutions as we can discover, ignoring the differences as irrelevant to our study; and so what a historian wishes to bring out is what is specific, unique in a given character or series of events or historical situation . . . The historian is concerned to paint a portrait which conveys the unique pattern of experience, and not an X-ray photograph which is capable of acting as a general symbol for all structures of a similar type.

(Berlin 1997: 22)

History in some ways is the most challenging of disciplines. Historical scholarship usually requires detective work, tracking down documents, pictures or other artefacts that are lost or forgotten, tucked away in dusty archives or sitting unlabelled on a computer disk. History involves interpreting, sifting through, juxtaposing and comparing many different sources of information, written, visual and oral, to build up a picture of a certain set of events. Perhaps more than any other discipline, it requires imagination, judgement and the ability to weave all the disparate elements into a coherent tale about why and how change and transformation has occurred. No organizations, communities or societies are static or without a history although that history is often ignored.

Nowadays, history books are best sellers. They set people and events in a wider context, sometimes offering a romantic view of the past, making it seem much more interesting than our own colourless, muddled times.

At worst, though, historians and history books glorify the past in order to justify certain actions in the present. Eric Hobsbawm, a distinguished economic historian, argues that history has been used ideologically to justify nationalistic or religious interpretations of events, so it is very important that historians 'tell the truth' and, to the best of their ability, establish the 'facts' (Hobsbawm 1997). For example, both Jews and Muslims argue that 'history' supports their claim to ownership of the holy city of Jerusalem. The evidence suggests that the history of Jerusalem was more muddled and complex than either version will allow. A few historians have claimed that the Holocaust of Jews and gipsies in Nazi concentration camps never took place. Disputes of this magnitude illustrate how important it is to establish the historical accuracy of events and the range of perspectives involved. Modern historical scholarship is generally very painstaking, although, of course, historians themselves may emphasize or favour one interpretation of the facts over another. The evidence may not be crystal clear, or may even have been falsified or destroyed. But positivism and relativism are not quite the battleground that they are in some other disciplines.

The history of childhood

The history of childhood, now a lively subsection of history, tells us how expectations of children's capabilities and behaviour have changed.

Philippe Ariès, a French historian, is credited with making historians take childhood seriously. In his famous book *Centuries of Childhood* (1962), he claimed that childhood did not really exist until the sixteenth or seventeenth century. Before that, children had been treated as small and inadequate adults. He considered they were often maltreated, and that today we are much more careful about protecting children. He substantiated his claim partly by using pictorial evidence. Pictures and illustrations that remain from that time often depict children as little adults: small but with adult proportions and adult clothes.

While historians recognize the importance of Ariès' work, many now dispute his claim that children were not allowed to be children. Linda Pollock, for example, claims that parents have always shown a range of emotions towards their children, from great fondness and indulgence to punitive coldness (Pollock 1987). Nicholas Orme has written an illustrated history of children in medieval times (Orme 2001). He also suggests that children were part of everyday life – they played, annoyed their elders and betters, and were loved by their parents. Paula Fass, an American historian has edited an encyclopaedia of children and childhood (2004), which gives a useful overview of the range of debates about the history of childhood, although from a USA perspective.

There was a spectrum of opinion about childhood in all the historical periods that we know about. But at certain periods or among certain groups or classes, particular ideas were very powerful. In Chapter 1, I quoted the example of well-to-do children in Tudor times. The learning that was expected of them was phenomenal by today's standards – oral and written fluency in several languages; a sophisticated understanding of rhetoric, law and religion; exquisite handwriting; an appreciation of art; an ability to play an instrument; and the physical dexterity to step out in intricate sixteenth-century dances such as galliards. And if that was not enough, they might well ride, hunt and fence. All this by age 11 or 12.

There was a widespread view among the well-to-do in Victorian England when universal education was under discussion that the poor were not fit to learn. Offering them education would mislead and confuse them and give them ideas above their station. Hugh Cunningham has written a history of the way that poor children have been treated in England (1991). As industrialization swept through England, families moved from the country into the towns and cities. Instead of helping out in the fields or with animals in the homestead, children were left to fend for themselves in the streets. Children just hung around with not much to do (and probably not much to eat). There were constant complaints by the middle classes about the children of the poor. They were always in the way. They formed unruly gangs. They were out of control. In the eighteenth and nineteenth centuries, the predominant public view was that these children should be put to work and not idle about in the streets. There were many attempts to set up industrial schools for them, where they were found small repetitive jobs, for example, knitting and nail-making. The trouble was that these schools were expensive and did not make enough money to cover their costs. The children did not earn enough or work fast enough to make it worthwhile.

As more industry became established, poor children were put to work in factories and mines. A small proportion of children were employed as chimney sweeps. Because they were so small, they could climb up chimneys more easily. But social reformers were concerned about what work did to children. Children spent very long hours in harsh conditions, with very few breaks. They became stunted, pale and tired. The child chimney sweeps attracted a lot of attention. They were more visible – and very dirty and sooty – and they were compared to slaves. Books and poems were written about their plight. The poet William Blake, in 1789, in *Songs of Innocence*, wrote a very famous poem about child sweeps:

> When my mother died I was very young,
> And my father sold me while yet my tongue
> Could scarcely cry 'weep! weep! weep!'
> So your chimneys I sweep and in soot I sleep.

Gradually legislation was introduced to restrict the number of hours children worked, first of all to 10 hours a day. But as children worked less, they hung around again. Middle- and upper-class children had been attending school for a long time, although in Victorian times, boys were much better educated than girls. Perhaps schools could also keep poor children off the street, and give them a smattering of education? Universal education was finally introduced in 1872 (much later than in many other European countries), but it only ever had limited aims. Schools were like education factories for poor children. It kept them from being idle and a public nuisance. It gave them just about enough of an introduction to the three 'R's – reading, writing and arithmetic – to enable them to be more employable. Children were allowed to bring their younger brothers and sisters to school – otherwise they would have had to stay at home and look after them.

As Robin Alexander (2000) has pointed out, this mean-spirited conception of education has dogged education in England to the present day. We still use the Victorian education-factory buildings in the cities and we still have narrow aims for education. We still want to keep poor children off the streets. (The history of education is rather different in Scotland, where education was more highly valued and private schools were less common.)

The debate about the poor has always been with us in the UK. At the beginning of the twentieth century, many people, including some very eminent psychologists, like Francis Galton, a founding father of the study of psychology, believed in eugenics or population control. There were arguments about whether the poor were a degenerate strain of the population whose rights needed curtailing (a eugenic argument that took a different, and terrifying, turn in Germany). In 1938, the magazine *Nursery World* reported a conference organized by the National Council for Mental Hygiene at Central Hall Westminster on the topic 'Is our national intelligence declining?' The organizers concluded that it was, since the more intelligent had fewer children, and the poor bred uncontrollably (1938: 237). The recent Sure Start programme (see below) was aimed at poor children. A key component of the programme is to educate parents so that they bring up their children not to be a nuisance. A historian might say *plus ça change* . . . 'nothing changes'.

One of the biggest changes in our attitude to childhood has been in expectations of survival, at least in the North. Nowadays if a young child dies it is a catastrophe (but it is still an everyday event in the South). Children's survival rates used to be very low everywhere – on average perhaps 50 per cent of children might survive into adulthood. In the UK, public health measures (sanitation, clean milk supplies, immunization, and so on) were gradually introduced in the nineteenth and twentieth centuries, which brought down the death rate. Until then everyone had frequent experience of the death of friends and relatives. Stepmothers and stepfathers, stepbrothers and sisters were very common. Trying to make sense of death was a normal experience for children and their parents.

Religion was a primary source of explanation for, and an attempt to come to terms with, death (spiritual explanations, spells, witchdoctors and malign fates are still common explanations in countries with high infant mortality). Many books for children were about death and the meaning of death. Bedtime stories might include an account of the death of a good child, with angels hovering; or the death of a naughty child facing everlasting torment in hell. Heaven and hell were part of every child's vocabulary. Religious understanding was an important aspect of education – the UK magazine *Nursery World* used to carry regular religious features. These speculations about life and death and the meaning and conduct of daily life have largely dropped out of current thinking about childhood.

Stoicism and resilience were necessary survival skills for children. (They still are for many millions of children in the South.) These aspects of character were highly valued. The Victorian writer Charles Dickens always portrayed children in this way, bravely putting up with adult wickedness and cruelty. But as children's survival becomes more or less assured, society values other attributes of childhood besides stoicism and obedience. Concepts of risk have changed dramatically – children are now protected against every eventuality. Contemporary parents in the North invest a great deal of time, money and effort in individual children. As they have become the focus of intense parental attention, children have become more cosseted and shielded against the tasks and duties of everyday life. They have become more 'childlike'. Zelitzer, in a famous book called *Pricing the Priceless Child* (1985), gives an account of the changes in views about the economic value of children. She gives examples of various insurance scams involving the illness and death of children. In a subsequent paper (2002), she argues that although children still work and make an economic contribution to the household, although much less than previously, we do not see and do not rate such contributions. Instead children are regarded primarily as consumers, and targeted ferociously by advertisers.

Charles Dickens was familiar with scams involving children. In the following extract from *Nicholas Nickleby*, first published in 1839, Squeers, the proprietor of Dotheboys Hall, a boys' school, explains how he paid for his own family's medical bills:

> The fact is we have only one extra with our boys, and that is for doctors when required – and not then unless we are sure of our customers . . . After my medical bill was run up, we picked out 5 little boys (sons of tradesmen as was sure to pay) that had never had the scarlet fever, and we sent one to a cottage where they'd got it, and we put the four others to sleep with him, and they took it, and then the doctor came and attended 'em once all round, and we divided my total among 'em and added it on to their little bills, and the parents paid it. Ha . . . we always do it. Why when Mrs Squeers was brought to bed . . . we ran the whooping cough through half a dozen boys and charged her expenses among 'em, monthly nurse included. Ha.

This may seem like horrific cruelty now, but there is a comparison to be made in current thinking about the status and worth of children. For example, some economists (and some leading psychologists such as Sandra Scarr – see Chapter 3), routinely calculate the financial trade-off between investment in childcare and outcomes for children. If investing in childcare makes little difference to how children perform later in life, it is not worth making the investment. Poor childcare is 'good enough'. It does not matter if many young children are cooped up together with bored caregivers. The quality of children's lives in the here and now, and the pleasures they might get from their daily life, are of no consequence in this economic reckoning. This economic argument is used as a justification for avoiding regulation in the USA. Children have been termed by the journal *The Economist* as 'negative equity', in an article suggesting that the public should be compensated for the trouble they cause to others. In this article, 'Mum's the Word', the anonymous author argued that children should be charged more for air travel because they are a nuisance to sit next to on a fight, they wriggle, cry and make a mess (*Economist*, 5 Dec. 1998: 20).

Children have always had their own subculture, their own rhymes, games and plays that get passed on from one generation to the next. This subculture has been described by Peter and Iona Opie (1959). They collected rhymes and games from school playgrounds, and traced some of them back over several centuries. More recent studies, such as that of Bishop and Curtis (2001) on school playgrounds, suggest that these rhymes and games are still practised, even although the places that children can play have become much more restricted because of worries about safety.

Changes in our understanding about childhood happen before our eyes. Some people argue that children nowadays are profoundly affected by consumerism. (This subject is dealt with in more detail in Chapter 9.) The Canadian author Stephen Kline has demonstrated how children have been ruthlessly targeted by advertising. In his book *Out of the Garden* (1993), he illustrates how children's favourite domestic objects have changed. Children's toys used to be relatively simple and homemade – as they still are in most parts of the world. But in rich countries children have come to judge happiness by what they possess – the latest toys or trainers or computer games.

Studying the history of childhood illustrates just how much what we think of as normal is particular to a time and a place. The history of childhood gives us yet another angle to understand the present. Child development as a discipline tends to assume that understanding about childhood is cumulative and scientific; and that the knowledge that we have today is the best of all and supersedes that of the past. This is unlikely to be the case, for the reasons that have been explored here and in previous chapters.

The history of policy-making for young children in the UK

What follows is the history of policy-making for early education and care in the UK. History is about particularities, not about generalities, so in this chapter I am focusing on one example, the UK. In other European countries this history would be different; even more so in the southern hemisphere. The common thread is perhaps the disregard which governments show towards young children, and the persistence of this failure of compassion in English-speaking countries.

Historical methods can also be usefully applied to childcare policy and practice. Those who make the rules and regulations for nurseries and other forms of provision and training for young children are influenced by a number of factors. They try to take what is best from the 'scientific' understanding of the child development of their day. William Kessen, one of the most famous of American developmental psychologists, described the history of child development as 'a history of rediscovery . . . with some modest advances towards truth' (1965: 2).

Christine Hardyment (2007) has shown just how much scientific advice to mothers has changed over the years. In the twentieth century, there has been a complete turnaround. She contrasts Truby King, writing in the 1930s, who said that science showed children should be brought up with the utmost regularity, with the liberal advice of Benjamin Spock. King said babies should be fed on time, put out in the fresh air for a regulation amount of time, and never indulged. Half a century later, Spock was recommending the opposite. Babies should be fed on demand and looked after in a thoroughly relaxed way.

Upper- and middle-class mothers of the eighteenth century were expected to be genteel ladies of leisure. They employed nannies and governesses for their young children. The nannies were mainly working-class girls, for whom looking after children was a form of domestic service. Yet, as Gathorne-Hardy (1972) points out, these nannies were entrusted with the upbringing and education of the young children in their care.

The role of women in the family is a recurring theme in the history of childcare and early education. The emancipation and economic independence of women and the gradual dismantling of sexual stereotypes are some of the greatest historical changes of the last century. The perception of women, their inclinations and capacities – their noble, but submissive character – as mothers, childcarers and teachers, shaped the availability and scope of provision for young children.

Well-to-do women expected someone else to care for their children. Friedrich Froebel, an Austrian teacher, argued that it was a noble role for women to teach children. Froebel is credited with developing the first nursery school, in 1836. He had a following in the UK, and some private nurseries were set up to demonstrate his ideas. He felt that children should have great freedom to play and to develop their innate spiritual responsiveness to nature. But he also thought it was a woman's job to bring up children. Trained and dedicated women would make excellent kindergarten teachers.

> She is in duty bound not only to watch the unfolding of the powers and capabilities of her pupils but also to teach them to love the good and hate the bad, to awaken in them new desires, to develop new interests, to arouse their higher instincts, and then to satisfy these cravings after higher ideals by opening up to them the wonderful world of nature, of art, of literature, and so give them a glimpse of the joys that await them and the rich heritage that may be theirs for the asking.
>
> (cited in Steedman 1988: 83)

The arguments about women's role in relation to children crop up again and again.

Nursery education has often attracted radical thinkers. Robert Owen provided the first workplace nursery at his factory at New Lanark in Scotland as early as 1818. He argued that children needed caring for in an enlightened way, and their mothers would work better knowing that their children were being well looked after. (His bottom line was the profit of his factory.) As well as Froebel's disciples, the Italian educator Maria Montessori also set up nurseries in the UK in the early twentieth century, some of which still continue. In 1927, ten years or so after Montessori visited the UK, the philosopher Bertrand Russell and his wife Dora set up an experimental school, Beacon Hill, that attracted a lot of attention. Russell was inspired by the new 'science' of psychoanalysis, somewhat contradictorily mixed with behaviouristic ideas about regular training to inculcate good moral habits. But the overriding idea was that repressing emotions and feelings in children would prove destructive in later life – especially sexual repression. 'Education consists in the cultivation of the instincts, not in their suppression.'

Russell spelt out his ideas in a book, *On Education, Especially in Early Childhood*, first published in 1926 and reprinted many times. He scandalized people with his psychoanalytical explanations about the dangers of repressing children's basic instincts. Outraged critics protested. 'If the old fashioned virtue of obedience is to be ruled out of a child's life . . . the children of the future will be exterminated by the process of eating what they like, going to bed when they like, playing with fire when they like' (*TES*, 27 Feb. 1926). Russell argued that the rich were at liberty – in fact had a duty – to pave the way for others with their experiments. In his book, he argued that we should start with values, the attributes that civilized people should encourage and foster. His values included vitality, courage, sensitivity and intelligence.

Perhaps the most famous of the radical nursery experiments was Malting House School at Cambridge, run by Susan Isaacs. Like the others, this was a school for the young children of professionals, mainly academics. One-third of the children were residential. The regime was inspired by the theories of the psychoanalyst Melanie Klein about childhood aggression and repression, and the need to fully express emotion. The job of the wise adult was to chronicle every nuanced step each child took on his or her emotional and intellectual journey. The school became legendary for the freedom it allowed to children. Reporters clustered on the doorstep for salacious copy. Susan Isaac's own tone was more sober. She scrupulously observed the young children under her care, and subsequently wrote two highly regarded books about this experience. She became a columnist for a popular magazine, and gave authoritative and dignified advice on childrearing to a generation of its readers, before finally becoming a Kleinian analyst.

While the well-to-do were experimenting, the poor were stuck. In 1900, more than half of all 3- and 4-year-olds were in school. Katherine Bathurst, an inspector for the Board of Education, castigated this system in a famous report published in 1905:

> Let us now follow the baby of three years through part of one day of school life. He is placed on a hard wooden seat with a desk in front of him . . . he is told to fold his arms and keep quiet . . . He is surrounded by a large number of babies all under similar alarming and incomprehensible conditions . . . A certified teacher has 60 babies to instruct, many of whom are hungry, cold and dirty . . . They are heavy eyed with unslept sleep . . . What possible good is there in forcing a little child to master the names of letters and numbers at this age? The strain on teachers is terrific.
>
> (*TES*, May 1905)

Her report shocked people. But the result of her campaigning was to exclude young children from school. In 1907, funding was withdrawn for children under 5 in schools. By 1910, the number of children under 5 in school was halved, and by 1920 it was down to only 15 per cent.

But leaving young children outside of school was no good either. Poor children had nowhere else to go if their mothers were working – as most then were. Margaret McMillan, a leading nursery education campaigner, did her best to argue for nursery schools:

> What young children require is fresh air, play and rest, and this is what the nursery school offers them. The development of nursery schools would tend greatly to raise the standard of physical health among the children.
>
> (*Nursery Schools: Advisory Committee on Education*, Labour Party, 1919)

In 1923, the Nursery Schools Association (NSA)[1] was formed to campaign for more nursery schools. It produced a series of pamphlets on nursery education, some of which sold more than 200,000 copies. It also issued an authoritative policy statement in 1927, arguing that nursery schools were places where children could be free and well looked after, unlike their cramped homes in cramped streets:

> Underlying all mental and bodily development lies the need for free activity. Without it neither healthy growth of body and spirit, nor training in self-control is possible . . . Free activity involves the provision of spontaneous and purposeful activity in spacious open-air conditions . . . as well as an atmosphere of love, joy and freedom . . . The daily routine must provide for the right alternation of rest and

activity through the day . . . It is undesirable to accept the hours of the ordinary school day as the limit for Nursery school.

(NSA 1927, BAECE/BLPES)

Despite this vigorous campaigning, by 1939, there were only 118 nursery schools; together with under-5s in infant schools they catered for 180,000 children.

The NSA campaigned for state nursery schools but there was an older, rival organization, with a different campaigning focus. The National Society of Day Nurseries (NSDN) was founded in 1906 to set standards and register day nurseries and crèches. It described itself as 'the only voluntary body specifically devoted to the problem of the care of young children whose mothers go out to work' (NSDN 1923). By 1914, 80 day nurseries were recognized, many of them mill nurseries. The officers of the Society met in the drawing rooms of Piccadilly, and held fundraising balls at the Carlton Club, the bastion of the Establishment. Despite their fashionable charitable image, they made serious efforts to support the training of girls for nursery work or to raise standards of private day nurseries and crèches. Their work eventually led to the founding of the Nursery Nurses Examination Board (NNEB).

At the beginning of the Second World War, it was important to evacuate children from the towns and cities because of the danger of bombing. The government tried to provide nursery centres for billeted mothers and evacuee children – to be staffed, if possible, by voluntary workers. It was also obvious that more needed to be done to encourage women workers in industry. There was an argument about funds, but once they were sorted out, nurseries were set up very quickly. By the end of the war there were 1450 wartime nurseries, each catering for children from birth to 5 years, and open from 7am to 7pm. Their cost was estimated at £10 million over the course of the war (Ferguson and Fitzgerald 1954: 203).

The disputes in the war about nurseries had been as much about mothering as about children. Mothers were working and childcare had to be provided. But after the war, mothers had to make way for returning soldiers. They were encouraged to give up their jobs and stay at home with their children. The theories of Bowlby about mother–child attachment provided a rationale for closing nurseries. By 1947, predictably, 700 nurseries – nearly half – had closed. Some of the remainder changed into nursery schools; others continued as social services day nurseries.

The NSA objected that nursery schools should not be closed. They still had a useful role to play providing outlets for emotion and instinctual expression in young children (BAECE/BLPES). During the war there was much concern about whether young children were learning to be aggressive; controlling aggression in children was regarded as being very important (see Chapter 3). Nurseries could support mothers in dealing with nervous, clinging children.

> The way of life [in nursery schools] organized for the children is simple and childlike and is planned in relation to the physical and psychological needs of children . . . Aggressive dominating 'toughs' discover the happiness that comes from friendly co-operation with others.
>
> (De Lissa 1945: 3)

The themes of aggression and loss, and inner emotional balance were explored in detail by John Bowlby in his theory of attachment (see Chapter 3). An article by a child guidance psychologist put it more romantically.

> We must remember that the child's inner world is a romantic one, peopled like a Breughel canvas with a crowded population of shining angels in armour wielding swords of justice on a host of goblins, dragons and bat-like figures with yawning mouths and scaly tails.
>
> (Bodman 1945: 17)

Dorothy Gardner, head of child development at the Institute of Education, argued that

> we cannot educate a very unhappy child, or one who is even temporarily in the throes of jealousy, anger or mourning. We are also coming to realise that emotional satisfactions lie at the root of all intellectual interests and that feelings are the driving force between all intellectual effort.
>
> (1956: 11)

But no sooner had Bowlby become the accepted wisdom of those working with young children than there was a new theoretical giant on the scene – Jean Piaget. As we saw in Chapter 3, Piaget revolutionized thinking about young children. The government in the UK commissioned the Central Advisory Council for Education to produce a report entitled *Children and Their Primary Schools* (1967). The Plowden Report, as it became known, after its chairwoman Lady Plowden, included nursery education. It endorsed the theories of Jean Piaget about the child as an individual, self-propelled scientist experimenting with the world. It highlighted educational inequalities, except this time working-class children were not physically stunted or unable to control their fierce emotional lives. They were now intellectually stunted, and the job of the nursery and primary schools was to reawaken intellectual curiosity (HMSO 1967).

Plowden was influenced by Bowlby as well as by Piaget. She was hostile to working mothers – although she herself used nannies. Her report maintained that it was no business of the state to provide services for working parents.

Nursery education from then on (as it still is today) changed from offering all-round full-time care, education and healthy living. It became a part-time service, with the more limited objective of fostering children's intellectual development. The hours of nursery education became shorter than those of any other comparable European country, between 12 and 15 hours per week.

For half a century after the war, from the 1950s to 2000, working mothers and their children were an unpopular cause. Simon Yudkin, a paediatrician, wrote a widely supported report (1967) that detailed the large numbers of (mainly working-class) women who went out to work and the lack of affordable childcare they faced (and still do in the UK). He said there was no evidence for the common view ascribed to Bowlby, that working mothers harmed their children. He recommended a proper government investigation into what he considered was an intolerable situation, which weighed heavily against poor families; and in particular against black children. The proportion of black working mothers, particularly from Afro-Caribbean backgrounds, was far higher than that of any other group.

Instead, Margaret Thatcher, then Minister for Education, firmly endorsed the educational approach and commitment to nursery education set out in the Plowden Report. The government committed itself to providing 250,000 new nursery places within 10 years, for 35 per cent of 3-year-olds and 75 per cent of 4-year-olds, plus an additional 15 per cent of full-time places. Urban aid would be used to fund the first tranche of nursery places, and some local authorities drew up plans for expansion (Department of Education 1978. Circular 2–73).

Meanwhile, the shortage of nursery education places had prompted a mother, herself a teacher, called Belle Tutaev, to set up a campaign for more nursery education. She encouraged mothers to start their own schools – or playgroups. The Preschool Playgroup Association (PPA, now known as the Preschool Learning Alliance) was founded in 1961. Mothers acted as volunteers, helping out in the playgroup.

Jerome Bruner was persuaded by the government to leave the USA for a few years in the 1970s to take up a post at Oxford University as director of a project that explored British policy on early years. He and his team provided a useful picture of the state of early education and care in Britain, but his policy recommendations showed up his prejudices. He thought mothers should stay at home, and playgroups – volunteerism – was the best way forward for early years services. 'No long term benefit could accrue by making early pre-school care seem like the domain of professionals. It would surely have a corrosive effect on the self-confidence of parents and reduce volunteer efforts' (Bruner 1980: 231).

Bruner's assumption of maternal involvement through volunteering was implicitly based on a traditional view of domesticity. Women stayed at home to look after their children; and, indeed, looking after their children was their prime, if not always fulfilling, function. As one contributor to the PPA magazine *Contact* put it: 'I seem to be fighting a battle between the part of me that is determined not to be a domestic cabbage and the part that wants to do well the job of looking after husband, children and home' (October 1965). For such middle-class full-time housewives, playgroups fitted the bill exactly. For the poor working mothers, the lack of childcare was a major problem. Lady Plowden, who had become chairwoman of PPA, now argued that state provision was completely unnecessary:

> It's no large overall system which is needed . . . only in the last resort is there need to provide a substitute for those who are completely unable to manage themselves . . . When we are planning for the care of our young children we must also enable care in its widest sense to be given to those who have the day to day responsibility, their parents and in particular, their mothers.
>
> (Plowden 1977: 9)

As a result of these attitudes towards women and the obsession with the misdemeanours of the poor, early education and childcare in the UK has always been characterized by a large voluntary and private sector.

Ten years of Labour Government, 1997–2007

The Labour Government came to power in 1997 full of good intentions about redressing the past. It would make nursery education widely available, it would integrate care and education, it would increase the number of childcare places for working women, it would support community initiatives to improve life for young children from poor backgrounds. From being a political backwater, the provision of early education and childcare became a popular campaigning issue. The government has sought ways to coordinate and increase the provision of early education and care, and to improve its quality. Responsibility for care services was transferred from the Department of Health to the Department for Education and Skills. A common regulatory system was introduced under Ofsted. A common core curriculum for all children under 6 has been introduced. A Minister for Children was appointed. A good account of the situation and subsequent changes is presented in various OECD reports (2000b, 2001, 2006), and in two National Audit Office reports (2004, 2006).

But the trajectory of the past, as always, persisted into the present. Instead of working out the long-standing contradictions within the different types of services, and arriving at a more coherent policy, politicians tinkered with existing arrangements, rather than grasping the nettle and substantially changing them. Nursery education has been extended to cover all children, although nearly 60 per cent of provision for 3-year-olds is in the private and voluntary sector. Essentially the part-time offer of two and a half hours a day free nursery education for 3- and 4-year-old children – compared for example with 5–8 hours per day in most European countries – has not changed. Whereas the two and a half hours of nursery education is supply-side funded (the money goes directly to the service), the childcare is still demand led and parents must pay at the point of use, often a very hefty sum (although more subsidies are available). So nursery education and childcare remain essentially separate regimes, as before. Vulnerable children are still catered for under targeted area arrangements, although these have changed their names according to the latest initiative – variously centres of early excellence, neighbourhood nurseries, Sure Start for under-threes, children's centres. There were also a variety of short-lived local coordinating arrangements – first, early years development and care partnerships (EYDCPs); then a reinstatement of local authority control and management. At the time of writing local 'Children's Fund' committees are being proposed.

Policy has proceeded in a series of leaps and jumps, reorganizations, restructurings, and 'rebrandings'. There were a bewildering number of short-term initiatives that were withdrawn as it became apparent – predictably – that they were not working. At the same time there was a merry-go-round of the civil servants responsible for shaping the policies. The civil service has always been generalist, recruiting on the basis of varied administrative experience, rather than on expert knowledge. In a country like Sweden there are well-developed policies on early years, developed by a constant and stable group of experts in the Ministry. In the UK it is unusual for people to remain in the same post for long, and the lack of continuity among senior civil servants in turn impacted on the understanding of and delivery of policy.

Demand-led policies (providing childcare tax credits in order to enable mothers to work) has led to a sevenfold increase in the development of the for-profit (private) sector, which was previously very small. In particular, the corporate sector now has the biggest share of the childcare market. Some 15 companies between them provide over 50,000 places (Laing and Buisson 2007). The government considered that the private market – except in poor areas – was best placed to provide new places, as it could expand quickly and flexibly. As in many other areas of government, the importance of the private sector, and business methods, has dominated government thinking (Pollock 2004). The local authority role in respect of childcare has now shrunk to that of a mainly regulatory body. Far from local authorities leading an expansion of publicly funded, publicly provided provision, a model followed by various other European countries (OECD 2006), the duty of the local authority has been reduced to 'childcare market managers'. Their job is now to stimulate and coordinate the private and voluntary sector in meeting government targets for the provision of early years services. The government has commissioned a series of research reports to advise them about how it might be done (Harries et al. 2004: PriceWaterhouseCoopers 2007). Figures 6.1 and 6.2 give an indication of the extent of private sector provision.

The notions of choice and flexibility in order to compete in a global market have been a guiding principle of government action across the board (Giddens 1998). Because parents needs are seen to be so diverse, they need 'choice' in childcare (Waldfogel 2004). Choice is, however, a mirage. The private for-profit sector tends to operate a core hour service, e.g. 9–4pm because the profit margins are less for childcare outside these core hours (Laing and

NURSERY MARKET SIZE BY PROVIDER TYPE, UK 2006 [£Millions]

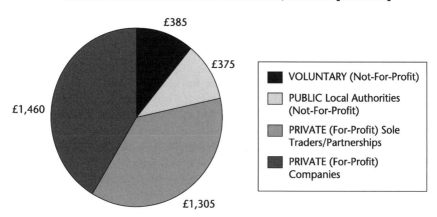

Figure 6.1 Share of childcare nursery market by provider.

Source: Laing and Buisson (2007), Children's Nurseries Conference.

Figure 6.2 Increase in the total value of the childcare nursery sector since 1990.

Source: Laing and Buisson (2007), Children's Nurseries Conference.

Buisson 2007). Cleveland et al. (2007) suggest that because parents are reluctant to travel with young children to use childcare, most provision, to be financially viable and attract customers, has to be local. If the local population of young children is not big enough, no choice is possible – a single centre-based provider will mop up all the demand. If the sole supplier of centre-based childcare is part of a large nursery chain owned by (as increasingly likely a private equity company), parents are not likely to have very much say in how it is run.

The government's aims were threefold: (1) to improve educational attainment; (2) to help parents of young children into employment, especially single mothers in receipt of state benefits; and (3) to combat child poverty. Judged by these criteria, the Labour Government policies have not made much impact.

Table 6.1 gives figures for changes in the employment of women in the workforce over a ten year period 1994–2004. These figures have changed relatively little over the life of the Labour Government. The government's stated aim in 1997 was to achieve a level of workplace participation by single mothers of 70%. As can be seen, it is someway short of that target.

Similarly, the measures taken to combat child poverty have only had a marginal impact. Child poverty reached an all-time high of around 1 in 3 children in the UK, 1980–1995, under the Thatcher Government, and after dipping slightly, is now increasing again (Brewer et al. 2007). The Sure Start programme for under-threes was the government's flagship attempt (in England) to combat child poverty. It was based on the premise that early childhood interventions in poor areas would make a difference to child outcomes, and the involvement of mothers would make sure that the changes taking place would endure. The government's own evaluation suggested that the development of local Sure Start programmes was very uneven and critics suggest the programme was misconceived in its aims and intentions, in particular, in its failure to address structural poverty (Clarke 2006; Rutter 2006). Social mobility, that is, the opportunities for poor children to succeed, has become less, rather than greater. Social stratification has intensified as a result of the government's policy of supporting the private market through childcare

Table 6.1 Full-time and part-time employment rates for mothers with dependent children

	Married/cohabiting mothers			Lone parents		
	Full-time	Part-time	Total	Full-time	Part-time	Total
1994	24	40	64	21	21	42
1997	26	42	68	22	23	45
2004	29	42	71	28	26	54

Source: Office for National Statistics, Labour Market Trends, July 2005 tax credits, and price has become a determinant of access (Vincent 2006; Vincent et al. 2007). Children who are born poor are likely to remain so. A UNICEF report described children in the UK as near the bottom in a league of child well-being (Bradshaw et al. 2002).

The UK Government fanfares would have us believe that, somehow, a corner has been turned and early education and care provision is much better under its ministrations. But the main change has been in the growth of the private, and increasingly the corporate sector. The most well-known and internationally admired tradition of nursery schools has all but been abandoned. A better knowledge of history would have valued tradition but also indicated how much more change is necessary to break away from the limited policies of the past.

Summary

This chapter has considered how history provides new insights on childhood and policies towards young children. It argues that history provides an essential and revealing context for understanding early childhood education and care, both in the way we see young children, and the way in which policies are derived.

Main messages from this chapter

1   History helps us understand the uniqueness and particularity of events.
2   History provides important perspectives about the way we understand young children.
3   History shows us that policies are not conjured out of a hat but draw on deep-rooted traditions.

What to read next

Fass, P. (ed.) (2004) *Encyclopaedia of Children and Childhood in History and Society.* New York: Thompson/Gale.

Penn, H. (2007) 'Childcare market management: how the UK Government has reshaped its role in developing early childhood education and care', *Contemporary Issues in Early Childhood*, V8(3).

Note

1   The Nursery Schools Association changed its name to the British Association for Early Childhood Education (BAECE) and more recently to 'Early Learning'. Its archives are listed under BAECE and held at the British Library for Political Economic and Social Science (BLPES).

7 Children's Rights

What is 'childhood'? What is a 'normal' childhood? These seemingly obvious questions have taken on a new slant over the past 20 or so years. The study of childhood in the twentieth century has been dominated by child development theory and the assumption that age is a key variable in understanding differences between children. In turn, these psychological ideas about development have been closely linked to ideas about healthy biological development (see Chapter 3). But from the mid-1980s, interest has rapidly grown in the idea of childhood itself. Children and childhood have been studied within and across a wide range of disciplines linked to the social rather than the natural sciences: sociology, media and cultural studies, anthropology, history, law, literature, geography, social policy, economics, international studies and philosophy. Concepts of the child, of childhood and adulthood and their relationship to one another, views about values, rights and ethics which need to be rethought in relation to children, methods of collecting and analysing data concerning children, have all been subject to scrutiny within these various disciplinary lens.

Although it is very difficult to generalize across different fields, each with their own focus and methodological history, very broadly, the emphasis has been on understanding the diversity and complexity of children's lives. Instead of seeking universal behaviour patterns, as in child development, researchers have been interested in children's circumstances, how those circumstances shape their lives, and how children themselves act within or manage to change their circumstances. As Fass has remarked, childhood is an artefact 'a pattern inscribed by culture through the ways in which dependency and age, sexuality and maturity, the body and mind were defined and delineated' (2007: 5). Interdisciplinary studies of childhood are much more alert to children's own voices and their own perceptions and engagement with their situations. This contrasts with a much narrower view of childhood in contemporary child development and education literature, where childhood is seen as a preparation for a particular kind of adulthood. Long-term goals of socialization have dominated contemporary Euro-American perceptions of young children.

The UN Convention on the Rights of the Child

Childhood studies have been given an extra impetus by the United Nations Convention on the Rights of the Child 1989 which declared children to be citizens of the world with rights – the rights to protection, provision and participation. The UN Convention on the Rights of the Child 1989 (UNCRC) took ten years to be written and agreed.

Important articles also urge governments:

- to encourage the mass media to disseminate 'material of social and cultural benefit to the child ... that promote social, spiritual and moral well-being and physical and mental health';
- to ensure wide publicity about the UN Convention to adults and children alike.

A convention is the strongest kind of international treaty. The UNCRC is by far the most widely endorsed treaty ever, ratified by 192 governments who thereby promise to implement it in law, policy and practice, and to report regularly to the UN on progress in so doing. These internationally agreed rights are specified below.

Provisions rights

- Care necessary for the child's well-being.
- Competent standards of care.
- The highest attainable standards of health and necessary health treatment.
- Periodic review for looked-after children.
- Adequate standard of living for physical, mental, spiritual and social development.
- Compulsory and free primary education.
- Education that is preparation for responsible life in a free society in the spirit of understanding, peace, tolerance, equality and friendship among all people.
- Rest and leisure.

Protection rights

- Physical or mental violence.

- Injury or abuse.
- Neglect or negligent treatment.
- Maltreatment or exploitation.
- Cruel, inhuman or degrading treatment.
- Unlawful deprivation of liberty.
- Discrimination.
- Rights to the promotion of physical or psychological recovery and social reintegration of child victims after neglect or abuse, cruel treatment or armed conflict.

Participation rights

- The right to life and survival.
- To a name, an identity, a nationality.
- To contact with parents and family.
- To play, and to participate freely in cultural life and the arts.
- To respect for the child's ethnic, religious, cultural and linguistic background, humanity and inherent human dignity.
- The child's right to express views freely in all matters affecting the child.
- The views of the child to be given due weight according to the age and ability of the child.
- The opportunity to be heard directly or through a representative during proceedings that affect the child.
- Freedom of expression and information.
- Freedom of thought, conscience and religion.
- Freedom of association and peaceful assembly.
- Disabled children should enjoy a full and decent life in conditions which ensure dignity, promote self-reliance and facilitate the child's active participation in the community with the fullest possible social inclusion.

The CRC recently commissioned a report on early childhood, which it then ratified at a special meeting in 2005 (CRC 2005). Within the wider framework of provision, protection and participation this also stressed the importance of respecting the capacities and integrity of young children as people.

Most recently, UNESCO, who coordinate and monitor the *Education for All* (EFA) goals, issued a new update which stressed the importance of taking a child rights approach to early childhood development (UNESCO 2007). *Education for All* is an international agreement, endorsed by all countries and by the UN and the World Bank. This endorsement is an important step, although, like so many of the international documents, its aims are aspirational rather than implementable and its statements on the worth for young children are a long way off realization.

Many people see modern rights in terms of 'Keep out! Don't interfere with me. I have the right to do whatever I like, as long as it doesn't harm anyone else.' In this view, no wonder children's rights are unpopular, a nightmare vision of the selfish unmanageable child, careless of parental love, and of responsibility, duty, loyalty or concern for others, the sort of child who ends up in a 'brat camp'. However, the UN Convention rights are different. They are about necessities, such as clean water, not luxuries. They involve concern for children's best interests, for public order, health and morals, and for parents' rights and duties. The preamble to the Convention asserts the importance of every child living 'in an atmosphere of happiness, love and understanding' – although no one can have the right to love because love cannot be enforced by law. Rights are shared equally: 'our rights' not 'my rights'. Children's rights respect the inherent worth and dignity and the inalienable rights of all members of the human family. They promote social progress and better standards of life in larger freedoms that lay foundations for justice and peace in the world. They are tools for change, when governments regularly report to the UN on how they are implementing the rights in law, policy and practice.

Concepts of the child, of childhood and adulthood

Because of the rise of child development and advances in biological sciences, it is commonly held that now we know, 'scientifically' what children are 'really' like. Our present knowledge about children surpasses all previous knowledge. But this can only be a partial truth. If children are treated differently, if expectations about them differ, they are likely to behave differently. The most arresting examples concern children's independence. There are innumerable examples, from historians, for example, or from anthropological studies, that children are capable of an extraordinary degree of independence; they can find their way and visit places on their own, they can handle equipment like knives, they can negotiate dangers; they can care for others; situations that we would consider, from a contemporary Euro-American perspective, to be positively hazardous and unsafe, children have learnt to cope with. This is not to say, of course, we should immediately retreat from our own standards and expectations about keeping children safe, or deny the complexities and very real threats of urban life. But it does indicate that there is a much wider range of possibilities than contemporary Euro-American understandings of childhood generally allow. Hewlett and Lamb have edited a collection of studies on hunter–gatherer children, and point out that

Western societies have developed elaborate structures and institutions to educate and socialize children and adolescents but it is abundantly clear that such institutions are not necessary in most societies and many cultures do not afford children the same kinds of explicit education or instruction.

(2005: 413)

In most of the groups studied in their book, children lead very social, and at the same time, independent lives. Alma Gottleib, an anthropologist working in Côte d'Ivoire, also comments on very young children's independence. She describes a girl of two years old in the village she studied:

Chantal, a feisty two year old in our compound, disappeared from our sight many mornings, only to emerge at noon for lunch and then again around 5pm for dinner preparations. Though too young to report on her day's travels, others would chronicle them for us: she regularly roved to the furthest ends of this very large village, and even deep into the forest to join her elder siblings and cousins working and playing in the fields.

(2004: 12)

Once children in such communities have been weaned, their daily lives are remarkably free from adult control, at least by the standards of industrialized countries. On the other hand, if children are a collective responsibility, and everyone, including other children, regards themselves as having some responsibility towards younger children, the dangers of such freedom are less, because everyone is watching out for all children. 'My child is your child' is an African proverb. Even if these anthropological findings mostly relate to small and relatively isolated communities, the *fact* is that most of the world's children do not grow up in the benign protected environments considered by early years specialists to be so essential, and they rarely have done.

Play is central to contemporary understandings of childhood, but it was not always so. Fass, a historian, has explored understandings of childhood in the USA (2007). She argues that in the USA until the twentieth century, childhood was seen as a time for apprenticeship. Children were junior workers, being trained to do everyday tasks, to be essential contributors to household economy. At the same time, children were expected to exercise more autonomy, more independence, and more self-reliance than contemporary explanations allow. Zelitzer (2002) argues that children still do make economic contributions to household economies in the USA, but when they do it is downplayed or ignored. Childhood is still characterized in many communities in the South as a time for learning the domestic and work skills that are necessary for living in tightly knit interdependent, households that survive in precarious economic conditions. In these circumstances children's play reflects the tasks they will one day do, and the division between work and play is often an arbitrary one (Katz 2004). Whereas in more industrialized countries, work and play are so separate, that children are rarely able to prefigure what it is that adults do at work, and their play is expected to be more trivial and toy orientated. One of the tensions of globalization is renegotiating understandings of childhood between North and South, especially in respect of work–play balance.

At the very least, this kind of data suggests that some of the claims to knowledge about children should be revisited. We tend to think of young children as very vulnerable because they are small and have relatively limited vocabularies. We think they lack competence or wisdom and cannot gauge the risks they face. Children are seen as essentially vulnerable and egotistical, and in need of adult protection. They 'need' unremitting benign care, attention and surveillance from those adults closest to them in order to protect them from all harm and danger, and indeed, need adults to help them learn. Both attachment theory and Vygotskian ideas about scaffolding underwrite this view of children who are essentially dependent for their physical safety, for their emotional development, and for their learning – for all aspects of their development in short – on the continuous presence of guardian adults.

Because we see children as vulnerable and dependent, childhood, especially early childhood, is seen as a time free from responsibility, and children's experiences are viewed as distinctly and qualitatively different from adult cares or concerns. Their lives are lived more or less separately from those of adults except in the intimacy of the home, and even that is assumed to be a partial and one-way intimacy – parents shaping children's lives, rather than, as is so often the case in reality, children shaping parent's lives. Early childhood in particular is a time consecrated to play. We are so grounded in consumerism, that we think children need an extraordinary amount of manufactured equipment to achieve their development potential, and we undervalue the everyday practical opportunities available in almost any environment. We believe that through play with specially constructed objects, a child is assumed to begin to learn how to relate to others, to develop an idiosyncratic, individualistic identity tempered by hard-learnt social graces. Play is seen as an unrivalled opportunity for a child-person to experiment – within carefully constructed adult limits – and to learn to exercise consumerist choices between a range of playthings and play opportunities.

These various understandings of childhood are written into discussions of quality provision in early childhood, so much so that they form the basis of the standard test of quality – the Early Childhood Environment Rating Scale. Yet if such very different understandings of childhood exist, how is this conceptual gap approached? One way is to assume that Euro-American ideas are indeed right and supported by science, and it is the job of international agencies and concerned persons to promote them, because of the benefits they bring. Many people do indeed hold this view and voice it firmly, despite the enormous task involved of converting many millions of parents in the world living in difficult circumstances to adopt such an approach (Grantham-McGregor et al. 2007). An alternative is to say if indeed children's lives, especially young children's lives do not conform to Euro-American expectations of a good life for children, are there lessons to be learnt from the way children experience and cope with their lives. This is the approach that many of those working in the field of childhood have adopted. For example, the *Young Lives* project is a longitudinal (15-year) study of poor children growing up in Anhar Pradesh in India, in Peru, in Ethopia and in Vietnam, in which children's own experiences and views about their circumstances will play a very important part (www.younglives.org.uk).

Within a UK and a European context, there has been a revision of conventional ideas about childhood, which critique for instance concepts of maturity, or capability or resilience (Boyden 2007). There are an increasing number of projects which explore children's ability, widely recognized or not, to contribute to the situations in which they find themselves. But above all, they are undertaken in a context which acknowledges that children – like all of us – are living in the present, in the here and now and daily experiences matter in themselves not as some nebulous future as a more productive adult, although of course adults do have the benefit of hindsight in trying to shape children's lives. By contrast in the field of the economics of early education and care, discussed in the next chapter, this perspective on children's present well-being has proved very hard to incorporate.

Basic aims and questions

Although, as we grow older, we become more experienced and informed, and perhaps more wise, children too can be profoundly experienced, informed and wise. Most western children are too carefully protected to encounter serious dangers, but researchers who are fortunate enough to listen to children who know about danger, such as refugees or those who face life-threatening illness (Alderson 1993), discover how intensely experienced young children can become and how maturely they can cope with complex and distressing information and decisions. The aim then becomes to explore how competent children can be. And taken-for-granted ideas about childhood can be turned into questions.

- How do people construct and reconstruct childhood as a life stage of being volatile or reliable, weak or strong?
- How can beliefs/theories about childhood be stretched to fit the

exciting newer evidence about how thoughtful and social very young children can be?

For example, researchers have examined children's work (MacKinnon 2003), the experiences of disabled children (Davis et al. 2000), children's contributions in their early years setting (Clark 2007) and how children actively take part in research (Clark and Moss 2001). Once they see children as people, researchers and practitioners can work respectfully with them to explore their complex and wide-ranging views and experiences (Greene and Hogan 2005).

> 'Traditional' child psychology, as mentioned earlier, tends to test and assess children in order to detect and potentially prevent and treat conditions that seem unhealthy or abnormal. Yet this can inadvertently harm children by showing them in such a negative light if the best a child can score is zero. A typical questionnaire asks parents to rate how much their pre-school child 'tells lies . . . has wet or soiled self this year . . . has stutter or stammer . . . has other speech difficulty [and] bullies other children'. Further questions ask if the child 'is so active it exhausts me . . . appears disorganised and distracted . . . has more difficulty [than other children] concentrating and paying attention.'
>
> (Abdin, cited in Grieg and Taylor 1999: 128–9)

There is no chance for children to give their views and perhaps reasonable explanations about their behaviour or to talk about their achievements.

A popular textbook about how to fit observations of children to 23 pages about 'milestones' of development sums up ten whole months in these words: 'Key features of 9–18 months: Growing independence can lead to rage when thwarted. Shows anxiety when left alone. Emotionally more stable but can be jealous of adults' attention to other children. Can be defiant – learns NO' (Sharman et al. 1995). No positive examples are given. Yet children aged 9 to 18 months have many lovely characteristics. The examples are biased in concentrating on children's unreasonableness and seeming limitations, which would make it hard to trust or respect the children or work with them as partners in solving their problems. Adults' positive questions, solutions and attitudes then risk being discouraged and even excluded from research and childcare.

Many books by early years specialists are positive, and give fine examples of competent children, their helpfulness and imaginative awareness of others. Yet phrases such as 'terrible twos' abound. Like racism, these are negative stereotypes of a huge and very mixed group of people, falsely grouped together for one biological feature, in this case, their age.

In recent years there have been a series of programmes on TV about children whose behaviour has become uncontrollable. For instance, BBC 3 has run a series *House of Tiny Tearaways*, a programme in which a psychologist, Dr Tanya Byron, gives advice to parents about how to control their young children's bad behaviour. This is now available as a book (Byron 2005). The programme purports to help parents, but the wider circumstances of these parents and children, their isolation or poverty or particular history are never really shown or commentated on. Instead, in a voyeuristic way, we are invited to view the extreme behaviour of these children in highly artificial situations, and to regard any solution to the problem as lying within the ability and self-determination of individual parents to solve. It is unclear what say, if any, children themselves have in taking part in such programmes, or how they might view their solipsistic appearances in retrospect.

Different tendencies between older and newer approaches to childhood could be summed up as follows. Older approaches tend to emphasize adults protecting and providing for children and research projects treat children as objects whose experiences can be manipulated to produce measurable outcomes; newer approaches are more likely to see children as active contributors who can be creative partners with adults. The next section looks further at these contrasting approaches.

Views about values and rights

Childhood researchers vary but they tend to endorse the following values. Children's lives are worthwhile and they matter now in the present, not simply for their future effects. Children are not merely developing and practising, they are also accomplishing and contributing competently. Their views and values can be valid in their own right, and adults are not always correct about what it means to be right or wrong, good or naughty. Adulthood is not the perfect endpoint and instead we all go on changing and learning, forgetting and making mistakes throughout our lives. These values link to views about children's rights.

Children's rights can benefit everyone. At the most basic level, when communities have clean water, food, security and safe spaces (none of which are likely to be available to many children in poor countries), everyone benefits, not just children. At the other end of the scale, reconceptualizations of children's autonomy also benefit their parents. For instance, 8-year-old Finnish children have one day a week off school while their parents are at work. All the parents take it for granted that the children can stay at home on their own all day or go out to play with friends, even on dark winter evenings. So when Scandinavian children have more rights and freedoms, so too can their parents. In Britain, after-school childcare stops children's freedoms of peaceful 'association and assembly' to wander freely around their district and play with friends when and where they choose. Childcare is also very expensive and a great contributor to child poverty. Beliefs have grown up in Britain that all children need constant adult supervision, and when children are no longer allowed to exercise certain rights and responsibilities they are seen as unable to do so (see Chapter 9).

Views about ethics

When children are seen as real people with rights, new questions arise about ethics in practice and research. These concern researchers, practitioners and students when they observe or test children, interview or assess them, or write case studies or records about them. Ethical research involves respecting people's privacy and confidentiality and their informed consent or refusal, besides many other standards that weave into all aspects of research (Christensen and James 2000). Too often, adults are respected but not young children, although the latter are even less able to challenge researchers, or get research methods improved or inaccurate reports corrected (Hill 2005). Children should have the same privacy rights as adults.

Informed consent to research involves telling people what the project is about, what you would like them to do to help you, why, how this could affect them, and what you will do with the data. It involves respecting children if they refuse or want to stop or withdraw from a project. Even young children can understand and talk about these matters. When are children old enough to be competent to consent? Much depends on each child's own experience and confidence, the type of research, and the skill with which researchers talk with children and help them to make unpressured, informed decisions. Children aged 3 years upwards have willingly taken part in research, not only as subjects but also as researchers.

Modern medical ethics has forced medical researchers to change their methods. They now do less risky research with children, and they inform, respect and protect children more. It is time for social and psychological researchers to take ethics more seriously. Unfortunately, distressing research, such as testing how upset babies become if their mother leaves them with a stranger, is still often carried out, although some psychologists criticize this and other methods where children are 'objectified' (Greene and Hogan 2005).

One-way mirrors, or secret records such as case studies made without asking for the person's permission, are unlikely to be tolerated today in research with adults. They are no more acceptable in research with children or when training students to study or work with children. Adults may argue that if they tell children what they are researching, such as bullying or racism, the children will hide their behaviours and the research will be impossible. Yet this negative deficit type of research can be counter-productive and is unlikely to produce helpful findings. Alternatively, involving the children as informed partners can produce much more useful results. For example, 7-year-old children decided to do a survey about bullying. Instead of asking the usual question 'Who bullies whom?', they asked 'When and where does bullying mainly happen?' Their survey helped the staff to know the danger areas where they needed to be in the playgrounds, and the rates of bullying fell (Highfield Junior School, Plymouth 1997). Similarly, research which asks children what they think racism means and how it affects them is likely to reveal ways for children and adults to work together to tackle racism (Alderson 1999).

Ethical research involves sensitive methods for discovering children's own views and meanings. In one study, children said the book area was the least popular place in their family centre. Were they immature or was the book corner inadequate? When they were asked why, the children explained that they disliked the way that the book corner was used – sometimes rather like a prison to keep them quiet and constrained, and also to read stories to large groups. So the use of the book corner changed, and there were smaller story groups (Miller 1999).

Ethical and rights-based research also takes account of children's own views about good and useful research and not only adults' views. It is concerned:

- to protect children from harm, abuse, anxiety, distress, and dishonest exploitation during the research;
- to be aware of risks of published research reports that could increase shame, stigma and disadvantage for whole groups of children (such as all refugee children or all children of single parents);
- to consider ways of preventing and reducing these risks.

There are three main ways of involving children in projects:

1 Unknowing objects of research who are not asked for their consent and may be unaware that they are being researched.
2 Aware subjects who are asked for their informed, willing consent to be observed or questioned, but within fairly rigid adult-designed projects such as questionnaire surveys.
3 Active participants who willingly take part in doing the research (see methods section below).

Asking ethical questions can help you to be a critical reader of other researchers' reports.

- What are the report's hidden values and standards relating to harm or benefit, honesty, fairness and respect?
- Who will the research recommendations mainly benefit – children or

certain adults such as educators or therapists who claim that research shows their services are needed?

- Are children seen as problems, victims or contributors?
- Do the researchers aim to rescue, or criticize, or respect children?
- Do the researchers thank the children who took part?

Children are not fully equal to adults, adults have far more power and resources and authority. But many children have strengths, capacities and good sense that are respected by ethical researchers and professionals.

Methods of collecting and analysing data

In the past, research about children tended to be done through:

- surveys of parents' or teachers', but not children's, views;
- standardized tests of 'representative' children;
- measuring children against assumed norms to show their abnormalities, failings and deficits;
- artificial laboratory tests with complicated methods that younger children often failed, and asking standards questions instead of questions about the child's own experiences.

Some of the newer methods are described below.

Asking for children's own views

This can be done through observing, talking and playing with them, and helping them to take photos and make diaries, maps and videos about their daily life. In semi-structured interviews, children tell stories about their lives, in which they are the experts. Or they take photos or make videos, maps and drawings. Children who cannot read or write can do all these activities, such as when young Nepalese children made maps of where they herded their animals and collected fodder and firewood (Hart 1997). Children have plenty of interesting and useful views about their education, their rights (or lack of rights) at school, and how they have improved their schools, such as through their skilled peer mediation and conflict resolution (Alderson 1999; Greene and Hogan 2005).

Taking account of context

Understanding childhood goes beyond the usual approach of looking at each child individually, by taking account of the social and political context. For example, approximately one in three children in Britain grows up in poverty, so that understanding childhood includes understanding how poverty affects children's lives and learning, and how children are seen and see themselves either as inferior beings or as respected, competent people. Children and young people helped to design and conduct a survey of nearly 3000 young Londoners' views which led to the Mayor of London working with children and young people to create his city-wide Children's Strategy (Hood 2001).

Moving away from testing failure

Other new research methods are moving away from testing children's failings to examining their own reasons for their beliefs and behaviours which can then often be seen as sensible – understanding each child's viewpoint, meaning and values. Susan provides a good example of the benefits of this method. Susan determined to be the first person in her family to go to university. She insisted on moving from her local reception class, when 4 years old, where she felt 'smothered and mothered', to be a weekly boarder at a special school. She is blind, though, like many children at that school, she is exceptionally far-sighted about life, values and, for some, politics, which they debate with great enthusiasm. Susan recalled how 'Mum had to drag me screaming down the [school] drive because I didn't want to go home.' Unlike many of her peers, Susan managed to keep a close friend at home. When Susan was 10, she visited several secondary schools and then chose what she believed was the best one, though she found it a hard choice to make. A year later she was very pleased with her decision, academically and socially. In some ways, Susan was the only person who could make a fully informed decision that took account of her experiences, values and plans. Like many other children I have met, her understanding was not linked to her age or assessed intelligence, but to her experiences (Alderson and Goodey 1998: 119–20).

Practical research with and by young children shows their competence. For instance, a run-down housing estate was being upgraded. Almost by chance, an adult asked children about the plans. Eventually, ten children aged 3–8 years did a survey of the other children's views. They wrote a report about their results, adding their photos, maps and drawings. They met senior council officers to discuss the report, and advised that the play area should not be put on the edge of the estate as planned, beyond a busy road. Instead, the play area was set in the centre of the estate, where children could safely play without needing adults to be with them (Newson 1995).

Summary

Childhood studies examine how children live in the present, how they achieve and accomplish activities besides learning and practising. Everyone is seen as having mixed abilities, instead of being an inferior child or a perfect adult. Being able to do things well can depend far more on a person's experience and knowledge (even as a baby) than their age. Nor is moral awareness necessarily linked to age. Young children can be kind and responsible, and adults are sometimes selfish. Early years staff have everyday experience of sensible, sensitive young children. We therefore need to rethink older ideas about incompetent children and see how we can listen to and involve children in many aspects of their lives and choices, also how we can adapt professional practices and policy-making to take greater account of children's informed views.

Main messages of this chapter

1   Babies and young children are competent people but too few people recognize this or act on it.
2   The UN Convention on the Rights of the Child has been a landmark in rethinking children and childhood.
3   Research with young children has undergone a sea change; the ethics of such research have been scrutinized and children are much more centre-stage.

What to read next

John, M. (2003) *Children's Rights and Power: Charging up for a New Century*. London: Jessica Kingsley.
Greene, S. and Hogan, D. (eds) (2005) *Researching Children's Experience: Approaches and Methods*. London: Sage.

Acknowledgements

This chapter is based on the chapter in the earlier edition by Priscilla Alderson. I am grateful for her permission to draw on it.

8 What it costs and what it's worth: the economics of early childhood.

Is it worth spending money on early childhood care and education? And if so, what is the best way to spend that money? Economics provides a methodology and rationale for understanding and making predictions and decisions about people's behaviour, for putting a value on it and costing their time and effort. Economic analysis can be applied to almost any area of human activity, including early childhood education and care.

Most of the discussion about early childhood in books and professional magazines takes as its starting point certain principles – for example, about how children learn or what kind of caring arrangements work best or how staff can be supported. But in economic terms, everything has a cost, and those costs inevitably must be balanced against other competing costs. Few people have enough money to spend as they want. Domestically, for most of us, there are practical and sometimes uncomfortable decisions to be made about how we spend our income. Do we buy designer clothes for the children, but scrimp on our own clothes to make them happy? Should we take out a loan to smarten up the bathroom? We have to weigh up the costs, and think about the consequences of our decisions. The decisions we make in the short term might be different from those we might want to make for the long term. Writ large (very large) these same kinds of decisions have to be made by governments. Should we buy more arms for defence or invest more money in wind technology? Should taxes be raised to pay for new services? Why indeed should money be spent on young children? Who benefits and who loses out?

What are the benefits of spending money one way rather than another? Those who run businesses *have* to make these decisions about values, assign costs and calculate benefits. Running a business and making sure that you make a profit and do not spend more money than you have, or waste it unnecessarily is called 'the discipline of the marketplace'. It is a discipline that many governments are keen to endorse.

The macro-economic view

Economics is theoretical, in the sense that it proceeds from certain assumptions about how people make decisions about money and increase their wealth. But it relies on quantitative data, a particular way of computing the consequences of transactions of goods and services between people. Economics as a discipline is said to have originated with the Scotsman Adam Smith, who in 1776 wrote a book entitled *An Inquiry into the Wealth of Nations*. Put very roughly indeed, the wealth of nations depends on encouraging individuals to make money. Smith argued that everyone acts in their own self-interest, to maximize their gain. The definition of self-interest varies considerably. Interpreted at its crudest, it means everyone wants to make a profit whatever the cost to others, a kind of economic Darwinism whereby only the fittest succeed. Adam Smith himself considered that self-interest included a notion of civic obligation, because it is in everyone's interest to live in a properly run society.

Everything we do involves some kind of commercial exchange with other people – from buying vegetable seeds to making a telephone call. This process of exchange is called 'the market'. If there is scarcity, the price goes up in the short term, but in the middle to long term, if there is enough demand for a product or service, then the market will expand to provide it. If there is no demand the market will shrink. In classical economics, supply and demand are in a state of continuous readjustment to reach a balance. If there is high demand for a product but a shortage of supply, prices will go up until demand and supply are in some kind of equilibrium. If there is overproduction and too much of a supply, producers will compete against one another to provide the best and cheapest products and prices will drop and/or producers will go out of business.

Competition drives the market forward. Some economists argue that the market should be left alone as much as possible to find its own levels of supply and demand, whatever the goods or services concerned. The key question is whether there are some services where competition has bad side effects, for instance high turnover and lack of stability, or where the information available is not sufficient for the consumer to make a rational choice, or whether there are special conditions which make it uneconomical to provide the service on a for-profit basis. Some people argue that early childhood education and care is a classic example of where 'the law' of supply and demand does not work, because it is very labour intensive, but ordinary people cannot afford the necessary costs in providing it.

We pay for the goods and services we use by working to earn money, through our physical or mental labour. In classical economical theory, if we earn enough to meet our needs, and we have accumulated a surplus, we can save it or invest it in *capital*, that is in plant, or premises or tools or technology which we can then use to generate more surplus money to reinvest. Hence the name 'capitalism'. Because the market is continually changing through competition, or because of new technologies or new products, or new regulatory conditions, business entrepreneurs are engaged in a continuous search for profitability. As well as marketing their business efficiently, they have to make their businesses more competitive or productive, for instance, by persuading their workforce to work harder or work longer or more flexible hours; or to work more efficiently by using new technology. Another way of becoming profitable is through economies of scale. Working on a large scale, or on multi-plant economies of scale, for example, in a car factories or food-processing plants, all the processes of purchasing, production, distribution and marketing can be streamlined and be made more efficient. But manufacturing is increasingly a poor analogy, because many jobs in what is called 'the knowledge economy' do not fit into these classical economic categories. It is the quality of the knowledge that counts as much as the effort put into a job.

In some jobs, productivity is very hard to define or achieve, partly because it is essentially labour-intensive. For instance, working with young children is a labour-intensive job. Even making economies of scale is problematic. If one of the desired attributes of nurseries is that they are local and responsive to community needs, being part of a large nursery chain (as most nurseries in the UK now are) where head-office decisions are made for many hundreds or thousands of children, may be counter-productive. The ABC nursery chain, based in Australia, now has over 3000 nurseries *worldwide* and over 1000 in the UK. This economy of scale is achieved because of standardization of many of the features about the way the nurseries are run – for instance, security arrangements, or reporting to parents. So its responsiveness to individual circumstances or individual locations is unlikely to be nuanced, and parents' say will necessarily be limited.

Even in a market economy, orthodox economists allow that the market may fail. If there is a monopoly, the market will not function properly – so there are rules against the formation of monopolies. State services are sometimes viewed as a monopoly, and therefore have to be broken up. If the information available is asymmetrical (insider knowledge) or inadequate, then the market cannot work properly – the economist Joseph Stiglitz won his Nobel Prize for showing that asymmetrical markets were very common, and mostly market knowledge is imperfect. Individual decisions may be at odds with those of the wider society. Individuals may not want to pay high taxes, but if they do so, it may mean a fairer distribution of those goods and services almost everyone needs and uses at some point and which are not really subject to the law of supply and demand. But what are these 'merit goods'? If the government provides them, will it just mean that more people will take advantage of them, when they might otherwise be prepared to do without? Public health services are regarded as a merit good in the UK, but not in the USA. Nurseries are a merit good in the Nordic countries, but not in the UK.

Economic theory then is the attempt to calculate and predict how the market works. Since there is a constantly changing range of goods and services, economics provides a method and a means of analysing and modelling how value is assigned, how money is spent and how goods and services are provided. In today's complex world, the market is immensely sophisticated, and it is not easy to understand the consequences of a particular economic policy on people's behaviour. For example, if taxes are put up, how will it affect small-time entrepreneurs just starting out on their businesses? Will high taxes be such a disincentive to those starting out, and outweigh the advantages of higher taxes to the Treasury (more money for the government to spend on arms or childcare!)? Should small businesses be given tax breaks to help them start up or might tax incentives be exploited by dodgy operators? One of the features of the current UK market is *private equity companies*. These are financial institutions which pay very low tax, a concession made by the government in order to encourage investment in new or risky businesses. Although they are not all dubious, they have earned a bad name for themselves because of their large or excessive profits, and financial manipulation, for instance, with pension funds. Several nursery chains are now run by private equity companies.

Economics is a set of theories which rely on quantitative data. The criticism levelled against economics is that although the maths is sophisticated, economists' approach to the social world is relentlessly positivistic. For the purposes of calculation, economists reduce social events to simplistic truths; and then claim that these truths are invariable, holding good in all contexts and all circumstances. Economics is sometimes seen to be synonymous with big business, a means of enabling the rich to justify their business practices.

In the nineteenth century, another famous political economist, Karl Marx, argued that raw capitalism and the unfettered market caused so much havoc, created so much exploitation, poverty and anguish, that there had to be another way. This theory led to communism, and the rise of Soviet Russia. The Soviets interpreted Marxism as meaning that governments could take charge of the economy, and plan it centrally so that the poor truly benefited. It is certainly the case that in communist countries literacy rates and infant mortality and other health indicators were very good, and, for that matter, free kindergartens of an amazingly high standard (with swimming pools and dance halls, for example) were routinely provided in many cities. But in the end central planning was a failure; it was too inflexible, and led to too much concentration and abuse of power, and because there was no competition and few incentives, individuals and organizations did not accumulate the capital necessary for reinvestment and continued economic growth. In 1989, communism finally collapsed. Partly as a result of this collapse, those that believed that the free market was the only economic way forward thought they had won the argument. Books appeared with titles like 'The End of History' (Fukuyama 1992).

In the 1980s and 1990s, the dominant view or paradigm in economics became 'neo-liberalism' a view that the state should interfere as little as possible, and should not arbitrate in the way people exercise their self-interest; businesses and entrepreneurs do best with competition at its rawest. The IMF (International Monetary Fund) and the World Bank were strong adherents of this point of view. People should be free to spend all their money exactly as they want, with minimum interference from anyone else, and that way they will work harder. Taxes should be kept to the barest minimum, so people can keep what they earn for themselves. The 'market' will automatically find its own level whatever the goods or services. State services are inefficient and people should be encouraged to buy what they need directly – even health or education or welfare – instead of the state providing it for them. The USA neo-conservatives in particular strongly believe in 'economic medicine' as abandonment of state services is sometimes called. These neo-liberal ideas were ruthlessly applied in developing and transitional countries as a condition for loans, and in retrospect appear to have badly damaged the welfare of people in many poor and transitional countries (Stiglitz 2006).

Adherents of this neo-liberal approach regard income inequality and the existence of the poor not as injustice but as a nuisance. The trouble with poor people, in these terms, is that they do not try hard enough and cause a lot of inconvenience and damage to others, especially through crime. Conversely people who have a lot of money are high achievers and deserve everything they earn – they should be especially lightly taxed because they generate wealth. The impact of neo-liberal policy on poverty, in particular, the poverty experienced by children, has been much discussed (Moore 2001; Phipps 2001; Vleminckx and Smeeding 2001). Basically there are many groups in society who are outside the labour market through no fault of their own, and cannot influence what happens or work harder or make a significant economic contribution – young children are the prime example. Should children pay the price for inequality or should all children be entitled to an equal start, whatever the social or economic position of their parents? In many countries, for example, within the OECD group of the 32 richest countries, the prevailing value is that children should have equal entitlements to education and care services, whatever their parents' circumstances. However, this view is not universally held. Neo-liberals tend to see children as the property of their parents, rather than as citizens in their own right. It is the parents' duty to buy the services their children need.

There has been a reaction to neo-liberal economic approaches, partly because they have been ineffective in promoting economic growth, especially in poor countries, and partly because they are intrinsically unpleasant in their rationales for human motivation and effort. The influential Nobel

Prize-winning economist Joseph Stiglitz, in his books *Globalization and its Discontents* (2002) and *Making Globalization Work* (2006), argues that neo-liberalism has been a near-disaster, and governments do indeed have an important role to play. The very rapid privatization in Soviet Russia after transition, and abandonment of state control and planning had disastrous results in terms of the rise of inequality and corruption, and in a shocking fall in indicators of well-being for children. Numbers of street children increased dramatically, and life expectancy plummeted. Neo-liberalism has also been very damaging to relationships between North and South, and has unfairly favoured the North, especially the USA. Neo-liberalism in effect helps the rich get richer, because those who already have money are in the best position to act on their self-interest and increase the money they have. Under these conditions the poor do not benefit from the increased wealth of the rich, they only get poorer. Neo-liberalism, in Stiglitz's view is an uninformed interpretation of the market, because it does not take account of the unfair conditions (hierarchy, class, colonialism, war, etc.) in the past which led to the accumulation of capital and ownership of assets.

Stiglitz argues that, on the contrary, both national governments and international institutions like the UN have a key role to play in the regulation of the market. Governments can analyse economic information more thoroughly than any one individual, and provide an overview. They can also redistribute money through taxation and through the provision and regulation of services, and mitigate the extremes of wealth and poverty especially for the young, the old, and the sick, those outside of the labour market who simply cannot change their circumstances. Some services – policing, health, education, sanitation – are for the benefit of everyone, and in order to provide them, or ensure they are delivered, the government must impose taxes to pay for them.

On an international level, the UN and other international institutions can act to prevent neo-liberal world trade free market rules from discriminating against the poor. Governments can prevent situations from becoming so unfair that they are self-defeating. If the poor have nothing to lose, then they may act recklessly, turn to crime, and make the lives of the rich difficult. Unequal countries like the USA and Brazil tend to have much higher crime rates than more equal countries like Sweden or Belgium. Stiglitz argues that neo-liberalism, far from being a panacea, is an inefficient economic system. Too much gets wasted, and too many people get hurt. Countries have to find a delicate balance between too much reliance on the market and too little.

There is an increasing number of economists who argue that neo-liberal economic theory is too simplistic in the way it views people's motives; so much so there is now a journal entitled *The Journal of Post-Autistic Economics*! This may be a politically incorrect title, but it has more than a grain of truth: it signifies a concentration on certain predictable, manipulable details, excluding everything else, because the big picture – especially poverty and suffering – is too complicated and messy and difficult to understand. Post-autistic or heterodox economists argue that there are many ways of exploring economic activity, without recourse to ideas of supply and demand or the market. The self-interested consumer who makes a careful considered free choice about what best suits his or her purse is a myth – economic experiments suggest that people are on the whole not rational and not well informed and do not exercise free choice (Ormerod 2007). Governments that emphasize the importance of consumer choice, in true neo-liberal fashion, are mistaken in assuming this is either desirable or possible.

These economic views are echoed by others, non-economists, whose research nevertheless documents the suffering experienced by children as a result of neo-liberal policies. The geographer, Cindy Katz, who has documented in some detail children's attempts to deal with the poverty of their circumstances, describes neo-liberalism as a policy of terror and revenge on those who threaten the security of the rich, and deplores its 'incessant victim-blaming rhetoric' (2004: 160) and 'visceral nastiness' (2004: 244). In the UK, it is well known that neo-liberal policies, promoted by the Thatcher Government, led to a considerable rise in child poverty. At the end of her period of government, an estimated one in three children was living in poverty – a level of child poverty that the subsequent Labour Government has been unable to redress very much.

Neo-liberalism has been partly discredited. Instead, the latest fashion in economic theorizing is called 'post-neo-classical endogenous growth theory', a phrase coined by Gordon Brown when he was Chancellor of the Exchequer (Finance Minister) in the UK. Growth theory explores how and why nations become wealthy. It relies on new economic statistical data collected over the past 20 years trying to measure wealth. Such data is rapidly improving – it provides estimates of wealth for countries going back over many centuries (Coyle 2007). International teams of economists are collaborating over providing the information – rather as scientists have been collaborating over the Genome Project (see Chapter 4). Endogenous growth theory suggests that education and new technology go hand in hand to provide the conditions for generating wealth – rather than, as in classical economics, growth being related to the accumulation of capital. But as with previous theories, it is a very general theory, and its precise application is a matter of gathering new evidence and devising new economical models to support the theoretical approach. Not that governments wait for theories to be proved!

The emphasis on 'human capital' – the importance of having well-educated citizens – in endogenous growth theory has been emphasized, for instance, by Nobel Prize-winning economists Amartya Sen (2000) and James Heckman (1999). Both of these economists consider that investment in early childhood education brings good returns, since it leads to better educational performance, and a better educated population (see below for the detail of the argument). This partly explains why a number of governments, including the UK Government, have decided to promote investment in early childhood.

To summarize this section, economics is a powerful discipline, and economists have been very influential in determining national and international policies. Economists use sophisticated methods, but draw heavily on theory, and the theories often do not tally, either with each other or with reality. This has led some economists, most notably Paul Ormerod in his book *The Death of Economics* (2000) to claim that economic theory has very little predictive power, and economists would do well to recognize their limitations, and to be more humble in their claims. Not unsurprisingly, this is a controversial point of view among economists.

The economics of early education and care: cost–benefit analyses

Economic theories rule the way we live our lives, although we do not always realize it. The rest of this chapter explores early education and care services from an economic perspective. What do early education and care services cost, how are the costs calculated, and what identifiable benefits might accrue? What economic policies should a country adopt to ensure the best deal for children? How will children, and society, benefit if such policies are adopted?

As economists know well, calculating costs and measuring benefits, especially in the fields of health and education, is problematic. Economists provide sophisticated and complicated economic analyses of a complex range of data, in which many assumptions and judgements are made about the basis of calculations. In undertaking a cost–benefit analysis there are always arbitrary decisions to be made about what is included and what is left out. For example, if you introduce a new integrated programme for young children, what is the time frame of the cost–benefit analysis? When do the benefits begin to kick in? Now? In a year? In 10 years? What is the range of costs that are incurred? Do you include the opportunity costs of women's labour, what they could be paid if they were not looking after children? What are the outcomes that are measured? Children's exam performance when they get to school? Children's physical fitness as measured by number of visits to the doctor? Cost–benefit analysis provides a way of prioritizing and quantifying a potentially very large body of information, focusing on those outcomes that have the greatest potential benefits or costs from a particular perspective. In health there is now a large literature discussing how cost–benefit calculations might be calculated. In early education and care there is much less experience and much less consensus.

Some commentators argue that cost–benefit studies of early interventions represent a significant development in economic research and may play an important role in policy-making (Heckman 1999; Currie 2000, 2004). There are a group of economists, mainly based in the USA, who have become interested in trying to define the nature of investments in early education and care, and the outcomes which might be expected from such investment.

Heckman, a Nobel Prize winner for economics, who has written a great deal about the pay-offs of investing in early childhood, might be referred to as an 'autistic' economist. His article, 'The Productivity Argument for Investing in Young Children', reduces bringing up children to a single dimension, whether or not children when they grow up will contribute to society by making money:

> Education, perseverance and motivation are all major factors determining productivity both in the workplace and beyond it. The family is a major producer of these skills, which are indispensable for students and workers. Unfortunately many families have failed to perform this task well in recent years. This retards the growth of the quality of the labour force. Dysfunctional families are also a major determinant of child participation in crime and other costly pathological behaviour. On productivity grounds alone it appears to make sound sense to invest in young children from disadvantaged environments. An accumulating body of evidence suggests that early childhood interventions are much more effective than remedies that attempt to compensate for early neglect later in life.
>
> (Heckman and Masterov 2005: 2)

The assumption, carried over from neo-liberal economics, which underlies this extract is that in a society which is democratic and open to all, and where the supreme goal is wealth creation, the poor are the failures. They have failed to compete successfully in an open society through laziness or incompetence and they perpetrate this failure on their children. The poor are not victims; on the contrary, they are to blame for most of society's ills. But Heckman is also making the point, very forcibly, that investment in early childhood pays off. Pound for pound, dollar for dollar, you get more for your money if you invest in early childhood education, than if you invest in remedial education when children are older, or in custodial care when they are youths. Above all, this argument depends on taking a long-term view of benefits that might occur in the future, but aren't really obvious in the here and now. Since Heckman is a leading economist who has shown interest in early childhood, advocates for early education and care have seized on his claims, without always fully understanding the context of his remarks.

As part of the DfES Evidence Based Policy and Practice Initiative (EPPI), I worked with a group of colleagues to carry out a detailed examination of the claim that there is 'an accumulating body of evidence' which shows that early interventions are effective. In fact, there is surprisingly little evidence. There are *only three* robust studies which exist which have measured cost benefits over a period of longer than 10 years: the Perry High Scope, which was begun in the 1960s; the Abecedarian which was begun in the 1970s; and the Chicago Child-Parent Centers, which was begun in the 1980s. They all show some long-term benefits for children; but they are different programmes run for different age groups, for different amounts of time, and the benefits they show are not the same. But above all, these studies were carried out with African-American children at a time and in places where racism was pervasive, yet there is little or no acknowledgement that this might be the case, and that racism might have shaped both the research questions and the results. In fact, it makes one gasp to read the first High Scope study published in 1967; it would be unpublishable today, and the account has changed a great deal in the subsequent telling and retelling of the story (Penn et al. 2006; Penn and Lloyd 2007).

The figure quoted on the basis of these *three* studies is that investing 1 dollar in early childhood brings a return of 7 dollars when the children grow up, mainly because they are less likely to commit crimes or other misdemeanours. However, the crime rates among the African-American population in the USA, and levels of victim compensation, are far higher than anywhere else in the developed world, and these savings on crime account for between 40–60 per cent of the 7 dollars saved. This figure varies between the three studies, but in any case it is a ball-park figure which does not represent the range of variation within and between the three studies or the *highly specific* circumstances in which the studies were carried out.

It is *impossible* to extrapolate from these studies any clear idea of what programmes work best, or what should be replicated, despite some very heavy self-promotion from High Scope, which subsequently turned itself into a non-profit organization dedicated to promoting and selling the High Scope method. Yet these three, basically parochial, longitudinal studies are cited over and over again by economists and politicians and form the basis of their evidence. The niceties of extrapolation are overlooked and instead, these three studies have been used as a 'rational' basis for economic calculations. They crop up, for instance, in many World Bank early childhood documents, and have been used to support a particular model of early childhood development in situations and in countries which could not be more distant from the circumstances of the original three studies (Penn 2008).

Just as with the brain studies cited in Chapter 4, claims from these longitudinal studies have been misread because misreading and over-emphasis – we can change the lives of poor children by getting at them young – conveniently diverts attention from a more probing analysis of the causes and consequences of the poverty faced by so many children. Child poverty is low in many

European countries, and almost non-existent in Nordic countries, perhaps 1 in 50. In English-speaking countries it is still high. The rates of child poverty are 1 in 3 or 4 in the USA, 1 in 5 or 6 in the UK and a majority of all children in many countries of the South. Poverty on this huge scale is structural, not a matter of personal failings, and can only be addressed by rethinking ideas of economic justice and redistribution on a global scale (Stiglitz 2006). In these circumstances, targeted, compensatory services are inefficient since they will make a marginal difference to overall levels of poverty, even if they make a difference in the lives of a few children and families.

Jane Waldfogel, an economist specializing in families and social care, based at Columbia University in the USA, has been influential in summarizing the range of evidence on what are called 'early interventions' to pronounce on what kind of economic policies governments should adopt in early education and care. She argues pragmatically, and without recourse to any wider political or economic debate about inequality. Her analysis has been influential on the UK Treasury. She argues that if the government's stated aim in its recent legislation for children is to improve child outcomes (health, cognitive development, social and emotional development) for all children, and to narrow the gaps between disadvantaged children and others, then we need to know about the research findings from the two major types of early years policy – parenting programmes and early education programmes. Additionally, we need to know what role quality plays and how it can be measured; and whether policies are effective and, if they are not, how can local areas and programmes be held accountable? She sees the research findings as mostly straightforward and unproblematic, and their findings as universally applicable, whichever country (mostly the USA) in which the research was carried out.

She classifies parenting programmes as parent education (e.g. teaching parents to read with child); parent support (e.g. home visiting for new parents); and parent management training (e.g. training for parents of children with conduct disorders). She claims that the evidence suggests that parenting programmes might change parental behaviour, but that there is much less evidence that it changes child outcomes, with the exception of specific literacy programmes and behaviour management programmes for children with 'conduct disorders'. The results from parenting programmes on the whole do not provide a clear enough rationale for economic support.

She argues that the evidence from the USA and the UK about centre-based early childhood services is consistent on several points. First, centre-based interventions increase children's school readiness in a variety of ways; second, children from disadvantaged backgrounds benefit most; and third, higher-quality care is more effective than lower-quality care. Quality care is defined by good child/teacher ratios and good training of childcare workers/teachers. However, none of these results are unequivocal. There are a variety of factors which may influence the results; starting young (but not too young, which is a counter-indication of good socio-economic outcomes), the intensity of the service (or number of hours attended), the curriculum, class size, social mix, and what happens subsequently at school (Waldfogel 2004).

This kind of analysis partly explains recent government policy in the UK, and why money has been switched around so much as economic thinking about early education and care develops, and is then found wanting.

The role of the private sector in childcare

However, Waldfogel and most other economists operate from a US perspective in which a private market for childcare is the unquestioned norm and right-wing economic perspective currently prevails. So it is unproblematically assumed in the USA, and more recently in the UK, that these general policies will be delivered through a 'demand-led' policy, that is by providing subsidies to parents through tax or credits, so they can choose and buy their own services. Because quality control or regulatory measures are in place, the private sector can expand to meet demand. Parental demand can be stimulated by giving parents incentives and grants in the form of tax credits, so they can 'choose' how to spend their money. If parents demand childcare, then the market will expand to provide it. Waldfogel also argues for parental choice, on the grounds that parents lives are so diverse, that they need specific arrangements to suit their particular needs. As Cleveland et al. (2007) have pointed out, the argument of choice is something of a fallacy. At least in the UK it is, because it has proved unprofitable for private companies to offer the kinds of choice envisaged. A majority of private nurseries operate within relatively limited hours (9–4pm) and are unwilling to invest in poorer areas (Penn 2007b).

Like any other market commodity, nurseries are a saleable asset – they can be bought and sold, and indeed in the UK there are now estate agents that specialize in the buying and selling of nurseries. And like any other potentially profitable business, nurseries can expand. A profitable nursery can open a second or third branch, and then become a chain of nurseries. The UK magazine *Nursery World* provides a regular listing of the most profitable nursery chains. Around one quarter of all provision is now provided by such nursery chains, the equivalent of nursery supermarkets! Some 15 companies in the UK now provide 50,000 nursery places. The world's biggest chain, ABC nurseries, whose management is based in Australia has now taken over one of the British chains. It has bought out the 'Busy Bees' nursery chain, and added its 46 nurseries to its international portfolio of 2320 nurseries in Australia, the USA, Australia and New Zealand (*Nursery World*, 28 Dec. 2006). And just as nursery chains can expand, they can also go bankrupt, or decide to invest their assets elsewhere. The Laing and Buisson review of the profits of large chains in the

UK, each offering more than 1000 places, suggested that over half are currently operating at a loss (2007b: V5(8): 148). Almost every week now in *Nursery World*, there are reports of closures and takeovers, often leaving many children and many workers stranded. At very short notice, their parents have to find other childcare, and workers have to find new jobs.

Recent studies in Canada and the USA also suggest that the for-profit sector is characterized by high turnover of staff *and* high turnover of nursery providers, whether small one-off businesses or large commercial enterprises (Kershaw et al. 2005). In cities such as London, where land and property prices are very high, turnover is also very high, since opportunity costs (what it costs *not* to sell valuable assets such as land or property) are so considerable. There is more money to be made by selling than by holding on to valuable assets.

Most recently Sosinsky et al. (2007) reviewed some of the data from the USA large-scale longitudinal study from *The National Institute of Child Health and Human Development Study of Early Childcare and Youth Development*. This study has provided a unique bank of data of about children growing up in the USA and the kind of care they have experienced right from birth. The particular study examined the relationship between childcare quality, cost and type of provision. The study distinguished between for-profit corporate care, for-profit small providers, non-profit care and church-based non-profit care. I'm summarizing some complex and nuanced findings but very approximately the research found that it was the type of provision that determined the quality of the care:

- Non-profit centres paid higher wages than for-profit centres.
- Staff turnover rates in corporate chains was higher than in any other centre.
- Non-profit centres had better educated staff than for-profit centres.
- Non-profit centres had less turnover than for-profit centres.
- Non-profit centres showed better quality, especially for preschoolers.
- Quality was lowest in for-profit corporate chains, although not all chains were poor quality.
- Church or religious-based centres were next lowest in quality.

These findings reflect the particularities of the US market which is less regulated than in the UK. The authors say that stricter regulation would almost certainly put prices up and regulation on its own is not enough. The real difficulty is that, in economic terms, no market works well if there is imperfect information. Parents have insufficient information, and often don't know how to assess it. They are often not in a position to know how to exercise choice – it is their child who experiences the childcare when they are not there. For example, the US authors cite one study which showed that parents were misled by very clean vestibules, and tended to rate the quality of the centre as higher, depending on the entrance area.

The notions of supply and demand, competition, productivity, profit, and the marketplace, and how they should be interpreted and regulated by economic policy, increasingly underwrite thinking about childcare and education – and most other services – in the UK. This change has been insidious rather than open and debated (Pollock 2004). In the past 10 years, despite a Labour Government, there has been a decided shift towards pro-market policies and abandonment of state services.

The financing patterns for early care and education have changed dramatically since 1997. The investment has gone up, but the patterns of expenditure are changing. In 1997, private nurseries were rare and local authority or non-profit voluntary nurseries were common. Now it is the other way round. Almost all the very recent expansion in childcare and nursery education places has been in the private sector (Laing and Buisson 2007a). For instance, some 20,000 new nursery education places have been provided *outside* the state sector. As pointed out in Chapter 6, in England, the DfCSF now requires local authorities to be 'childcare market managers' and have sponsored research to explore how local authorities can best sponsor and support private sector early childhood education and care entrepreneurs.

Yet, as in the health service, there has been no real public discussion or analysis about whether parents would actually *prefer* private for-profit childcare to state services or subsidized non-profit services; or indeed, whether demand-led services – giving money to parents in the form of tax credits so they can choose and buy their own childcare – meet the government's own stated economic aims of improving social mobility and reducing inequality by getting more women into the workforce. The parent is technically a consumer, although choice is essentially limited to whether to buy the service or not. It has just been assumed by the Treasury that demand-led childcare policies and sponsorship of for-profit care are the only rational way to proceed.

There appears to be no direct relationship between the amount parents pay and the quality of service they receive, although studies elsewhere suggest that in general for-profit centres offer poorer quality (Goelman et al. 2000; Cleveland et al. 2007). The UK has a comparatively tight regulatory and inspection system for all centres. Therefore – the argument runs – all providers, whether profit or non-profit, can offer similar services to parents. The private sector argues that these standards constrict profits. From a private provider's point of view, regulation is too heavy-handed for all but the most robust operators:

> Business pressures are building up across all trading sectors, large or small operators, and throughout the UK. These pressures have been catalysed by the government's agenda to manage childcare provision

and funding, in order to deliver adequate, affordable and flexible childcare for parents. Without a change to this agenda, the sustainability of the existing private and voluntary children's nurseries sector is seriously threatened. This threat has already prompted a national 'Save our Nurseries' campaign by the Conservative Party.

(Laing and Buisson, conference leaflet 2007a)

So are the UK Government's economic policies of stimulating demand through the private sector succeeding? Economic decision-making is of course closely intertwined with political decision-making. Politically the government's stated aims are to reduce inequality, to increase social mobility and, above all, to reduce child poverty. The poorest families are workless families. So the strategy has been to encourage women, especially single mothers, to go to work, since they will be less dependent on state benefits, and instead once in work, they will contribute to tax revenues. Since childcare availability and costs are a major barrier to women working, the Treasury has offered childcare tax credits and subsidies as an incentive to get women back into work. It has assumed that not only will the private sector expand the supply of childcare to meet increased demand for places, but that increased private sector involvement is in itself a positively valued outcome. Where the market does not work well – in poorer districts where investment is unattractive – the government offers a top-up strategy, subsidizing capital investment, as in the new children's centre programme.

The success of these government strategies has been partial at best. The for-profit childcare sector has expanded considerably, but it is highly problematic, as the discussion above suggests. More mothers work, but low-wage employment at the bottom end of the market is likely to be the least flexible and sympathetic to the needs of working parents (Dean 2007), and combining work and childrearing is hard. Private childcare has led in many ways to increased inequality. Costs for parents are prohibitive. Two recent studies by Vincent (2006) and Vincent et al. (2007) for example, show that childcare provision in London is almost entirely stratified by social class, even in mixed social areas. Similarly recent research (Brewer et al. 2005) suggests that the childcare tax credit mainly benefits middle-class families, and is barely claimed by working-class families. Unskilled women or lone parents are deterred from working, since the low wages they are likely to earn will not necessarily compensate for the benefits they lose by working. Child poverty rates, having dropped, are now increasing again (Brewer et al. 2007). Government targets for reducing child poverty cannot now be met.

And at the end of the day, as Lister (2006) points out, the government agenda is not for children in the here and now. It exists primarily in order to realize other future-oriented government economic aims.

Summary

Economics offers a set of concepts – the market, competition, profit, productivity, consumer choice etc. – and a methodology for making sense of the social world. Governments base their decisions partly or mainly on their economic analysis. I have suggested that in the case of early childhood education and care in the UK, the economic analysis is flawed, in the sense that it has not achieved the desired political or economic outcomes.

Yet these outcomes, low levels of child poverty, good outcomes for children, social mobility, and high percentages of working mothers in the workforce, have been achieved in some countries, most notably in the Nordic countries. This has been achieved partly through redistribution of tax and benefits. High earners pay much higher taxes, but these taxes are spent on services, including early education and childcare services. Local, well-funded high-quality services (including as a sine qua non generous outside playspace, and fully trained staff) affordable and flexible, and are used by almost everyone. The planning and provision of services are undertaken locally and in consultation with service users. The private for-profit sector is rarely used.

The OECD report *Starting Strong II* (2006) reviewed early childhood education and care in 20, mainly European, countries. One of its findings is that although the private market can be seen as more flexible and responsive to changing levels of demand – but that too may be questionable – it is also likely to increase inequality. Once access to provision becomes dependent, or partially dependent, on ability of parents to pay, it becomes segregated and accentuates social divisions. Those countries which have universal publicly funded provision do not experience such inequalities of access. Economists are now beginning to explore the implications of providing universal early education and care services, in terms of improving child outcomes and increasing single parent access to the workforce. But the shibboleth of for-profit care has not so far been addressed. It is seen as politically acceptable and economic sense to allow parents to buy the services they can afford. To do otherwise would be an admission that 'the market' and 'supply and demand' and 'consumer choice', lynch-pin concepts of neo-liberal economics, do not work straightforwardly in the case of early childhood education and care, and indeed in other key service areas. The economic arguments are by no means over.

Main lessons from this chapter

- Economic theories underwrite policy-making on early childhood education and care as much as psychological ones, and it is important

to have a basic grasp of economic arguments to understand policy decisions.
- Not all economists think alike – there are many theories about economic growth.
- Profitability and sustainability are elusive in the for-profit sector, once regulation is introduced.
- Equal access and absence of social segregation are best achieved in universal, publicly funded early childhood education and care provision.
- Long-term cost benefits are very hard to calculate.

What to read next

Children in Europe (2006) *Managing the Mix: Public and Private Provision*, No. 11. English language edition available from Children in Scotland, Edinburgh.

9 Practice makes no difference

I have a postcard from an exhibition which says 'Practice makes no difference'. Yet it is a common-sense axiom that 'practice makes perfect'. Does doing things over and over again make you more skilled or more bored? Practice has a triple meaning. It means constant repetition – the sense in which it is meant in the postcard. It also means a repertoire of ideas and skills on a particular topic which are brought together by a group of people to create what is called a practice, or sometimes a community of practice. And thirdly it means doing things, as opposed to hearing or reading about them, as when you 'put your ideas into practice'. Sometimes all three meanings are conflated. The idea of 'practice' sounds straightforward but it is not. Most of the chapters in this book have been devoted to exploring ideas and approaches that have underpinned or informed practice (in the sense of a body of ideas and skills), even though they may fall outside of conventional thinking about child development. Now it is time to look at what people do in practice (in the sense of doing rather than reading or thinking) and whether practice (in the sense of repetition) leads to improvement or change.

Practitioners working in early childhood have accumulated a lot of experience, individually and collectively. For those who go to university to improve their learning and skills, this experience of practice should provide a rich seam to draw on. For many students, however, their experience seems to be irrelevant. Doing things, and doing things often, does not necessarily enable people to talk about them in any kind of abstract way. Linking practice and theory does not work easily. There are several reasons why this might be the case.

Book learning, especially for those who have been out of education for some time, is like learning another language. The language, expectations and conduct of university life are so different from everyday working life in a nursery that students sometimes have great difficulty in translating from one to another.

After working in the childcare field for many years, as an employee, then latterly as an employer, I felt I could draw on my skills and knowledge. I thought the degree would allow me to offer my services to others in the profession, and open doors to further opportunities. I soon discovered the lecturers spoke a different form of the English language when it came to allowing students to share their specialized field.

(Joan)

I have been working with children for six years and in a wide range of settings (I work for an agency) and I reflect on what has been said here, and try and put it into practice and match it up with what I do. I'm accumulating knowledge, it's there in the back of my head. I should have approached the lecturers more. I looked on them as aliens, they are above me, and I forget they are as human as me.

(Cynthia)

Like Joan and Cynthia, students may be very competent in their everyday dealings with parents and children, but analysing those actions and then writing about them are very different processes. Moreover, as this book has been at pains to show, many of the ideas about child development are highly specific or very subtle, or just plain contentious. They cannot be turned easily into prescriptions for practice in a classroom or nursery. On the other hand, if I thought that students did not benefit from learning, thinking, discussing and writing, there would be no point in writing this book.

Learning about child development, from an academic point of view, may give some insights into how children behave, but it does not tell you about the rules and regulations, explicit and implicit, which govern everyday practices with children. A nursery or childcare setting could be described, in the phrase of the cultural psychologists (discussed in Chapter 3) as a 'community of practice'. There are traditional ways of doing things that can only be understood as an outsider by analysing the significance of particular actions and events, and working out their meaning to those involved. The people involved often cannot explain what they are doing because they take it completely for granted, beyond explanation. Yet, to the outsider, those actions may be strange and unfamiliar.

A well-known example is the study by Joseph Tobin and his colleagues described in Chapter 2. He videoed daily life in nurseries in China, Japan and the USA and asked the staff to comment on each other's practices. In each country the nursery staff thought that what they did was drawn from the best available knowledge. They were well trained, and were putting their training in child development into practice. Yet each group of staff was shocked at what they saw elsewhere. In the Japanese nursery there was enormous reliance on peer pressure. In the Japanese class there was one child whose behaviour was very disruptive. Instead of correcting him, the teachers said again and again to the children, you must sort it out, you must deal with it. Japan is a conformist society, and the teacher's intention was that the children should learn how to make errant members of the group conform. In the Chinese nursery, on the contrary, the teacher was firmly in charge, and all the children obeyed her without any quibbles. The emphasis was on doing things *together*, as efficiently as possible. In the US nursery the children were aggressive and individualistic, and the teacher emphasized all the time the right, or necessity, of each child to make his or her own choices. When the staff saw each other's videos, and then met to discuss them, there was lively discussion. But basically, each group thought that their own practices were right, and those of the other groups was misinformed.

What we take for granted as standard – for example, the *developmentally appropriate practice* approach described in Chapter 1 – turns out not to be normal or standard at all, but a reflection of a particular, North American philosophy about childhood. Similarly, my friends in Central Asia are learning, painfully, that what they took to be hard scientific knowledge, proven and tested, is seen as old-fashioned and downright wrong elsewhere. As one indignant parent said to me, 'They tell us that everything Russian was wrong. Well, I think it was a good education and what we have now is far worse.' Meanwhile, the sunny philosophy of the best European nurseries described in the OECD reports (2001, 2006) holds yet another set of underlying principles about child autonomy and collective action.

As a researcher, I have been fortunate to visit nurseries and other early years provision in rich and poor countries. I have mostly conducted reviews for governments or international agencies such as the EU, the OECD, the Asian Development Bank and Save the Children. The methods I used were those of official investigators: interviews with key people; analysis of documentation (including financial statistics); and ethnographic observations in nurseries and other settings. As an official visitor I also saw a lot of performances by children, sometimes put on for my benefit, sometimes coinciding with an event such as a special holiday or end of term. I have spent months working in Italian and Spanish nurseries; I carried out official reviews of Belgian nursery classes and of the Canadian system of early education and care. I have a particular interest in South Africa. My work for Save the Children in particular has enabled me to become familiar with nursery education and childcare provision in many places in southern Africa. I have also spent time in Central Asia and Eastern Europe, initially for Save the Children, and subsequently for the Asian Development Bank. I have come to know the ex-Soviet system of kindergartens, which was, as Bronfenbrenner (1965) once commented, the most comprehensive system of early education and care ever devised.

I have, then, had a bird's eye view of many policy documents and many practices. Early education and care practices are constructed at different levels and in varying contexts, as well as constantly changing in time. On a micro level, the way practitioners understand, interpret and reconstruct early childhood learning and development is intrinsically linked to their beliefs, knowledge and experience as well as to the contextual factors in which they operate. On a macro level, different local and national pressure groups, donors and political parties compete to influence education and development policy in relation to global and national interests. The formal and informal policy texts – the curricular guidelines, the health and safety guidelines, the training and practice manuals etc. – reflect a compromise of views, struggles and influences of the policy writers. While policy texts are written in a language that is understood and acceptable to the public and appealed to common sense, they are not necessarily coherent in practice and for specific contexts, representing as they do a rich amalgam of influences. The consequences of policy texts emerge only when it is enacted within the *context of practice*. Policy writers cannot control how their texts will be interpreted and practitioners reinterpret and recreate it in relation to the resources they have available. What practitioners actually *do* is more complicated than following the guidelines they have been set.

What I propose to do is to explore some key topics of practice and discuss how they are viewed in different countries or in different systems of early education and care. It is a very incomplete list verging on anecdote and I will only skim through it. But it may give readers some rather different ideas about practice from outside their own particular community of practice. These topics are interrelated. I have introduced them to give some idea of the range of practices – and the range of assumptions that underlies them. To give them snappy titles, they are:

- *Holistic and whole* – some examples of practice which claim to offer children an all-round experience.
- *Suppleness, strength and stamina* – physical education and how it is undertaken in different countries.
- *Aunts, angels and teachers* – views about the role of staff in nurseries.
- *Catalogues of toys* – objects used in nurseries and their perceived use in 'stimulating' children.
- *Listening, speaking and singing* – who listens, who speaks, who sings, and when.
- *Learning your colours* – ideas about art and aesthetics.
- *Skeletons of frogs* – ideas about maths, science and the environment.
- *Grannies on the doorstep* – parents, grandparents and the wider community and their influence.

Finally, I discuss what facilitates 'good' and 'bad' practice.

Holistic and whole

'Holistic' is a word much used in practice. Holistic is taken to mean providing for a range of children's needs: for cognitive development, emotional development, social development and physical development. As I suggested in Chapter 3, these categories are themselves problematical.

Addressing 'the whole child' is a goal that many countries have adopted, perhaps nowhere more than in the ex-Soviet states. The interpretation given to holistic in the Soviet system indicates, by comparison, the limited way in which it is used in many English-speaking systems.

The Soviet state believed that if society was to fundamentally change, it would have to begin with the collective upbringing of young children (Kirschenbaum 2001). The Soviets also believed everybody could, should and wanted to work, men and women alike. Work and family life were reconciled by the provision of widespread childcare. Psychologists, doctors and many other experts worked on the development of the kindergarten programme, which was extended to some of the poorest and remotest regions in the world, for example, on the steppes, or in the Gobi Desert (Penn and Demberel 2006). Children were set tasks appropriate to their age, and they were encouraged and monitored by their teachers in undertaking those tasks. Sometimes the tasks were arduous by western standards. For instance, children regularly gave end-of-year performances, or performances for special occasions, in which the level of performance – playing a simple musical instrument like a drum, or singing, or reciting poetry, or dancing – was of an exceptionally high standard and required collective discipline. Children had to perform together as well as separately. I have been privileged to see and hear some of these performances. It is a humbling experience to visit a kindergarten in a rough and remote desert area, and see immaculately costumed children singing, reciting and dancing; and also to watch their very proud parents.

Because the intention of the kindergarten was also to offer 'a good upbringing', there was a considerable emphasis on the class doing things together, in a disciplined way. No one could excel, or be individualistic, or different, but nor could anyone fail. No child fell behind her companions; all were expected to do and complete the same tasks, with extra help if necessary from the teacher or from other children. Bronfenbrenner wrote:

> From the very beginning stress is placed on teaching children to share and to engage in joint activity. Frequent reference is made to common ownership: *'Moe eto nashe; nashe moe'* (mine is ours, ours is mine). Collective play is emphasized. Not only group games, but special complex toys are designed which require the co-operation of

two or three children to make them work. Music becomes an exercise in social as well as sensory-motor articulation. As soon as children are able to express themselves, they are given training in evaluating and criticizing each other's behaviour from the point of view of the group . . . Beginning in the second year of nursery (age 2) and continuing through kindergarten, children are expected to take on ever increasing communal responsibilities, such as helping others, serving at table, cleaning up, gardening, caring for animals, and shovelling snow. The effects of these socializing experiences are reflected in youngsters' behaviour, with many children giving an impression of self-confidence, competence and camaraderie.

(1965: 23)

Bronfenbrenner also pointed out that there was congruence between the way parents treated their children and the way the kindergartens treated children; deliberately so. Both at home and in kindergarten, children were disciplined by withdrawal of affection. If a child was naughty, the mother, or the teacher, appeared hurt, as if saying, 'How could you behave like this to me?' This emotional disapproval, consistently applied, was extremely effective. The fact that the kindergarten discipline was based on traditional Russian upbringing meant that although parents did not spend much time at the kindergarten, they and their children did not experience discontinuities between home and kindergarten.

As the kindergartens were also providing care for working parents, they were open for long hours, from 7 or 8 in the morning to 5 or 6 at night. In some kindergartens, catering for shift workers, or for very poor parents, children would board during the week and go home at weekends. These long hours meant that great attention was also given to children's physical development. They received carefully monitored diets, with agreed portions of meat and vitamins. They slept every afternoon – most kindergartens were built with separate restrooms. Each kindergarten had exercise routines. These physical routines are discussed further below. Many kindergartens had their own swimming pools, gyms and dance halls.

The kindergartens held clinics, and children had health checks from doctors and nurses at least weekly. Medicines were issued at the kindergartens, and most kindergartens had a full-time nurse in attendance.

Bronfenbrenner, Kessen, and other eminent American psychologists visited kindergartens in Russia and China in the 1960s and 1970s. They were impressed, not only by the extraordinary level of investment, unmatched in any non-communist country at the time, but also because, to their psychologists' eyes, the children seemed relaxed. They appeared to show none of the signs of stress and disruptive behaviour so common in nurseries in the USA. Kessen concluded that although this level of conformity was not the

American way, nevertheless it offered children a security and a predictability that benefited them at least in the short term. Table 9.1 summarizes the differences between the Soviet and Anglo-American regimes.

After transition in 1990, communist regimes fell apart. Kindergartens, like many other social services, closed down. Many kindergartens had been attached to state factories and farms, which were sold off or simply shut. In Kazakhstan, for example, more than 50 per cent of kindergartens were closed (MONEE 2001), and the rest had to introduce fees which in effect put them beyond the reach of poor families (Penn 2004a). Other ex-communist countries also struggled to maintain what they once had. Teachers' salaries fell or failed to rise with the exponential rise in the cost of living post-1990. Initial and in-service training more or less ceased. Buildings were not maintained. Worn-out equipment was not replaced. Visiting these countries now, in Eastern Europe and in the ex-Soviet Union and its satellite states such as Bulgaria and Mongolia, what remains is the wreckage of an extraordinarily ambitious – and holistic – system.

Table 9.1 Comparison of the Soviet and Anglo-American regimes

Soviet	Anglo-American
Historical role for a society trying to achieve radical change. Kindergartens have a key role to play in bringing about societal change	Kindergartens/nursery a peripheral service with no particular role to play in understanding society
Dual care and education. Starting point is care for working mothers which is also at the same time profoundly educational	Education and care as separate systems. Cognitive development a separate and distinct issue from the provision of daycare
Knowledge consciously defined and prescribed by the educational system, to be learnt by child	Emphasizes the individual construction of knowledge: constructed by the individual in her own particular way
Importance of educators in delivering knowledge. Importance of educational institutions over the family. Child as product of kindergarten	Care of young children a marginal occupation. Emphasizes the roles and responsibilities of the family. Child as product of parenting
Collective character of education: the group is more important than the individuals within it	Education is the education of individuals not a welding of the group. Young children are seen as individuals for whom group life is an imposition

Source: Adapted from Penn (1999: 34)

The system in transitional countries could legitimately have been called holistic. It provided for mind and body in an encompassing way. It once seemed to be an outstanding system to visitors like the psychologists from the USA. Now it is widely perceived as repressive and institutionalized, and certainly not a model to be encouraged in the new global capitalist environment. For sure, not everyone remembers kindergartens kindly. One of my Kazakh colleagues described them as being like army camps. Physical punishment was not unknown, especially when children expressed reluctance at having to sleep for two to three hours every afternoon. (This was said to be neurologically necessary for brain growth.) The Soros Foundation – and many other consultants – recommended that staff be retrained in western, Piagetian models, where children had freedom to choose what they wanted to do, and individuality was encouraged. The irony of this suggestion, that Piaget replace Vygotsky as a theoretical model, escaped them. Or perhaps, as suggested in Chapter 3, many of those consultants recommending change were experiencing a time-lag, and harking back to their own remembered training.

However, the question these experiences raise is, what is meant by holistic, or catering for the 'whole child'? Can provision that is available only for two or three hours a day, and that offers neither food nor exercise – as in much of the UK and other English-speaking countries – be described as holistic? In these countries, 'holistic' usually means trying to think broadly about what a child needs, and child well-being. But at what point does catering for the whole child slip over into being unacceptable and encroaching on the rights and duties of parents? Where I have spoken to parents, for example, in focus groups in countries as diverse as Bulgaria, Kazakhstan, Mongolia and China, it is evident that they still have a high regard for the Soviet model. Those who can no longer afford to pay for kindergarten care feel bitterly excluded; conversely, the most wealthy gladly pay the cost (Penn 2005).

Suppleness, strength and stamina

I was recently the rapporteur (writer) of an OECD team carrying out a review of Canadian early education and care. What struck the team very forcibly was the immobility of the children in most education and daycare environments. They seemed to be encouraged for the most part not to take any risks, not to move about too much, for fear of endangering themselves or other children. Canada is the land of the great outdoors, a challenging environment for hiking, climbing, skiing, canoeing and biking. Yet such is the lack of exercise in children that child obesity is a major health problem. Similarly in Australia, another country with vast amounts of space. Perhaps it is not so surprising after all. A leading Australian manual for young children gives safety checklists that insist on a pristine, hygienic environment (Greenman and Stonehouse 1997). It reads like that of a sterilized hospital ward for intensive care. The emphasis is on removing all conceivable hazards, rather than enabling children to deal with them. (I first came across these guidelines in a training manual in southern Africa. It was especially poignant to see them there, since there was no possibility such standards could be reached in a resource-poor country.)

It also seems likely that, from a medical point of view, the manual may be plain wrong. Children may need small exposures to risky environments to develop their immune systems, to control their body temperature, to improve their circulation. All these physiological systems may depend on exposure to challenges so that young bodies can adapt to changing environments, just as children learn how to adapt their thinking and learning by encountering novel situations.

Young children spending their days in nurseries are often very restricted in their movement, and protected against every possible – and impossible – contingency. The policy guidelines are interpreted very cautiously by practitioners, for a variety of reasons. In one daycare nursery I visited in the UK, the only exercise children had was to go to a carpeted exercise room, where they were allowed to walk on a beam 6 inches off the floor, provided they held the hand of a childcare worker while doing so. Staff, recruited mainly from welfare backgrounds, regarded children as intrinsically threatened and vulnerable. The staff were so concerned about risk and their reputation as carers that children were forbidden *any* physical activity or challenges (Penn 2002a).

An exaggerated notion of risk is only part of the problem. Physical activity is not conceived of as exercise but as a means to an end – learning. So children learn 'hand–eye coordination', 'manipulative skills' and the like. Rarely does one read in the Anglo-American literature of exercise for the joy and pleasure of movement itself. John Muir, the Scottish explorer who founded the National Parks movement in the USA, describes in his autobiography how, as a young boy of 8 or 9, he and his friends would run 12 miles or more for the sheer joy of it:

> In the winter, when there was little doing in the fields, we organized running matches. A dozen or so of us would start out on races that were simply tests of endurance, running on and on along a public road over the breezy hills like hounds without stopping or getting tired . . . we thought nothing of running right ahead ten or a dozen miles before turning back; for we knew nothing about taking time by the sun and none of us had a watch in those days.
>
> (1996: 23)

John Muir's energy seems inconceivable to us now. We would simply not expect children to run long distances for the sheer fun of it. Yet most small children are naturally exuberant. A 3- or 4-year-old will often run or gambol rather than walk. Our understanding of children's physical energy and capacity is very much bound by time and place.

Do other countries see physical activity differently? In Nordic countries, where winter weather is sometimes harsh, the view is that children must learn to adapt to their environment. In Norway, kindergartens organize outside camps in winter. In Finland, children typically spend more than 13 hours a week outside, and they are encouraged to play vigorous games. In winter, they may do cross-country skiing or tobogganing. In Denmark, children may build huts, light camp fires, or swim in the sea in their forest kindergartens (OECD 2006). In these countries the outdoor life is valued for itself, for the pleasures it offers, and in order to cope positively with a sometimes harsh environment. They are not merely a means to improved intellectual performance.

In the Soviet and Chinese systems, a great deal of attention is paid to physical fitness. Soviet kindergartens – which were usually very big so there were economies of scale – were routinely supplied with dance/gym space, and many had swimming pools. In Sofia, in Bulgaria, in 1998, 90 per cent of children in the relevant age group still attended kindergarten, and most of these kindergartens had their own swimming pool. The kindergartens offer programmes for various kinds of highly specific physical exercises, including foot strengthening exercises (for children with flat feet), breathing exercises, and so on. In the freezing Soviet winters, some kindergartens even offered cold outdoor bucket showers – an old Russian tradition for improving the circulation. To those of us who live cosseted existences in rich countries, this seems positively barbaric, but one of the kindergartens I visited which had a cold showers regime was a special kindergarten for children with weak health. The doctors at the kindergarten claimed high success rates (Penn 2005).

In Chinese kindergartens, the emphasis was on callisthenics, exercises to develop strength, suppleness and stamina. These kindergartens, especially in cities, tended to be very big, about 200–300 children. After each lesson period, all children would come into the playground. Each stood on the spot which had been allocated. Loudspeakers would then relay the music and instructions for the movements. The children would bend, stretch, turn, balance, and so on, all on their marked spot. Again this is derived from an old Chinese tradition, Tai Chi or shadow boxing. Groups of elderly people in the parks would be doing similar exercises. The result of callisthenics was that small children were fit, moving in supple, graceful and controlled ways. I have a video I made at a kindergarten in Beijing, which I sometimes show to English audiences. The children look extremely graceful, with the exception of a small American girl who was also attending the kindergarten; she seemed bemused and clumsy by comparison. For a long time after I came back, English children seemed to me to be poorly coordinated. They seemed to have relatively little awareness of or control over their bodies in comparison with the Chinese children.

In Africa, by comparison, nurseries and crèches are often makeshift affairs, with untrained care staff and little in the way of equipment. Yet dancing and singing in many nurseries are second nature. Children learn to dance rhythmically very early on. Dance has a particular status in society, as a collective expression of emotion. I watched a trade union demonstration for increased public sector pay in Swaziland, where the demonstrators danced their disapproval of the government. The government official who was watching the demonstration with me, said, 'They have been dancing for three hours now, soon they will be tired and go home' (Penn 2005). All ritual occasions in the calendar require collective dancing in this small southern African kingdom, as in many other African societies. Children are not taught how to dance, but, as with the Guatemalan weavers' children described in Chapter 3, they join in adult dances, for a little bit, then for longer and longer until they are full participants.

In both the Soviet and Chinese kindergarten systems, activity is complemented by rest. In poor homes, children are unlikely to have their own rooms, and will go to bed when the family goes to bed. So rest regimes are deemed especially important. In the southernmost European countries there is also a siesta tradition – early afternoon is the hottest period of the day.

The body needs exercise and rest, but it also needs fuel. In the Soviet and Chinese systems, food is plain, local fare (partly prepared by the children in China, for example, shelling peas), but it is nutritionally sound and always freshly cooked. Cook–chill and other forms of food processing, the norm in rich countries, are unknown and in any case would be too expensive in poor countries. But food – and its digestion – are also important in many European countries. One nursery I visited in Valencia in Spain had its own properly laid out restaurant, and the cook went round the classes each day to discuss the menu with the children. This may be an extreme case, but food in these nurseries is much more important, and part of a traditional way of life, than is the case in the UK or other English-speaking countries.

In all the communities and societies I have described, the physical regimes and expectations of physical prowess and body maintenance have a wider resonance beyond the nursery or kindergarten. It is undeniable, however, that the Anglo-American childcare tradition underplays physical activity and the need for rhythms of rest, activity and replenishment. On the other hand, children are regarded as vulnerable and fragile and in need of constant protection and surveillance. Children are cocooned into inactivity.

Mark Dudek (2005) has brought together a series of articles by practitioners and academics wanting to provide a more stimulating and eco-friendly environment for children. Environmental issues are now high on most people's agendas. Care of the body is now seen as the other side of the coin to care of the environment; both need to be cared for sensibly, and guarded against stress, pollution and degradation.

Aunties, angels and teachers

In many societies, perhaps in a majority of societies, children are expected to be deferential – to older children, to those within their families, and to older people in their community. It is simply not tolerated to answer back or to disobey. Robert Serpell (1993) describes the way children are brought up in rural Zambia. He asked parents to define intelligence. For them an intelligent child was a helpful child, one who understands and anticipates the needs of others around him or her, a child who obeys instructions with alacrity. I have described elsewhere how nomadic families in Mongolia handle their children in order to make them constantly aware of the needs of others, to be alert to the effect their behaviour has on non-family members as well as on their mothers, fathers and siblings. Young children are shy, but extremely considerate (Penn and Demberel 2006).

Children, then, are taught to relate to adults in different ways depending on where and when they grow up. Here is a very different example, from observations in a Spanish nursery where daily life was like an ongoing party:

> In this nursery the pleasure the staff take in one another's company, and in the children, is palpable. There seems to be an implicit view amongst most staff that of all the places in which one could choose to spend one's time, this is it. There is a kind of *joie de vivre* which expresses itself not only in the staff spending much more time in the nursery than they are contracted to do, staying on to help on each other's shifts, but also with much physical affection and laughter. I watch a young member of staff and an older cleaner stroll up and down the courtyard, their arms around one another, deep in conversation. One member of the staff in particular gives enthusiastic kisses to every child, and to some of the parents, and their accompanying children, as well as to other staff. 'Handsome' she says to a small boy, and gives him a wet kiss, then kisses his older sister who is on her way to school; 'you are a delight' she says to another child as she bestows a kiss.

> . . . Although this particular member of staff is extravagant with her kisses, almost everyone shows physical affection uninhibitedly. A toddler strays into the kitchen, the cook picks him up, kisses him and passes him outside, where he is passed around amongst several staff and children, all of whom also kiss him. The children often solve

arguments and seal their peace with hugs and kisses, boys as well as girls.

(Penn 1997: 82)

Reading the official documents, the legislation and the local authority guidelines, you would not predict such jollity and conviviality. But for the staff it was a 'natural' way to behave, culturally sanctioned. This was an unusual nursery in many respects and I do not wish to claim that its practices should be copied. But I am using it to show the range of ways of relating to children, from expecting instant and unquestioning obedience to this kind of partying.

Much of the practice in Anglo-American countries, especially with very young children, harks back to attachment theory. Attachment theory postulated that there is a tight bond between an adult carer and a young child. Without this bonding a child may grow up badly, either indiscriminately affectionate or affectionless. Nursery nurses and care workers often see themselves as substitute carers in this bonding process. In this scenario, just as children are viewed as physically vulnerable, so they are seen as psychologically vulnerable. Nursery nurses and care workers are often themselves vulnerable young women, taking up care work as a relatively safe and academically undemanding occupation. Being with young children weaker and more dependent than themselves gives them some kind of status (Penn 2000a).

I have sometimes heard the expression 'he needs a bit of one-to-one' to describe the attention a nursery nurse gives an individual child, usually a naughty or disobedient one, who is made to sit down with her to undertake some small task. Nurseries are often organized to have 'key workers' who are, in principle, linked to a small group of children in order to be able to offer them the continuity of care and surveillance of a bonded relationship. In practice, staff turnover and staff absences, and irregular attendance by children, mean that key workers are frequently unavailable at the moment when one-to-one care might possibly make a difference. A senior government official in the UK, who had a 1-year-old child in an expensive nursery in London, confessed to me that she felt relieved if she saw the same member of staff more than once when she took her child to and collected him from the nursery. The fiction of continuity enables very poor practices to continue.

The argument has been made that in ordinary life, at least in rich countries, children get too much adult attention rather than too little. Non-intervention techniques, and a gentle distancing by mothers and carers, may be better for young children than a direct interaction initiated by an adult. Petrie and Owen (2005) discuss the work of Emmi Pickler, widely admired in Hungary, whose disciples now lead *Resources for Infant Educarers* (RIE), a movement based in California:

> The child expects to be the centre of attention all the time. He likes it. He of course doesn't do anything else any more; someone else is always busy doing something with him ... Such an infant will, in time, become increasingly whiney and cling to adults in an unhealthy way. He is only interested in adults, in having them around him, talking to him, doing things with him. None of this, however, gives him a feeling of joy and satisfaction, of quiet and well-being – at least not one of lasting duration. It leaves him restless and in need of excitement. It is precisely this kind of excitement a child gets accustomed to. He likes it. He cannot and will not do without it. We adults cannot do without lethal narcotics, once we have become addicted to them. In the same way, the infant who has gotten used to this kind of excitement does everything to be the centre of attention for adults.
>
> (Pickler 1969, cited in the *Bulletin of the Sensory Awareness Foundation*, 1994)

These words echo those of LeVine (2003), writing in entirely different circumstances, and drawing on his work in Africa. The attention it is assumed that adults need to pay to children, the 'stimulation' that is regarded as essential to their development (and if you believe the claims, to the development of synaptic connections in their brains), warrants a much more critical, and comparative, investigation.

Who else does a child relate to if not an adult? As Judy Dunn (1993) suggested (see Chapter 3), very young children relate intimately to each other. A key question when children are together in groups is how children might be expected to relate to other children. Are they fierce individuals who must be taught to 'share'? Or are they natural allies in a mysterious and hostile world of adults? The sociology of childhood, expounded by authors such as Berry Mayall (2002), suggests that children see and do things differently from adults not so much for reasons of immaturity and lack of experience, but because adults wield power and children do not. Generational differences are important in understanding childhood. The solidarity and subversiveness of children are posed against the authority of adults. Certainly for slightly older children in a school classroom where one teacher faces 20 or 30 children, this is likely to be the case. Maintaining control in a classroom is no easy task for a teacher, even in those countries where children are expected to be obedient. Devolving power to children and enabling them to support and regulate one another, so that the teacher is a kind of classroom resource, is a means of handling the imbalance between adults and children. This happens in a variety of ways, for example, in the Japanese classrooms described by Tobin and his colleagues (1989) or the systems of group controls in the Soviet system, or in a few innovative schools in the UK where children are in charge of classroom discipline (Alderson 1999).

Carers are commonly women, although there is a growing literature on men as carers. Most of this is descriptive (the numbers of men working in different circumstances) or rhetorical (why more men should work with young children). There are various arguments put forward for men to work with young children. These include providing equal opportunities for both men and women to be represented in the profession; and offering boys male role models. Yet gender is a highly problematical area. How (and if) men differ from women in the way they treat children is an open question. As Harty (2007) has pointed out, there is hardly any evidence to show that young children in nurseries respond to – or even notice – the gender of their carers. Other aspects of the personalities of their carers – friendliness, respect, etc. are more likely to be commentated on.

Listening, speaking and singing

There are many communities in the world that are still mainly oral. Talking, listening, remembering and recounting, declaiming, reciting and singing, people have learnt to rely on memory and performance. Some of the greatest ancient Greek literature, for example Homer's *Iliad* and *Odyssey*, tales of Greek heroes, were composed in this way. But oral communication is essentially collective and public rather than individual and private; it requires speakers and an audience.

In her book *Ways with Words* (1983), Shirley Brice Heath describes young black children growing up in an essentially oral community in the south of the USA. People used to gather around the doorstep in the evenings to chat and entertain themselves. In order to be heard and noticed in a group, young children, especially boys, had learnt to perform, to express themselves vividly and amusingly. When they got to school, their verbal wit was regarded as showing off, and their way of speaking was regarded as impertinent.

The skills of listening and speaking have to be taught and practised, just like the skills of reading and writing. In some communities this is a respected tradition. Certain people, for instance, the elders in First Nation communities in Canada, are given the task of making representations on behalf of the group they belong to. The praise singers of Mali and Senegal are a semi-hereditary group whose job it is to be the official memory of a community – a tradition translated to the North in the popular singing of Baaba Maal and Youssou N'Dour.

In some systems, most notably the Soviet system, there was considerable emphasis on memory and performance. When I first saw some of these extra-ordinary performances in remote places, where young children recited poems, sang and danced, I thought they were embarrassing demonstrations designed to showcase the kindergartens. I think now in retrospect that they were much more important, an attempt to recognize and preserve heritage and tradition, as well as a useful training in listening, memorizing and speaking.

In some countries the routine of the nursery or crèche or childcare setting regularly includes 'circle time', an opportunity for children to come together and to listen to one another. But this opportunity for self-expression within a group, important as it is, is only a start. Oral fluency, listening and memory are skills that are essentially collective rather than individual and private. My grandson took part in a rather chaotic end-of-term performance at his nursery. His group were dressed up as animals and the children had to learn songs as part of the performance. Several weeks later, when his parents and I were on a long journey in the car, he began to sing one of these animal songs. 'Who are you singing the song for?' I asked. 'I'm singing it for us,' he replied.

In some European countries, particularly those where school does not begin until 6 or 7 years of age, the pre-school curriculum emphasizes the skills of listening and speaking as a necessary precursor to reading and writing. The evaluation of the primary school outreach project by the National Theatre in London in the UK suggests that children who have taken part in dramatic performances also do better in their school work (Mayall et al. 2003).

Catalogues of toys

In one nursery school I visited in the UK, a spacious building with a big garden, I counted over 100 different activities that were available to the children. Some of them were innovative, for example, making a sand tray into a desert, with desert animals and shrubs; or the boot box where children could try on different sizes and colours of Wellington boots; or sorting and grading apples fallen from an apple tree in the garden for sale or for jam. This was besides the more usual nursery activities: many different kinds of bricks for building; painting with different types and thicknesses of paint; outside workstations with clipboards for writing and drawing. The nursery school in the UK has a long tradition of providing a stimulating environment for children. Margaret McMillan, one of the pioneers of nursery schools, saw children romantically as creatures of nature, and insisted on removing the barriers between inside space and outside space in her famous nursery school in Deptford. She believed children benefited from having great scope for autonomy and freedom of movement (Steedman 1990).

This practice has endured within nursery schools, although nursery schools themselves are being dismantled by a short-sighted UK Government. (It is quite unlike the separate UK care tradition which, as pointed out above, regards children as vulnerable and in need of surveillance.)

This wealth of activities pre-dated Piaget, but Piaget's theories lent them additional legitimacy. But alongside the theory, parents and childcare workers alike have absorbed the consumerist messages of the societies to which they belong. They have come to believe that nurseries should resemble shopping malls, in their reproduction of continuous multiple choice. Writing about American pre-schools, Tobin comments that

> Consumer desire is reproduced by the material reality of our pre-schools. The variety of things and choices offered by middle-class preschools is overwhelming to many children. We create over-stimulating environments modelled on the excess of the shopping mall and amusement park . . . We have become so used to the hyper-materiality of our early childhood care settings that we are oblivious to the clutter; settings that provide more structure and are less distracting seem stark or bleak.
>
> (Tobin 1995: 232)

Brian Sutton Smith, in his important book *Toys as Culture* (1986), suggests that young children have proved a lucrative market for the exploitation of caregiver and parental inadequacy. Parents, especially busy or absent parents, fear that they are not doing enough to promote their children's development. All manner of toys are marketed as 'educational' to tap into those fears. The statement below is a typical marketing ploy.

> Our mission is to provide families with a HUGE selection of creative and stimulating products in a customer-friendly entertaining and interactive shopping environment because we believe kids learn best when they're having fun.
>
> (Toyshop brochure, quoted in Kenway and Bullen 2001: 82)

Stephen Kline (1993) documents how marketing to children of toys, foods and other products increased in the second half of the twentieth century in rich countries. He illustrates the enormous sophistication, complexity and reach of market campaigns aimed at children and their parents. Advertisers of commercial products encourage children to demand and challenge in order to obtain what they want (or what is being promoted) and at the same time play on the guilt feelings of their parents. Kline claims that TV is used relentlessly to make sales pitches towards children. Although commercial toys have been advertised and sold in increasing numbers for the last century or so, it is in the past 25 years that the process has accelerated. For example, in 1987 (the last year Kline quotes), American toy manufacturers spent $350 billion on toy advertising. The commercialization of childhood extends to nurseries. Beatrix Tudor Hart, writing in 1938, gave a simple and ingenious list of toys that she used in her (very good) nursery. Today's nurseries are grossly overprovided by such standards. Magazines which aim at early childhood practitioners are replete with advertisements for new toys and equipment that are apparently indispensable for learning. Advertising pressurizes parents into buying all kinds of non-essential items for their children.

Seiter comments that children's vulnerability is exploited by the makers of cartoons and commercials:

> Children's cartoons and commercials portray an abundance of the things most prized by children – food and toys; their musical themes and fast action are breathtakingly energetic, they enact a rebellion against adult restriction; they present a version of the world in which good and evil, male and female, are unmistakably coded in ways easily comprehended by a young child; they celebrate a community of peers.
>
> (1995: 11–12)

A recent Australian study suggested that although children, even as young as 3, were knowledgeable and capable of exercising some scepticism about the claims to reality of what they saw on TV, videos, and computer games, they did not question at all the market culture that gives rise to such advertising and promotion. They took it as normal that such goods would be provided for them, and that they would have endless opportunity to choose among them (Kenway and Bullen 2001).

If this seems a bleak picture, there are also contraindications that children continue to create and pursue their own interests and identities independently from those of adults when time and space permit. In 1969, Peter and Iona Opie recorded children's games in close-to-home spaces – driveways, pavements, streets, car parks. They identified more than three thousand games played by children. They argued that this rich children's culture was carried on in the interstices of everyday spaces, the 'child-to-child complex of people going about their own business within their own society . . . fully capable of occupying themselves under the jurisdiction of their own code (Opie and Opie 1969, cited in Moore 1986: xiv). Indeed, they were dismissive of the idea that this children's culture could be shaped or controlled by adults in any way.

Although it is now much less likely that children would be allowed to play out and find spaces for their own use, recent evidence suggests that 'schoolyard lore' or 'childlore' is still vibrant in school playgrounds. Despite the overwhelming contemporary pressures to which they are subject, children, as they have done since time immemorial, have their own games, rhymes, chants and crazes, their own ways of amusing themselves. This child-lore is still the daily currency of the playground for most children (Blatchford et al. 1990). It has been charted in Australia, Britain, continental Europe and North America, and in ethnographic studies in the South. Child-lore and childplay reveal dimensions of creativity, artistry, musicality and complexity. Some of it, such as ball and skipping games, is highly active and requires dexterity and physical coordination. It is 'performative, carnivalesque, subversive and parodic' (Bishop and Curtis 2001) including elements of parody of the very features of advertising that seem so threatening. It includes narratives, epithets, jeers, taunts, riddles and dirty jokes. It is fun, but not necessarily all the time for all of the children taking part, and it sometimes verges on bullying (although bullying, too, is subject to interpretation). The persistence of such child-lore, despite all the concerns to the contrary, suggests that there are overwhelming reasons for its continuance. Brian Sutton Smith, the guru of children's play, argues that

> childlore deals with behaviour that has traditionally been regarded as non-serious, but as this behaviour appears to be a systematic part of the human repertoire, to think, therefore, it is unimportant might be a mistake.
>
> (1970: 4)

Marc Armitage claims that the layout of playground space inadvertently affects the nature of the games that are played in it. He carried out 90 play-audits of school playgrounds over a five-year period. He pointed out that designating an area as a particular kind of playspace is no guarantee that it will be used in that fashion; on the contrary, the most unlikely – or, to adults, unsuitable – places will be commandeered for games. Playgrounds have shrunk, as land has proved more profitable for other uses; and playtime has shrunk as teachers have become more obsessed with curricular and supervised activities. Playgrounds with nooks and crannies – round the back of steps, in corners – are commandeered for games, for example, marbles on drain covers, cops and robbers games by metal grilles or fences. Games of imprisonment were a feature which occurred in all the play audits, and witches frequently prepared potions in gaol-like places.

Armitage comments that:

> The primary school children of today can quite easily be left alone on the playground and their spontaneity will do the rest. This is in fact what already happens. But for them to be able to make use of this spontaneity to the best of their ability, and to do so without the need for direct adult intervention in their play, the environment provided for them as a place to play must respect the finding that children themselves are informally organizing their available spaces and features to meet their own needs. As adults, our role should be to support this and provide an environment that caters for what children actually play as opposed to what they should or could play, or even what we think they play.
>
> (2001: 55–6)

The debate about consumerism and toys is a debate from the rich world. Toys are simply not manufactured or available in the South, and the avenues for advertising do not exist. Rossie has made several studies of children's use of toys in the South (Rossie 1999). For more well-to-do children, imported toys have status, but for the majority of children age-old homemade toys are in frequent use. Goldschmied and Jackson (1996), in *People Under Three*, describes her 'treasure basket', a collection of household and natural articles, such as corks, chains, a sponge and fircones, that she offers children and which she claims interests babies far more than any manufactured toys.

Learning your colours

Art is as old as mankind. Decoration and images are present in the oldest archaeological sites. Even today, the art of Aborigine groups in Australia, or the San people in southern Africa serve to remind us of the veneration and ritual involved in creating representational art such as pictures of animals. Art is also functional and takes many forms besides the trendy conceptual art of rich countries: the weaving of South America; the carpet making and embroidery of the Middle East; the pottery and tiles of North Africa; the calligraphy of Arabic countries, to name but a few.

An Italian artist, doubling up as an infant teacher in an English nursery, said to me indignantly that she was expected to teach children their colours. 'There are more than 150 shades of blue. Which one is the blue that I should show to the children? Sapphire? Indigo? Aquamarine? I am teaching them to blur their colours, not to tell their colours apart.'

Neuroscientists such as Steven Rose have argued that children see the world very vividly, but that they learn to screen out the intensity of their perceptions in order to take in essential information more efficiently. My Italian colleague felt strongly that aesthetic information – in this case, colour – was important and that its importance should be recognized. In her view, adults should be required to know, and children should be required to learn, about gradations of colour, texture and pattern. I have described elsewhere (Penn 2000a) working with another reception teacher (another artist supporting herself by teaching) who insisted on obtaining raw pigments and on grinding the colours herself with her groups of South London children – who under her tutelage found the task fascinating.

There is no doubt that young children are capable of very fine visual discrimination. Children who are required to look after herds of cows (or in the steppes, of herds of horses) can easily discriminate among several dozen – or even more – animals which to an outsider appear as a blur of brown, grey and white. The distinguished writer on Central Asia, Owen Lattimore (1962) described the visual acuity of some of the nomad tribes with whom he worked. For them, being able to see, and judge what they saw, was a survival mechanism.

Languages with ideographic (picture) scripts have a different pattern for every word. In order to become literate in Chinese, a child would have to learn to recognize about 2000 different patterns – as opposed to the 26 letters of the English alphabet. Accuracy in pattern making is therefore very important. Chinese children are taught to copy very carefully, and a less than good copy is discarded because it might mean something else. The drawings of Chinese children tend to be very detailed and realistic and to display a sophistication that is regarded with some disbelief by Anglo-American colleagues. Similarly, in the Soviet kindergarten accurate representation is valued above self-expression.

By contrast, in Anglo-American nurseries children are encouraged to be expressive, and all expressions are valued and, if possible, displayed, careless blobs and blurs as they may be. At the same time the commercial pressures described above have led to a proliferation of kitsch cartoon images. Many nurseries in the UK and the USA are immediately recognizable because of their friezes of cartoon figures such as Donald Duck and Mickey Mouse; a recreation of a make-believe world that is supposed to have a special attraction for children. It is a very curious practice to use cartoon figures so ubiquitously, and it persists despite rarely appearing in any training guides.

There is a debate among architects about whether the creativity and design of the buildings in which children are taught and cared for contribute in any way to the children's own creativity. Mark Dudek's book (2000) *Kindergarten Architecture* provides an overview of the range of buildings that are used for children, from the grimly functional to the fantastic – fairytale castles and grotesque attics.

Paints, felt-tip pens, Plasticine, colouring books and the other staples of 'creativity' are simply not available in poor countries. On the other hand, everyday life may offer unparalleled artisan opportunities, of weaving, thatching, carving, pottery, and so on.

Skeletons of frogs

I recently visited a nursery in the island of Mauritius. The nursery was not very interesting in the sense of its having only a limited range of activities and training materials. But someone had gone to town on mock-up biology. On one table was a set of dissected plastic frogs; the pieces of the frogs' skeletons and organs could be dismantled and reassembled. On another table was a similar set of plastic digestive organs. The digestive tract could also be taken apart and reassembled. I do not know, and did not have the chance to ask, where these biology models came from, whether they were an unsolicited gift or whether a misinformed teacher had ordered them from a catalogue. Then I thought that perhaps I was being unfair, and the 5- and 6-year-old children at least could grasp the concepts involved.

Those growing up in rural environments (or whose fathers are butchers) are likely to be more familiar with slaughter and dissection. Mothibi, my grandson, was playing in his African grandmother's yard with the chickens, throwing them pieces of corn, and then chasing them. Two of the chickens were for the pot. His African grandmother wrung their necks, then chopped off the heads and took the chickens away to be plucked. Mothibi picked up the chicken heads and went on playing with them. This familiarity and unconcern with the processes of animal husbandry are widespread in some societies. Animals are herded and milked, they are fed, they reproduce, and they are slaughtered.

Similarly, as Barbara Rogoff (1990) described in relation to South American Indian communities, rural peasant children are involved in everyday horticulture. They help sow, weed, water and pick and prepare the plants that will be their food. They learn about cycles of growth, water conservation, and insect depredations not as special subjects but as part of their lives.

Science is the systematic investigation of natural phenomena. It must be more difficult for those children who only experience nature second-hand, and whose understanding of it is a sentimental one in which, for example, ducks dress up in sailor hats and mice wear shorts. But in all countries there is some kind of natural life to observe. Below is Mothibi's drawing of a dead grasshopper. Its serrated and immensely strong legs are accurately drawn. Mothibi noticed that ants swarmed over the corpse of any dead creature, so after he finished drawing the grasshopper, he insisted that we put it back outside for the ants to eat. (We did find another dead grasshopper, and dug a hole to bury it in the vegetable bed. Mothibi muttered a prayer over it, but then dug it up the next day to see how far it had decomposed.) These kinds of minute natural phenomena are everywhere to be explored.

Grannies on the doorstep

'Parents' is a gender-blind word, used in the name of equal opportunities. It is almost always mothers who make and take part in childcare arrangements; men are regarded as a special catch if they take part in such arrangements. There is invariably ambivalence about how men should be treated, so I will use the word 'mother' rather than parent as a more accurate reflection of the situation.

In the Soviet system, as I have noted, mothers and grandparents value kindergartens very highly. But they do not have very much to do with them. The teachers are the experts to whom they willingly defer. In the

Figure 9.1 This drawing of a grasshopper by my 5-year-old grandson illustrates the fascination children can have with the natural world. The life, death and decomposition of the grasshopper preoccupied him for days.

Anglo-American tradition the relationship between care workers, nursery nurses, teachers and parents is more ambivalent.

The mantra 'the parent is the child's first educator' is often used as a covert attempt to educate the mother into replicating the activities of the crèche or nursery or school at home.

Typically, in the UK, a child will have three or four different experiences of childcare before starting school: a childminder, a playgroup, a private nursery, a part-time nursery class. Because provision is ad hoc and often expensive, and turnover of staff is high, the goal of parental involvement is a paradoxical one. The mother may have to go to great lengths to find and/or pay for suitable daily arrangements (Skinner 2003). Often these arrangements are less than satisfactory. Yet she is required to acquiesce in these arrangements, and to appear to endorse them, by becoming 'involved'.

One rationale for parental education is that, because of the shrinking of family size and the increased mobility of families, mothers have little prior experience of children and few people to turn to. Often they do not know what to do with their children, and are puzzled by their behaviour. There are no grannies on the doorstep to fulfil their time-honoured role of giving advice and helping out. Some kind of non-judgemental advice from an experienced person might be useful to combat the isolation many mothers experience.

But in the case of low-income mothers or 'multi-problem' families, the mothers are considered as more than a little bemused by the responsibilities of motherhood. They are regarded as perpetuating 'a cycle of poverty'. This view that poor mothers are basically ignorant, and this ignorance can be addressed by education about parenting, stems from a concept of poverty as a personal failing. It permeates much of the literature on early childhood in the USA, and in turn reappears in a good deal of the World Bank and UNICEF literature.

Mothers who do not understand and apply basic hygiene, or do not talk to or 'stimulate' their children, run the risk of endangering their children's lives and atrophying their brains.

Another rationale for parental education is that it offers an opportunity for mothers to catch up on lost educational opportunities. Early childhood offers a 'window of opportunity' when mothers are newly conscious of the effects that they might have on another human being and are therefore especially willing to learn about new things. The emphasis in the UK is now to get mothers off benefits and back into the labour force as a saving to the economy. The government subsidizes many education programmes alongside crèche facilities for mothers seeking to return to work. Childcare is regarded as an appropriate work avenue for relatively unskilled women, and a good deal of the training available is to encourage women to become childminders or nursery nurses by undertaking some kind of basic vocational training.

This emphasis on parental education arises mostly in unequal societies with high levels of poverty, since inequality is justified by the assumption that the poor are inadequate rather than exploited. In those countries that have universal early education and childcare services and redistributive incomes, there is very little concern about parental education or parental involvement. The emphasis instead is on democratic participation. The curriculum for early years settings in Nordic countries, for example, is very broad and general and it is left to committees of parents and staff to flesh it out. Similarly the famous nurseries in Reggio Emilia in Italy are constructed around concepts of community and co-construction.

The above discussion, and indeed much of the book, have assumed that age-related institutions are the norm for children. Children are segregated from older children with specially trained people to educate and care for them, who do no other work while with the children. Like schooling, nurseries are based on the ideas of age segregation and specialized people. This enables children to learn. In this sense, nurseries are an extension of school, places devoted to children's learning.

Nurseries and kindergartens are not 'normal'. It is more normal, historically and geographically, for children to grow up in communities where life is lived publicly, rather than privately behind closed doors. There are typically many different activities being undertaken by people of all ages, and many different kinds of conversation to tune into. The children take part in some of these activities, and listen to some of the conversations. The extract with which this book began, from Flora Thompson's *Lark Rise*, illustrated such an environment. This kind of community life has more or less disappeared from modern industrialized societies, but what kinds of substitute exist? Children in nurseries and kindergartens more often than not lead narrow and safeguarded lives. Nurseries are devoted to play and learning – child development – but are divorced from work and adult conversation and interests.

They can be deeply boring places for adults and children alike. There are some attempts to develop intergenerational projects, and to create spaces for generations to mix and to engage in real activities, but these are few and far between.

Good and bad practice: one system for everybody?

Most countries try to provide some guidelines for good practice. These are contained in regulatory and/or curriculum documents. Often these documents have legal status. The 1989 Spanish Education Reform Act (LOGSE), for example, included a broad curriculum that gave a framework for those working with children aged 0–3 and 3–6. In the Nordic countries, where staff are well trained and the services are well financed, there is considerable autonomy within the system. The ministry provides loose guidelines, but nurseries are expected to make up their own curriculum and set and monitor their own standards with parents. In those countries where there is a large private or non-profit sector, such as the UK or Canada, regulations are highly prescriptive, and there is an inspectoral system to make sure they are carried out. In these countries, practitioners cannot be fully trusted to act on their own. In the ex-Soviet countries and China, the curriculum was also highly prescriptive – in China, it used to run to 18 volumes. But, paradoxically, staff were also well trained, and their job was to 'perform' the curriculum, to make it as interesting as possible, rather like actors interpreting a script.

Internationally the most widely known guidelines for practice and training are those compiled and distributed by the US National Association for the Education of Young Children (NAEYC). These guidelines, called *Developmentally Appropriate Practice*, have been distributed throughout the world.

They are much quoted by the World Bank and other donor organizations. *Developmentally Appropriate Practice* offers sensible advice about how to handle children and what activities to pursue with them at each age or stage of development. It cites research in child development (almost all of it from the USA) to back up the practices it advocates. It is a thoughtful and comprehensive booklet, and has been revised considerably over the past ten years to take account of its critics, especially over its sensitivity – or previous lack of it – to multicultural issues.

In the USA, early education and care provision is on an ad hoc basis through a variety of providers, mainly private. Many of these providers are likely to be untrained, and they need to make money from looking after children. In this context, where educated practitioners are not the norm, and the turnover of staff and children in childcare is high, simply stated instructions, referring with authority to 'research' in child development, are a useful tool to encourage good practice and to admonish bad practice. But the authors of *Developmentally Appropriate Practice* are only concerned with micro-level interventions. They implicitly assume that good practice is context-free and can be applied anywhere; and value-free, since it is based on 'scientific research'. Anybody can achieve it, in whatever kind of setting, by following the guidelines.

Developmentally Appropriate Practice is not of course value-free. It continually stresses individuality, self-assertiveness, personal choice and the availability of possessions. It is the job of the adult looking after the children to make sure that children can exercise choice between many different objects, and assert their rights over them. It takes individualistic consumer behaviour as its unwritten norm. It ignores the inequalities of society and the effects that these might produce on children. It also continually stresses the importance of adult–child affectional bonds, and downplays child–child bonds.

Other international organizations that have reviewed early education and childcare practices pay more attention to context and values. The European Union Childcare Network, a ten-year project to explore childcare across member states, produced a series of discussion booklets and a video on practice in kindergartens and nurseries. *Quality in Services for Young Children* suggests how certain questions arise from adopting certain value bases about practice including equality of access for all children. This discussion paper was followed up by a set of recommendations which stressed the role of governments in setting the necessary framework for services to develop; to provide an adequate funding base and systems for research and evaluation.

The OECD has produced useful statistics on education and economic indicators which are widely used throughout the world as benchmarks. It has recently been reviewing early education and childcare across its member states. Countries that have contributed to the review include the USA, Canada, Australia, the UK, most European countries, Korea and Mexico. The reviews are carried out on a peer-review basis; a small team of experts made up from contributing countries undertake the review of individual countries. These reviews are published by the OECD, and there are also international seminars held on key topics. A synthesis report (2006) *Starting Strong: Early Childhood Education and Care* summarizes the findings and makes general recommendations.

The OECD report gives comparative statistics, but focuses its discussion on practice at the level of policy. Like the EU, it argues that equality of access and quality of practice are important goals for services, but that they can only be achieved by adequate public funding and by a good infrastructure of planning, evaluation and training. By these criteria, the USA performs very poorly indeed, almost bottom of the class. Nordic countries do particularly well. It is therefore ironic that the US model, which stresses individual improvement at a programme level, is so enthusiastically adopted by the World Bank and other international donors.

I began the chapter by exploring the notion of practice. What people do they always do within a context, and never in isolation. Of course, good practitioners exist, and there are some wonderful ways of encouraging and supporting the development of young children. But dull practice is not just the responsibility of dull practitioners. The chain from theory to policy to practice is a complex one, and all sorts of requirements and precepts are introduced on the way (Aubrey 2007). Practice, that is doing the same thing over and over again, makes little difference without a critical eye. Nor is it likely to change easily. Practitioners, parents, policy–makers and academics, can all become complaisant with their particular status quo – and young children are both beneficiaries and victims of well-intentioned efforts to inform practice. This book has aimed to make people gaze more carefully at how we work with young children and how young children themselves might respond.

Summary

This chapter gives an overview of practice across the world. In particular, it contrasts the once comprehensive systems of the Soviet Union and other transitional countries, and China, with North American and European early education and care. It traces how practice grows out of political and economic conditions and traditions rather than from scientific research into child development. It suggests that, in some ways, practice in the UK, the USA and other English-speaking countries is poor, although practice in these countries is also characterized by tremendous variation, in the absence of coherent and sustained government intervention.

Main messages from this chapter

1   There are many ways of looking after children. Policy and practice are too often parochial.
2   In many countries of the North, practice is very consumption orientated, based on the premise that the more toys you buy, the more children can choose between lots of toys, the better the education. This is nonsense (except to toy manufacturers) and not based on any scientific research.
3   We have forgotten that young children are intensely physical and enjoy using their bodies. Too much practice focuses on keeping children still.

4　We underrate the pleasure that children get from each other's company and overrate the contribution of adults.

What to read next

OECD (2006) *Starting Strong II: Early Education and Care in 20 Countries*. Paris: OECD.

Postscript – an interdisciplinary approach?

It must be obvious to anyone who has read this book that I think it is important to take an interdisciplinary approach to understanding early childhood. I
mean by that there are many kinds of ideas about how the world is understood
and what the place and status of young children is within it. Familiarizing
yourself with a range of ideas about how to study early childhood is to enrich
your understanding. Delving into ideas and thinking about them deeply is
important. Knowledge and scholarship are wonderful human gifts; the notion
that we can pursue any topic in depth and with extraordinary precision. The
poet William Blake wrote 'to see a World in a Grain of Sand, and a Heaven in a
Wild Flower', as a wonderful metaphor for this extraordinary gift of insight
and imagination, detail and richness that is a human inheritance.

What this book has tried to do, in a very imperfect way, is give an overview of some ideas about the contexts in which early childhood is understood.
I certainly don't believe prescriptive content and learning outcomes can cap-
ture the nature of what we need to do to understand and relate to children – or
for that matter to anyone else. Perhaps the dull half-baked kinds of courses
now being promoted as training in early years offer a small starting point, but
even reading William Blake or learning how to use a microscope, practising
how to sing in harmony, or rowing a boat, would be an improvement on their
narrowness. Its not that I favour a return to a liberal, creative arts syllabus; but
I do think being open-eyed about knowledge and thinking deeply about what
we see and do are important in addressing almost any topic, or in dealing with
almost any person.

Early childhood is a relatively new subject, and has not really established
any disciplinary boundaries, if indeed it can. Its boundaries are arbitrary, and
differ from country to country, both in terms of what is taught to practitioners
and in terms of what is provided for children. It raises profound questions
of gender, culture and context. It draws on a wide range of sources – and
leaves others out – and the end result is not necessarily compatible or coherent. This book has been cast more or less within the framework of ideas current in the UK, and tries to track and comment on them, but recognizes their
particularity.

However, by inter-disciplinary, I don't mean multi-disciplinary or multi-
agency, which is one of the ways in which the notion of inter-disciplinarity
has become understood. Multi-agency is the new, or not so new idea that
professionals need to work together in the interests of the child, because if

they didn't make a special effort to understand each other's professional distinctiveness, and work together, they would somehow leave out or ignore the child.

I return below to the point that professional barriers are such that they impede rather than enable cooperation. But I would argue that the relationship between parents and those who in some capacity work with children needs some clarifying. From my perspective as a mother (or now as a grandmother), professionals are very peripheral to my daily life. What can 'professionals', doctors, or health visitors or teachers or social workers, or nursery workers possibly know about my own and my children's joys and dramas and struggles, about the particular intricacies of our lives? Indeed, I might argue, how dare they presume to know? What boundaries exist between what is intimate and confidential, and what is public? What kind of reciprocity exists in a relationship between parent and professional, when one is paid to help the other?

While I would be grateful for technical help, in diagnosing or treating an illness, or in learning maths, or some other kind of skill, the most I would expect is polite cooperation, rather than any kind of personal relationship. The idea of a 'team of professionals' around my child would make me very paranoid indeed. BUPA, the private health company, ran an advert saying 'Doctor, the patient will see you now' a reversal of the usual assumption about who is in charge and who sets the pace of the professional–client relationship. It is not too much of a generalization to claim that in the system of provision for young children in the UK, middle-class mothers can summon up (and pay for) the help they need; on the whole, the poor have help imposed upon them.

Burman (2007) has pointed out the conceptualization of the child as deserving a special focus of attention for adults has slipped into a notion of the child as a social problem; if concerned professionals do not help the child to achieve better outcomes, then who knows what kind of failure the child might become. Similarly, Burman argues, the mother (referred to mysteriously as 'parent' as if gender disparities have completely disappeared) has become the guilty party. Through being insufficiently sensitive, or insufficiently concerned with her child's well-being or development, mothers are putting their children's future life at stake. Mothers (parents) need the support of professionals, especially 'hard-to-reach' mothers.

I have a book at home called *Nurses for the Needy*. Published at the end of the nineteenth century (by someone who describes herself only as L.N.R.) it describes a home-visiting programme '*supplying the missing link between the comfortable classes and those who lack all comforts . . . helping our poor to help each other*'. The nature of the support and the advice being given is not so very different from today except that the terminology has changed; there is less emphasis on the bible as a source of guidance, although equally moralistic views about what the poor should be doing to better themselves and stop being poor!

This is not to deny that there are many mothers and many children who live their lives in pain and loneliness. There are many reasons why that might be so, chief among them living a precarious financial existence. Poverty is relative, but deeply experienced. 'Multi-agency' work implies that professionals can work together to alleviate personal pain, rather like the Nurses for the Needy, without addressing or changing the conditions that produce it, by concentrating on the interior lives of mothers and their children, rather than on the exterior circumstances that shape those lives. There are of course some very sophisticated models of inter-professional working that challenge existing conceptualizations of what it means to be a professional and solve problems (Engestrom 2008) but the early years literature is on the whole unsophisticated about help and support, because of the overpowering normative and sentimental concepts of childhood and mothering that Burman highlights.

This is not to deny too, that many children are in need of help, because of a recognized or unrecognized disability, or that children themselves may choose to relate to others besides their immediate family. At the very least one wants to ensure that children are treated with the alertness, with the humour, and with the reciprocity they, like anyone else, deserve.

But multi-agency work, bringing people together with different skills to work with (that mysterious normative being) 'the child' is an apologia for a muddled system of education and care for children. The Sure Start programme in England was an attempt to provide a multi-agency approach to the needs of young children in poor areas. But one of the things that happened was that the programme took more than twice as long to implement as planned, because of professional squabbles about who was in charge, how much they should be paid, how their hours of work might be reconciled, and how services might be organized (Tunstill et al. 2002). I remember being shown around a local Sure Start project office, and the official who took me round was proudest of the fact that the computer cabling and computer programs could be used by both health personnel and childcare personnel, a major achievement of cooperation in bringing professionals together!

In fact, in England, the Labour Government in its Childcare Act (2006) have ensured that even this minimal level of cooperation is going to be hard to achieve. At the time of writing, the original Sure Start programme has been replaced by a programme of 'Sure Start Children's Centres' which will have day nursery provision, or childcare for working mothers at its core. But although the bringing together of health, family support and other services required in a Children's Centre is being coordinated by the local authority, the day nursery provision or childcare element, must now be provided on a commercial basis, and be self-financing or 'sustainable'. Similarly schools are required to provide out-of-school or wrap-around care, and more often than not this is farmed out to an independent commercial or semi-commercial group, whose financial security is precarious, and whose company runs the risk of collapse. The growth of the private sector, in response to subsidies offered through the childcare tax credit system, has effectively negated or undermined possibilities for close professional work.

The net result of 10 years of Labour Government intervention in early years in England has been an increasingly muddled and unfair system, which exacerbates the social segregation between those who can pay for childcare and those who cannot, and those who are in work and those who are not. There has been a dramatic rise in for-profit care and an equally dramatic decrease in public sector care.

Does all this multi-agency working even need to exist in such a relatively small field as early years? As the OECD report *Starting Strong* (2006) suggests, many systems of early education and care are much more integrated. Providing early education and care on a universal basis, with a similar offer made to all children, does not undermine choice or impose bureaucratic restrictions on parents. The evidence suggests that it is unlikely that in England parents, except at the top end, have any real choice between providers, but why would they want it if there is good provision? In those countries where there are universal services, the private sector has very little footing; there is little or no demand for more 'choice'. Instead, in the UK, the government has acceded to every vested interest, and instead of making any hard decisions, has perpetuated the same inefficient and inappropriate systems that we have had for the past hundred years.

This diatribe is a reflection of profound disappointment with a government who promised so much and achieved so little. One has to work within a system, and to accept the limitations of the system in order to make improvements in it. On the other hand, we need to think with our eyes open. It is possible to have an integrated and interdisciplinary project of education and care, where children and adults work together as citizens for their mutual betterment and enjoyment. This is the kind of project outlined for instance by the Reggio Emilia nurseries, although their circumstances are privileged compared with most other places. It is the kind of project the most ambitious of Children's Centres in England aim for, although they are working in an unpropitious climate. It is what some of the unimaginably poor community projects in South Africa hope to achieve. In most countries there are pockets of collective, persistent, innovative, and articulate practice. But without knowledge, without a critical eye, and without articulation, the worst tends to repeat itself and the best (the many kinds of best) cannot flourish.

References

Abadzi, H. (2006) *Efficient Learning for the Poor: Insights from the Frontiers of Cognitive Neuroscience*. Washington, DC: World Bank.

Abley, M. (2003) *Spoken Here: Travels among Threatened Languages*. New York: Random House.

Ainsworth, M., Blehar, M., Waters, E. and Wall, S. (1978) *Patterns of Attachment: A Psychological Study of the Strange Situation*. New Jersey: Lawrence Erlbaum.

Alderson, P. (1993) *Children's Consent to Surgery*. Buckingham: Open University Press.

Alderson, P. (ed.) (1999) *Learning and Inclusion: The Cleves School Experience*. London: David Fulton.

Alderson, P. and Goodey, C. (1998) *Enabling Education: Experiences in Special and Ordinary Schools*. London: Tufnell Press.

Alexander, R. (2000) *Culture and Pedagogy: International Comparisons in Primary Education*. Oxford: Blackwell.

Ariès, P. (1962) *Centuries of Childhood*. London: Jonathan Cape.

Armitage, M. (2001) The ins and outs of school playground play: children's use of 'play spaces', in J. Bishop and M. Curtis (eds) *Play Today in the Primary School Playground*. Buckingham: Open University Press.

Aubrey, C. (2007) *Management and Leadership in Early Childhood Settings*. London: Paul Chapman.

Barnett, T. and Whiteside, A. (2002) *AIDS in the 21st Century: Disease and Globalization*. Hampshire: Palgrave Macmillan.

Bauman, Z. (1995) *Life in Fragments: Essays on Postmodern Morality*. Oxford: Blackwell.

Beck, U. (1992) *Risk Society: Towards a New Modernity*. London: Sage.

Begley, S. (1996) Your Child's Brain. *Newsweek*, 19 Feb., p. 55.

Belsky, J. (2006) Early child care and early child development: major findings of the NICDH study of early child care, *European Journal of Developmental Psychology*, 3: 95–110.

Bennett, M. and Hacker, P. (2003) *The Philosophical Foundations of Neuroscience*. Oxford: Blackwell.

Berlin, I. (1997) *The Sense of Reality: Studies in Ideas and Their History*. London: Pimlico.

Bion, W. (1962) *Learning from Experience*. London: Heinemann/Karnac Books.

Bishop, J. and Curtis, M. (eds) (2001) *Play Today in the Primary School Playground*. Buckingham: Open University Press.

Blatchford, P., Creeser, R. and Mooney, A. (1990) Playground games and playtime: the children's view, *Educational Research*, 32(3): 163–74.

Bodman, F. (1945) Aggressive play, in *Play and Mental Health*. London: New Era/ New Education Fellowship.

Bogin, B. (1998) Evolutionary and biological aspects of childhood, in C. Panter-Brick (ed.) *Biosocial Perspectives on Children*. Cambridge: Cambridge University Press.

Bornstein, M. (1991) *Cultural Approaches to Parenting*. London: Lawrence Erlbaum.

Botting, B. (ed.) (1995) *The Health of Our Children*, Decennial Supplement. London: OPSC.

Bowlby, J. (1952) *Maternal Care and Mental Health*. Geneva: World Health Organization. Later popularized as *Childcare and the Growth of Love*. London: Penguin, 1953.

Boyden, J. with Cooper, E. (2007) Questioning the power of resilience: are children up to the task of disrupting the transmission of poverty? Working Paper No. 73. Manchester: IDPM/Chronic Poverty Research Centre (CPRC).

Bradbury, B. and Jantti, M. (1999) *Child Poverty Across Industrialized Nations*, EPS 71. Florence: UNICEF Innocenti Centre.

Bradshaw, J. (2002) Child poverty and child outcomes, *Children and Society*, 16: 40–55.

Bredekamp, S. and Copple, C. (eds) (1997) *Developmentally Appropriate Practice in Early Childhood Programs*, 2nd edn. Washington, DC: National Association for the Education of Young Children.

Brewer, M., Crawford, C. and Dearden, L. (2005) *Helping Families; Childcare, Early Education, and Work-Life Balance. Election Briefing 2005*. London: Institute of Fiscal Studies.

Brewer, M., Goodman, A., Muriel, A. and Sibieta, L. (2007) *Poverty and Inequality in the UK, 2007*. IFS Briefing No. 73. London: Institute for Fiscal Studies.

Brewer, M. and Shaw, J. (2004) *Childcare use and mother's employment: a review of British data sources*. Working Paper No. 16. London: Institute of Fiscal Studies/ Dept of Work and Pensions.

Brewer, M. and Sheperd, A. (2004) *Has Labour Made Work Pay?* York: Joseph Rowntree Foundation/Institute of Fiscal Studies.

British Medical Journal (2002) *Global Voices on the Aids Catastrophe*, No. 7331 (special issue).

Bronfenbrenner, U. (1965) *Two Worlds of Childhood*. London: Penguin.

Bronfenbrenner, U. (1979) *The Ecology of Human Development: Experiments by Nature and Design*. Cambridge, MA: Harvard University Press.

Bruer, J. (1999) *The Myth of the First Three Years*. New York: The Free Press.

Bruner, J. (1960) *The Process of Education*. Cambridge, MA: Harvard University Press.

Bruner, J. (1980) *Under Five in Britain*. London: Grant McIntyre.

Bruner, J. (1982) Formats of language acquisition, *American Journal of Semiotics*, 1: 1–16.

Bruner, J. (1990) *Acts of Meaning*. Cambridge, MA: Harvard University Press.

Bruner, J. (1996) *The Culture of Education*. Cambridge, MA: Harvard University Press.

Bruner, J. (2000) Foreword, in J. DeLoache and A. Gottleib (eds) *A World of Babies: Imagined Childcare Guides for Seven Societies*. Cambridge: Cambridge University Press.

Burman, E. (2007) *Deconstructing Developmental Psychology*, 2nd edn. London: Routledge.

Byron, T. (2005) *House of Tiny Tearaways*. London: BBC Books.

Central Advisory Committee for Education (1967) *Children and Their Primary Schools: A Report of the Central Advisory Committee for Education (England)*. London: HMSO.

Chamoiseau, P. (1999) *Childhood*. London: Granta.

Children in Europe (2006) *Managing the Mix: Public and Private Provision*, No. 11. English language edition available from Children in Scotland, Edinburgh.

Chomsky, N. (2003) *Power and Terror*. New York: Seven Stories Press.

Christensen, P. and James, A. (eds) (2000) *Research with Children: Perspectives and Practices*. London: Falmer Press.

Chugani, H.T., Phelps, M.E. and Mazziota, J.C. (1987) Positron emission tomography study of human brain function development, *Annals of Neurology*, 22: 487–97.

Clark, A. (2007) To what extent have children's views shaped the development of children's services? Keynote paper given at Daycare Trust Conference, Lessons from Research on the National Childcare Strategy, 24 April.

Clark, A. and Moss, P. (2001) *Listening to Young Children: The Mosaic Approach*. London: National Children's Bureau.

Clarke, K. (2006) 'Childhood, parenting and early intervention: a critical examination of the Sure Start programme', *Critical Social Policy*, 26(4): 699–721.

Cleveland, G., Forer, B., Hyatt, D.I., Japel, C. and Krashinsky, M. (2007) *Final Report: An Economic Perspective on the Current and Future Role of Non-Profit Provision of Early Learning and Childcare Services in Canada*. Ottowa: Report to Human Resources and Skills Development Canada.

Clifford, J. and Marcus, G. (1984) *Writing Culture: The Poetics and Politics of Ethnography*. Los Angeles: University of California Press.

Cole, M. (1996) *Cultural Psychology: A Once and Future Discipline*. Cambridge, MA: The Belknap Press.

Cole, M. and Cole, S. (2006) *The Development of Children*, 5th edn. New York: W.H. Freeman.

Convention on the Rights of the Child (CRC) (2005) *Implementing Child Rights in Early Childhood*. General Comment No 7. New York: UN.

Corsaro, W. (1985) *Friendship and Peer Culture in the Early Years*. New Jersey: Ablex.

Coyle, B. (2007) *What Economics Really Do and Why it Matters*. Princeton, NJ: Princeton University Press.

Cunningham, H. (1991) *The Children of the Poor: Representations of Childhood Since the Seventeenth Century.* Oxford: Blackwell.

Currie, J. (2000) *Early Childhood Intervention Programs: What do We Know?* Arlington, VA: National Science Foundation, Joint Center for Poverty Research.

Currie, J. (2004) Viewpoint: child research comes of age, *Canadian Journal of Economics*, 37(3): 509–27.

Davis, J., Watson, N. and Cunningham-Burley, S. (2000) Learning the lives of disabled children: developing a reflexive approach, in P. Christensen and A. James (eds) *Research with Children: Perspectives and Practices.* London: Falmer Press.

Dawkins, R. (1976) *The Selfish Gene.* Oxford: Oxford University Press.

Dawkins, R. (1988) *The Blind Watchmaker.* London: Penguin.

Deacon, T. (1997) *The Symbolic Species: The Co-evolution of Language and the Human Brain.* London: Allen Lane.

Dean, H. (2007) 'Tipping the balance: the problematic nature of work-life balance in a low-income neighbourhood', *Journal of Social Policy*. October.

De Lissa, L. (1945) *Education up to Seven Plus*, NSA pamphlet. BAECE archives London: BLPES.

DeLoache, J. and Gottleib, A. (eds) (2007) *A World of Babies: Imagined Childcare Guides for Seven Societies.* Cambridge: Cambridge University Press.

Dennis, C. and Gallagher, R. (2001) *The Human Genome.* Hampshire: Palgrave/ Nature Publishing Group.

Department of Education (1978) *Nursery Education*, Circular 2/73. London.

Department for Education and Science (2003) *Every Child Matters*, Green Paper, 8 September 2003. Available at: www.dfes.gov.uk

Donaldson, M. (1978) *Children's Minds.* London: Fontana.

Dudek, M. (2000) *Kindergarten Architecture.* London: Spon.

Dudek, M. (ed.) (2005) *Landscapes for Children.* London: Architectural Press, pp. 178–94.

Dunn, J. (1984) *Sisters and Brothers.* Cambridge, MA: Harvard University Press.

Dunn, J. (1988) *The Beginnings of Social Understanding.* Oxford: Blackwell.

Dunn, J. (1993) *Young Children's Close Relationships.* London: Sage.

Edelman, G. (2006) *Second Nature: Brain Science and Human Knowledge.* New Haven, CT: Yale University Press.

Edwards, A., Barnes, M., Plewis, I. and Morris, K. et al. (2006) *Working to Prevent the Social Exclusion of Children and Young People: Final Lessons from the National Evaluation of the Children's Fund.* Research Report 734. London: DfES.

Eldering, L. and Leseman, P. (1999) *Effective Early Education.* London: Falmer Press.

Engestrom, Y. (2008) *From Teams to Knots: Studies of Collaboration at Work.* Cambridge: Cambridge University Press.

European Commission Childcare Network (1994) *Quality in Services for Young Children: A Discussion Paper*, DGV/B/4. Brussels: European Commission.

European Commission Childcare Network (1996) *Quality Targets in Services for Young Children*, DGV/B/4. Brussels: European Commission.

Evans, D. and Zarate, O. (1999) *Introducing Evolutionary Psychology.* Cambridge: Icon.

Fass, P. (ed.) (2004) *Encyclopaedia of Children and Childhood in History and Society.* New York: Thompson/Gale.

Fass, P. (2007) *Children of a New World: Society, Culture and Globalization.* New York: New York University Press.

Faulkner, W. (1964) *Short Stories.* London: Penguin.

Faulkner, W. (1965) *Uncle Willy and Other Stories.* London: Penguin.

Ferguson, S. and Fitzgerald, H. (1954) *History of the Second World War: Studies in Social Services.* London: HMSO.

Fitz-Gibbon, C. (1996) *Monitoring Education: Indicators, Quality and Effectiveness.* London: Cassell.

Fukuyama, F (1992) *The End of History and the Last Man.* New York: Free Press. 2006 edition.

Gardner, D. (1956) *The Education of Young Children.* London: Methuen.

Gardner, H. (1983) *Frames of Mind: The Theory of Multiple Intelligences.* New York: Basic Books.

Gardner, H. (1993) *The Unschooled Mind.* London: Fontana.

Gathorne-Hardy, J. (1972) *The Rise and Fall of the British Nanny.* London: Hodder and Stoughton.

Geertz, C. (1973) *The Interpretation of Cultures.* London: Fontana.

George, S. and Sabelli, F. (1994) *Faith and Credit: The World Bank's Secular Empire.* London: Penguin.

Giddens, A. (1991) *Modernity and Self-identity: Self and Society in the Late Modern Age.* Cambridge: Polity Press.

Giddens, A. (1998) *The Third Way.* Cambridge: Polity Press.

Goelman, H., Doherty, G., Lero, D., LaGrange, A. and Yougas, J. (2000) *You Bet I Care! Caring and Learning Environments: Quality in Childcare Centres Across Canada.* Guelph: Centre for Families, Work and Well-Being.

Goldschmied, E. and Jackson, S. (1996) *People Under Three.* London: Routledge.

Goleman, D. (1996) *Emotional Intelligence: Why It Can Matter More than IQ.* London: Bloomsbury.

Gopnick, A., Meltzoff, A. and Kuhl, P. (1999) *How Babies Think: The Science of Childhood.* London: Weidenfeld and Nicolson.

Gorard, S. and Taylor, C. (2004) *Combining Methods in Educational and Social Research.* Maidenhead: Open University Press.

Gottlieb, A. (2004) *The Afterlife Is Where We Come From: The Culture of Infancy in West Africa.* Chicago: The University of Chicago Press.

Gould, S.J. (2000) *The Lying Stones of Marrakech.* London: Jonathan Cape.

Grantham-Mcgregor, S., Cheung, B., Glewwe, P., Richter, L., Strupp, B. and the International Child Development Steering Group (2007) Developmental potential in the first 5 years for children in developing countries, *The Lancet*, 369, 6 Jan.

Greene, S. and Hogan, D. (2005) *Researching Children's Experience: Approaches and Methods*. London: Sage.

Greenman, J. and Stonehouse, A. (1997) *Prime Times: A Handbook for Excellence in Infant and Toddler Programs*. Sydney: Longman.

Grieg, A. and Taylor, J. (1999) *Doing Research with Children*. London: Sage.

Hardyment, C. (2007) *Dream Babies*, 2nd edn. London: Frances Lincoln.

Harries, T., La Valle, I. and Dickens, S. (2004) *Childcare: How Local Markets Respond to National Initiatives*. London: HMSO DfES Research Report RR 526.

Hart, R. (1997) *Children's Participation: The Theory and Practice of Involving Young Children in Community Development and Environmental Care*. London: Earthscan/ UNICEF.

Harty, R. (2007) 'Men as carers in nurseries', *New Zealand Journal of Early Childhood Education*, V.10 pp. 183–190.

Heath, S.B. (1983) *Ways with Words: Language, Life and Work in Communities and Classrooms*. Cambridge, MA: Harvard University Press.

Heckman, J. (1999) *Policies to Foster Human Development*, Working Paper No. 7288. Cambridge, MA: National Bureau of Economic Research.

Heckman, J. and Masterov, D. (2005) *The Productivity Argument for Investing in Young Children*. Available at: http://jenni.uchicago.edu/human-inequality/papers/h.

Heussler, H., Polnay, L. and Katz, M. (2000) The times are they a'changing? *Children and Society*, 14: 254–66.

Hewlett, M. and Lamb, M. (eds) (2005) *Hunter-Gatherer Childhoods: Evolutionary, Developmental and Cultural Perspectives*. London: Aldine Transaction, pp. 65–91.

Highfield Junior School, Plymouth (1997) *Changing Our School: Promoting Positive Behavior*. London: Institute of Education.

Hill, M. (2005) Ethical Considerations in Researching Children's Experiences, in S. Greene and D. Hogan (eds) *Researching Children's Experience; Approaches and Methods*. London: Sage, pp. 61–86.

HMSO (1967) *Children and Their Primary Schools: A Report of the Central Advisory Council for Education (England)* (the Plowden Report). London: HMSO.

Hobsbawm, E. (1997) *On History*. London: Weidenfeld and Nicolson.

Hood, S. (2001) *The State of London's Children*. London: Office of the Children's Rights Commissioner for London.

Horrobin, D. (2003) *Not in the Genes*. Available at www.guardian.co.uk. 12 Feb. 2003. Comment Column.

Hrdy, S. (1999) *Mother Nature: Maternal Instincts and How They Shape the Human Species*. New York: Ballantine Books.

Hrdy, S. (2005) Comes the child before man: How co-operative breeding and pro-longed postweaning dependence shaped human potential, in M. Hewlett and M. Lamb (eds) *Hunter-Gatherer Childhoods: Evolutionary, Developmental and Cultural Perspectives*. London: Aldine Transaction, pp. 65–91.

Huxley, A. (2000) *Brave New World*. London: Penguin.

Isaacs, S. (1929) *The Nursery Years: The Mind of the Child from Birth to Six Years*. London: Routledge.

Isaacs, S. (1930) *Intellectual Growth in Young Children*. London: Routledge.

Jahoda, G. and Lewis, I. (1987) *Acquiring Culture: Cross-cultural Studies in Child Development*. London: Academic Press.

James, A., Jenks, C. and Prout, A. (1998) *Theorizing Childhood*. Cambridge: Polity Press.

Jardine, L. (1999) *Ingenious Pursuits*. London: Little, Brown.

Johnson (1999) *Developmental Cognitive Neuroscience: An Introduction*. Oxford: Blackwell.

Jones, S. (1999) *Almost Like a Whale: The Origin of Species Updated*. London: Doubleday.

Kagan, J. (1984) *The Nature of the Child*. New York: Basic Books.

Kagan, J. (1998) *Three Seductive Ideas*. Cambridge, MA: Harvard University Press.

Kaldor, M. (1999) *New and Old Wars: Organized Violence in a Global Era*. Cambridge: Polity Press.

Kapuscinski, R. (2001) *The Shadow of the Sun: My African Life*. London: Allen Lane.

Katz, C. (2004) *Growing Up Global: Economic Restructuring and Children's Everyday Lives*. Minneapolis: University of Minnesota Press.

Kenway, J. and Bullen, E. (2001) *Consuming Children*. Buckingham: Open University Press.

Kershaw, P., Forer, B. and Goelman, H. (2005) 'Hidden fragility: closure among licensed child-care services in British Columbia', *Early Childhood Research Quarterly*, 20(4): 417–32.

Kessen, W. (1965) *The Child*. New York: John Wiley & Sons, Ltd.

Kirschenbaum, L. (2001) *Small Comrades: Revolutionizing Childhood in Soviet Russia, 1917–32)*. London: Routledge.

Kline, S. (1993) *Out of the Garden: Toys, TV and Children's Culture in the Age of Marketing*. London: Verso.

Kotulak, R. (1996) *Inside the Brain: Revolutionary Discoveries of How the Mind Works*. Kansas City: Andrews McMeel.

Laing and Buisson Ltd (2007a) *2007 Annual Children's Nurseries Conference: A sector under pressure*. London: Cavendish Conference Sector, 1 March.

Laing and Buisson Ltd (2007b) *Nursery and Childcare Market News*, February, 5(8). London.

Lamming, G. (1979) *In the Castle of My Skin*. London: Longman.

Lattimore, O. (1962) *Nomads and Commissars: Mongolia Revisited*. Oxford: Oxford University Press.

Lave, J. and Wenger, E. (1992) *Situated Learning: Legitimate Peripheral Participation*. Cambridge: Cambridge University Press.

Laye, C. (1959) *The African Child: Memories of a West African Childhood*. London: Fontana.

LeDoux, J. (1998) *The Emotional Brain*. London: Weidenfeld and Nicolson.

LeVine, R. (2003) *Childhood Socialization: Comparative Studies of Parenting, Learning and Educational Change.* Hong Kong: Comparative Education Research Centre.

LeVine, R., Dixon, S., Levine, S., Richman, A., Leiderman, P., Keefer, C. and Brazleton, T. (1994) *Childcare and Culture: Lessons from Africa.* Cambridge: Cambridge University Press.

LeVine, R. and New, R. (eds) (2008) *Anthropology and Child Development: A Cross-Cultural Reader.* Oxford: Blackwell.

Lister, R. (2006) Children (but not women) first: New Labour, child welfare and gender, *Critical Social Policy*, 26(2): 315–35.

MacCulloch, D. (1999) *Tudor Church Militant: Edward VI and the Protestant Reformation.* London: Allen Lane.

Machel, G. (2001) *The Impact of War on Children.* London: Hurst.

MacKinnon, D. (2003) Children and work, in J. Maybin and M. Woodhead (eds) *Childhoods in Context.* Chichester: John Wiley, pp. 173–218.

Malinowski, B. (1967) *A Diary in the Strict Sense of the Term.* New York: Harcourt Brace and World Inc.

Marshall, R. (1940) *Arctic Village.* London: Penguin.

Mayall, B. (2002) *Towards a Sociology of Childhood: Thinking from Children's Lives.* Buckingham: Open University Press.

Mayall, B., Turner, H., Wiggins, M., Hood, S. and Dickinson, R. (2003) *Evaluation of the National Theatre Education Department's Drama Work in Primary Schools. Interim Report.* London: Social Science Research Unit, Institute of Education.

Mead, M. (1975) *Growing Up in New Guinea.* London: Pelican.

Meade, A. (2001) One hundred billion neurons: How do they become organized? in T. David (ed.) *Promoting Evidence Based Practice in Early Childhood Education: Research and its Implications.* London: JAI, pp. 3–26.

Mental Health Foundation (1999) *Bright Futures.* London: Mental Health Foundation.

Midgley, M. (1998) One world but a big one, in S. Rose (ed.) *From Brains to Consciousness? Essays on the New Sciences of Mind.* London: Penguin, pp. 246–70.

Miller, J. (1996) *Never Too Young: How Children Can Take Responsibility and Make Decisions. A Handbook for Early Years Workers.* London: NEYN/SCF.

Miller, J. (1999) *Young Children as Decision Makers: On Raising Children's Rights in England.* London: SCF.

MONEE (2001) *Ten Years of Transition.* Project MONEE, CEE/CIS/Baltic Republics. Regional Monitoring Report No. 8. Florence: UNICEF.

Montagu, A. (1978) *Learning Non-aggression.* Oxford: Oxford University Press.

Moore, K. (2001) *Frameworks for Understanding the Inter-Generational Transmission of Poverty and Well-Being in Developing Countries.* Working Paper No. 8. Manchester: Chronic Poverty Research Centre.

Moore, R. (1986) *Childhood Domains.* Berkeley, CA: MIG Communications.

Muir, J. (1996) *The Wilderness Journeys*. Edinburgh: Canongate. First published in 1913 as *Story of My Boyhood and Youth*.

Murray, L. and Andrews, L. (2000) *The Social Baby: Understanding Babies' Communication from Birth*. Richmond: Children's Project Publishing.

Mustard, J. (2006) *Early Child Development and Experience-based Brain Development: The Scientific Underpinnings of the Importance of Early Child Development in a Globalized World*. Washington, DC: Brookings Institute. Available at: www3.brookings.edu/views/papers/200602mustard.pdf

Myers, R. (2000) *Thematic Studies: Early Childhood Care and Development*. World Education Forum Education for All Assessment. Paris: UNESCO.

Nabokov, V. (1967) *Speak Memory: An Autobiography Revisited*. London: Weidenfeld and Nicolson (2000 edition).

National Audit Office (2004) *Early Years: Progress in Developing High Quality Childcare and Early Education Accessible to All*. London: National Audit Office.

National Audit Office (2006) *Sure Start Children's Centres*. London: HMSO.

Newson, C. (1995) The patio projects, *Co-ordinate*, 10–11 January.

NSA (1927) Nursery School Education: Statement of Policy, BAECE archives. London: BLPES.

NSDN (1923) Address to the First International Conference on Day Nurseries, BAECE archives. London: BLPES.

Nursery World 52 (1938) p. 237.

Oakley, A. (2000) *Experiments in Knowing: Gender and Method in the Social Sciences*. Cambridge: Polity Press.

Ochs, E. and Schieffelin, B. (1984) Language acquisition and socialization, in R. Shweder and R. LeVine (eds) *Culture Theory: Essays on Mind, Self and Emotion*. Cambridge: Cambridge University Press.

O'Connor, F. (1963) *My Oedipus Complex and Other Stories*. London: Penguin.

OECD (1999) *Norway: Early Childhood Education and Care*. Country Note, 1 June. Paris: OECD. Available at: www.oecd.org

OECD (2000a) *United States: Early Childhood Education and Care*. Country Note, 1 July. Paris: OECD. Available at: www.oecd.org

OECD (2000b) *Starting Strong: Country Note UK*. Paris: OECD.

OECD (2001) *Starting Strong: Early Childhood Education and Care*. Paris: OECD.

OECD (2006) *Starting Strong II*. Paris: OECD.

Opie, P. and Opie, I. (1959) *The Lore and Language of Schoolchildren*. Oxford: Oxford University Press.

Orme, N. (2001) *Medieval Children*. New Haven, CT: Yale University Press.

Ormerod, P. (2000) Death of Economics Revisited, keynote address given to the Association of Heterodox Economists, 29 June 2000. Available at: www.volterra.co.uk/docs/dofer.pdf

Ormerod, P. (2007) Shun the rational agent to rebuild economics, *Post-Autistic Economics Review* 40, 56–60.

Peacock, J. (1986) *The Anthropological Lens: Harsh Light, Soft Focus.* Cambridge: Cambridge University Press.

Penn, H. (1997) *Comparing Nurseries: Staff and Children in Italy, Spain and the UK.* London: Paul Chapman.

Penn, H. and McQuail, S. (1997) *Childcare as a Gendered Occupation.* London. DfEE Research Report RR23.

Penn, H. (1999) Children in the majority world: is Outer Mongolia really so far away?, in S. Hood, B. Mayall and S. Oliver (eds) *Critical Issues in Social Research.* Buckingham: Open University Press, pp. 25–39.

Penn, H. (2000a) Is working with young children a good job?, in H. Penn (ed.) *Early Childhood Services: Theory, Policy and Practice.* Buckingham: Open University Press, pp. 115–30.

Penn, H. (2000b) Policy and practice in childcare and nursery education, *Journal of Social Policy,* 29(1): 37–54.

Penn, H. (2001) Culture and childhood in pastoralist communities: the example of Outer Mongolia, in L. Alanen and B. Mayall (eds) *Conceptualizing Adult–Child Relationships.* London: Falmer Press, pp. 86–98.

Penn, H. (2002a) The World Bank's view of early childhood, *Childhood,* 9(1).

Penn, H. (2002b) Maintains a good pace to lessons: inconsistencies and contextual factors affecting OFSTED inspections of nursery schools, *British Educational Research Journal,* 28(6): 879–88.

Penn, H. (2004b) Round and round the mulberry bush: private and public in the history of early education and care, in R. Aldrich (ed.) *Private and Public: Studies in the History of Knowledge and Education.* London: Woburn Press.

Penn, H. (2005) *Unequal Childhoods.* London: Routledge.

Penn, H. with Demberel (2006) Nomadic education in Mongolia, in C. Dyer (ed.) *The Education of Nomadic Peoples: Issues, Provision and Prospects.* London: Berghahn Books.

Penn, H. (2007) 'Childcare market management: how the UK government has reshaped its role in developing early education and care', *Contemporary Issues in Early Childhood,* 8(3): pp. 192–206.

Penn, H. (2008) 'Working on the impossible; early education and care policies in Namibia, *Childhood,* December forthcoming.

Penn, H. and Lloyd, E. (2009) Richness or rigour? A discussion of systematic reviews and evidence based policy in early childhood, *Contemporary Issues in Early Childhood,* (7)1: pp. 3–18.

Petrie, S. and Owen, S. (eds) (2005) *Authentic Relationships in Group Care for Infants and Toddlers: Resources for Infant Educarers.* London: Jessica Kingsley.

Phipps, S. (2001) 'Values, policies and well-being of young children in Canada, Norway and the United States', in K. Vleminckx and T. Smeeding (eds) *Child Well-Being, Child Poverty and Modern Nations: What Do We Know?* Bristol: Policy Press.

Piaget, J. and Inhelder, B. (1969) *The Psychology of the Child.* New York: Basic Books.

Pickler, E. (1969) *Peaceful Babies, Contented Mothers*. Original in Hungarian. Cited in *Bulletin of Sensory Awareness Foundation*. (14) Winter 1994.

Pieterse, J. (2004) *Globalization and Culture: Global Melange*. Oxford: Rowman and Littlefield.

Pinker, S. (1995) *The Language Instinct*. London: Penguin.

Pinker, S. (1998) *How the Mind Works*. London: Penguin.

Plowden, B. (1977) Opening address. Children and parents: self-help and the voluntary role, in *0–5: A Changing Population. Implications for Parents, the Public and Policy Makers*. London: Voluntary Organizations Liaison Committee.

Pollock, A. (2004) *NHS plc*. London. Verso.

Pollock, L. (1987) *Parents and Children over Three Centuries*. London: Fourth Estate.

Porter, T. (1995) *Trust in Numbers: The Pursuit of Objectivity in Science and Public Life*. Princeton, NJ: Princeton University Press.

PriceWaterhouseCoopers (2006) *DfES Children's Services: The Childcare Market*. London: PriceWaterhouseCoopers.

Punch, S. (2001) Negotiating autonomy: childhoods in rural Bolivia, in L. Alanen and B. Mayall (eds) *Conceptualizing Adult–Child Relationships*. London: Routledge, pp. 23–36.

Rahnema, M. (ed.) with Bawtree, V. (1997) *The Post-development Reader*. London: Zed Books.

Ramey, C. and Campbell, F. (1991) Poverty, early childhood education, and academic competence: the Abecedarian experiment, in A. Huston (ed.) *Children in Poverty: Child Development and Public Policy*. Cambridge: Cambridge University Press, pp. 190–221.

Rawls, J. (1999) *A Theory of Justice*, 2nd edn. Oxford: Oxford University Press.

Richards, M. (1998) The meeting of nature and nurture and the development of children; some conclusions, in C. Pantner-Brick (ed.) *Biosocial Perspectives on Children*. Cambridge: Cambridge University Press, pp. 131–58.

Ridley, M. (1999) *Genome*. London: Fourth Estate.

Riley, D. (1983) *War in the Nursery*. London: Virago.

Roberts-Holmes, G. (2005) *Doing Your Own Early Years Research Project: A Step by Step Guide*. London: Paul Chapman.

Rogoff, B. (1990) *Apprenticeship in Thinking: Cognitive Development in a Social Context*. Oxford: Oxford University Press.

Rorty, R. (1989) *Contingency, Irony and Solidarity*. Cambridge: Cambridge University Press.

Rosaldo, R. (1993) *Culture and Truth: The Remaking of Social Analysis*. London: Routledge.

Rosaldo, R. and Xavier, J. (eds) (2002) *The Anthropology of Globalization: A Reader*. Oxford: Blackwell.

Rose, H. and Rose, S. (eds) (2000) *Alas Poor Darwin*. London: Jonathan Cape.

Rose, N. (1989) *Governing the Soul*. London: Routledge.

Rose, S. (ed.) (1999) *From Brains to Consciousness? Essays on the New Sciences of the Mind*. London: Penguin.

Rose, S. (2003) *The Making of Memory: From Molecules to Mind*. London: Vintage.

Rosemberg, F. (2000) The doctrine of national security and the Brazilian Early Childhood Care and Education Programme, paper given at the EECERA conference, Institute of Education, London, August.

Rosetti-Ferreira, M., Ramon, F. and Barriero, A. (2000) Improving early child care and education in developing countries, State of the Art lecture given at the International Congress of Psychology, Stockholm, Sweden.

Rossie, J. (1999) *Toys, Culture and Society*. Halmstad: Nordic Centre for Research on Toys and Educational Media.

Russell, B. (1926) *On Education, Especially in Early Childhood*. London: Allen and Unwin.

Rutter, M. (2002) Nature, nurture and development: from evangelism through science towards policy and practice, *Child Development*, 73(3): 1–22.

Rutter, M. (2006) Is Sure Start an effective preventative intervention? *Child and Adolescent Mental Health*, 11(3): 135–41.

Said, E. (1999) *Out of Place*. London: Granta.

Scarr, S. (1992) Developmental theories for the 1990s: development and individual differences, *Child Development*, 63: 1–19.

Scarr, S. (1993) Biological and cultural diversity: the legacy of Darwin for development, *Child Development*, 64: 1333–53.

Scheper Hughes, N. (1993) *Death Without Weeping*. Los Angeles: University of California Press.

Scheper Hughes, N. (ed.) (1998) *Small Wars*. Los Angeles: University of California Press.

Schuman, J. (1998) Childhood, infant and perinatal mortality in 1996: social and biological factors in the deaths of children aged under three, *Population Trends*, 92: 5–14.

Seiter, E. (1995) *Sold Separately: Children and Parents in Consumer Culture*. New Jersey: Rutgers University Press, pp. 11–12.

Sen, A. (2000) *Development as Freedom*. Oxford: Oxford University Press.

Serpell, R. (1993) *The Significance of Schooling: Life Journeys in an African Society*. Cambridge: Cambridge University Press.

Sharman, C., Cross, W. and Vennis, D. (1995) *Observing Children: A Practical Guide, Case Studies*. London: Cassell.

Singer, I.B. (1977) *A Crown of Feathers and Other Stories*. London: Penguin.

Skinner, B. (1974) *About Behaviourism*. London: Jonathan Cape.

Skinner, C. (2003) *Running Around in Circles: Co-ordinating Childcare, Education and Work*. Bristol: Joseph Rowntree Foundation/Policy Press.

Sosinky, L., Lord, H. and Zigler, E. (2007) 'For-profit/non-profit differences in center-based child care quality: results from the National Institute of Child Health and Human Development Study of Early Child Care and

Youth Development', *Journal of Applied Developmental Psychology*, 28(5): 390–410.

Steedman, C. (1982) *The Tidy House*. London: Virago.

Steedman, C. (1988) Mother made conscious: the historical development of a primary school pedagogy, in M. Woodhead and A. McGrath (eds) *Family, School and Society*. London: Hodder and Stoughton, pp. 83–95.

Steedman, C. (1990) *Childhood, Culture and Class in Britain: Margaret McMillan 1860–1931*. London: Virago.

Stephens, S. (1995) *Children and the Politics of Culture*. Princeton, NJ: Princeton University Press.

Stiglitz, J. (2002) *Globalization and its Discontents*. London: Penguin.

Stiglitz, J. (2006) *Making Globalization Work*. London: Penguin.

Street, B. (1999) Meanings of culture in development; a case study from literacy, in F. Leach and A. Little (eds) *Education, Cultures and Economics: Dilemmas for Development*. Brighton: Falmer Press.

Sutton Smith, B. (1970) Psychology of childlore: the triviality barrier, *Western Folklore*, 29: 1–8.

Sutton Smith, B. (1986) *Toys as Culture*. New York: Gardner Press.

Sutton Smith, B. (1999) The rhetorics of adult and child play theories, in S. Reifel (ed.) *Advances in Early Education and Day Care*. London: JAI Press, pp. 149–62.

Thompson, F. (1939) *Lark Rise*. Oxford: Oxford University Press.

Time Magazine (1997) How a child's brain develops, 13 Feb.

Titmuss, R. (1943) *Birth, Poverty and Wealth: A Study of Infant Mortality*. London: Hamish Hamilton.

Tobin, J. (1995) Post-structural research in early childhood education, in J. Hatch, (ed.) *Qualitative Research in Early Childhood Settings*. Greenwood, CT: Praeger, pp. 223–43.

Tobin, J., Wu, D. and Davidson, D. (1989) *Preschool in Three Cultures: Japan, China and the United States*. New Haven, CT: Yale University Press.

Tucker, N. (1977) *Childhood*. London: Fontana.

Tudor Hart, B. (1938) *Toys in the Nursery*. London: Country Life.

Tunstill, J., Allnock, D., Meadows, P. and McLeod, A. (2002) *Early Experiences of Implementing Sure Start: Report and Executive Summary*. London: DfES.

UNESCO (2007) *EFA Monitoring Report*. Paris: UNESCO.

UNICEF (2007) *The State of the World's Children*. New York: UNICEF.

van Eyken, W. (ed.) (1973) *Education, the Child and Society: A Documentary History 1900–1973*. London: Penguin.

Vincent, C. (2006) *Childcare Choice and Class Practices: Middle Class Parents and their Children*. London: Routledge.

Vincent, C., Ball, S. and Braun, A. (2007) Local child care cultures: working class families and preschool childcare, paper presented at ESRC Final Report Dissemination Conference. London Institute of Education.

Vleminckx, K. and Smeeding, T. (eds) (2001) *Child Well-Being, Child Poverty and Modern Nations: What Do We Know?* Bristol: Policy Press.

Vygotsky, L. (1978) *Mind in Society*. Cambridge, MA: Harvard University Press.

Wadsworth, M. and Kuh, D. (1997) Childhood influences on adult health, *Epidemiology*, 11(1): 2–20.

Waldfogel, J. (2004) *Social Mobility, Life Chances and the Early Years*. London: Centre for the Analysis of Social Exclusion (CASE).

Watson, J. (1928) *The Psychological Care of Infant and Child*. London: Allen and Unwin.

Webster-Stratton, C. (2007) *The Incredible Years*. Available at: www.incredibleyears.com

Weikart, T. (1996) High quality preschool programs found to improve adult status, *Childhood*, 3(1): 117–20.

Wilson, E.O. (1998) *Consilience: The Unity of Knowledge*. London: Little, Brown.

Wolf, E. (1990) *Europe and the People Without History*. London: University of California Press.

Young, M.E. (1998) Policy implications of early childhood development programmes, in *Nutrition, Health and Child Development*. Washington, DC: Pan American Health Organization/World Bank, pp. 209–24.

Yudkin, S. (1967) *A Report on the Care of Pre-school Children*. London: NSCN.

Yudkin, S. and Holme, A. (1963) *Working Mothers and Their Children*. London: Michael Joseph.

Zelitzer, V. (1985) *Pricing the Priceless Child*. New York: Basic Books.

Zelitzer, V. (2002) Kids and commerce, *Childhood*, 9(4): 375–96.

Zuckerman, M. (1993) History and developmental psychology: a dangerous liaison, in G. Elder, J. Modell and R. Parke (eds) *Children in Time and Space: Developmental and Historical Insights*. Cambridge: Cambridge University Press, pp. 230–5.

Index

CRITICAL ISSUES IN EARLY CHILDHOOD
Nicola Yelland

> This book is a valuable contribution to the creation of a more critical and theoretically diverse approach to early childhood policy and practice. Through many vivid examples and a varied cast-list of authors, both academics and practitioners, it shows the potential of this approach for pedagogical work in early childhood institutions and the education of the early childhood workforce.
>
> *Professor Peter Moss, Institute of Education, University of London, UK*

This book challenges long-established beliefs about early childhood education. It offers readers the opportunity to think about the aspects of their profession that are fundamental to providing effective and equitable educational opportunities for young children in the 21st century. Well-known contributors explore issues that are not only 'critical' in terms of being fundamental to early childhood education, but also 'critical' in that they present alternative ideas and use frameworks that are not traditional to the field. Organized in three parts, the book considers:

- Contemporary views of early childhood education and teaching
- The rethinking of early childhood practices
- The emergence of new technologies and multiliteracies

The chapters in the book focus on aspects of early childhood education that have for a long time been accepted as truisms, or have been too hard to deal with and thus often ignored. For example, they include a consideration of issues that range from examining play that might be sexual in focus or learning how to cope with traumatic events in young children's lives, to the ways in which popular culture and new literacies impact on what young children are interested in and how they can be engaged in learning with information and communications technology.

Essential reading for students in all early childhood studies programmes, as well as early childhood practitioners who want to engage in more reflective practices around their work.

Contents
Against the Tide: New way in Early Childhood Education – Reconceptualizing the field (of early care and education): If 'western' child development is a problem, then what do we do? – Developmental theory and early childhood education: Necessary but not sufficient – How 'bad' can it be?: Troubling gender, sexuality and early childhood teaching – Preschool children's portrayals of their male teacher: A poststructural analysis – Who Can Speak? Silence, Voice, and Pedagogy – Freedom to choose: Examining children's experience in choice time – Learning to be a child: Cultural diversity and Early Years ideology – Questioning diversity – Secret children's business: Resisting and redefining access to learning in the early childhood classroom – 'Civilization and replicas': Disrupting multicultural pretend play props – Digikids: Young children, popular culture and media – Literarily Lost: the quest for meaningful literacy agendas in early childhood education – Curriculum, pedagogies and practice with ICT in the information age – Postmodernism, passion and potential for future childhoods.

2005   272 pp
978–0–335–21596–6 (Paperback)   978–0–335–21597–3 (Hardback)

YOUNG CHILDREN'S HEALTH AND WELL-BEING

Angela Underdown

The true wealth of a nation can be measured by the health of its youngest citizens and in the twenty-first century, children's health and well-being is largely determined by social, environmental and economic influences.

This book explores how factors such as parent-child relationships, family networks and social support, housing, poverty and the safety of the environment impact on children's early experiences and have consequences for their later health and well-being.

Topics include:

- Promoting infant mental health
- Family transitions
- Poverty, relative poverty and health inequalities
- Growth and nutrition
- Young children under stress
- Child public health
- Young children's involvement in health
- Research with young children and families

Underpinned by the United Nations Convention on the Rights of the Child and an ecological systems framework, this book takes difference and diversity into account to celebrate the rights of every individual child.

Young Children's Health and Well-Being is a comprehensive health text for students of early childhood. It is also important reading for student teachers, community practitioner nurses, social work students and others who work with young children and their families.

Contents

Foreword – Acknowledgements – A note on the text – Young children's health and well-being in context – The transition to parenthood – Foundations for emotional and social well-being – Health inequalities in early childhood – Growth and nutrition – The impact of family change on children's health and well-being – Child public health – Children under stress – Children's involvement in health – Listening to young children – Glossary – References – Index.

2006   216pp
978–0–335–21906–3 (Paperback)   978–0–335–21907–0 (Hardback)